The RHS Encyclopedia of Practical Gardening

WATER GARDENING

PHILIP SWINDELLS

Editor-in-chief Christopher Brickell

Philip Swindells currently practises as a consultant for botanical and historic gardens, specializing in water features. He has written extensively on the subject of water gardening, including a number of award-winning publications.

MITCHELL BEAZLEY

The Royal Horticultural Society's Encyclopedia of Practical Gardening © Octopus Publishing Group Ltd 1993, 1999

The Royal Horticultural Society's Encyclopedia of Practical Gardening: Water Gardening © Octopus Publishing Group Ltd 1993, 1999

First published in 1993
Reprinted 1994, 1995, 1996, 1998
New edition 1999

ISBN 1 84000159 3

Edited and designed by Mitchell Beazley, an imprint of Octopus Publishing Group Ltd
Michelin House, 81 Fulham Road,
London SW3 6RB
Produced by Toppan Printing Co., (HK) Ltd.
Printed and bound in Hong Kong

Contents

Introduction

Water is one of the most versatile and adaptable garden features. Not only does it offer the gardener an opportunity to grow a wide range of interesting plants, including colourful waterlilies, but running water creates sound and movement, while placid pools have a reflective quality which can bring peace to the garden. Even the smallest town patio can accommodate water in a tub or sink, and there are many plants that will prosper in the shallow water of these restricted spaces. A variety of water features can also be introduced indoors, adding an exotic, tropical touch to conservatories and sun rooms.

Water gardening has never been more popular due to the wide choice of inexpensive materials available for pool, stream and waterfall construction. Pre-formed units are easy to install, but the gardener is restricted to the shapes on offer, so a liner might suit his or her purposes better. With a liner, any configuration can be created, providing unlimited scope for imaginative design. Concrete can also be used; the beginner might wish to stick to simple shapes, while the accomplished do-it-yourself gardener can produce more complicated water schemes using wooden shuttering.

Moving water features are powered by pumps. These are available from garden centres, complete with comprehensive instructions on how much water they will move and how to use and install them. They enable the gardener to operate streams and waterfalls, fountains and water spouts.

Selecting plants is an exciting part of water gardening. Waterlilies are deservedly popular, but there are many other attractive deepwater aquatics which can also be grown. There are also numerous plants suitable for shallow water and marshy areas, namely marginal and bog plants. Fish breeding is a natural extension of water gardening for some pool owners. Koi carp fascinate many people, but more modest, affordable fish such as goldfish and shubunkins are colourful and attractive and can give as much pleasure.

All water features need to be well looked after. Given time, the ecosystem will become more established, encouraging wildlife to collect around the water; indeed, specially planted wildlife pools will often harbour threatened species, such as the great crested newt, and these pools can play a major role in nature conservation.

Water gardening is a rewarding and popular pastime, and it is well within the capabilities of both experienced and inexperienced gardeners to create an attractive pool, stream, waterfall or fountain.

Glossary 1

Acid A term applied to soil or water with a pH value of below 7.

Algicide A substance used for controlling algae.

Alkaline A term applied to soil or water with a pH value of above 7.

Annual A plant that completes its life cycle within one growing season.

Axil The upper angle between a leaf or leaf stalk and the stem from which it grows.

Barbel The spines or bristles hanging down from the jaws of certain fish.

Bare-rooted (plant) A plant lifted from the open ground (as opposed to a container-grown plant).

Basal At the base or bottom. A basal pool is below a wall fountain; a basal shoot on a plant is the bottom one.

Bladder A hollow sack-like organ on plants.

Bog An area where the soil is kept permanently damp but not waterlogged.

Bonemeal Bones ground to a powder and used as a fertilizer.

Bract A modified, usually reduced leaf that grows just below the flowerhead.

Bulbil A very small bulb which is formed above ground, in leaf and inflorescence axils.

Calyx The outer whorl of a flower, consisting of sepals that may be free to the base or partially joined.

Candelabra (flower) A flower stem with blossoms arranged in rings or whorls around it.

Carnivorous (plant) A plant able to trap and digest small insects.

Cast A tinge or shade of colour.

Caterpillar *see* Larva.

Caudal fin The tail fin of a fish.

Cement Fine grey powder, a mix of calcined limestone and clay, used with water and sand to make mortar, or with water, sand and aggregate to make concrete.

Chalice (flower) A cup-shaped flower.

Chameleon (waterlily) The term for a flower which changes colour with age.

Clump A plant that grows from clusters of buds.

Cluster Leaves, buds or flowers growing closely together.

Cocoon A protective envelope secreted by larvae in which the pupae develop.

Cold chisel A long, slim chisel used for cutting masonry.

Compost (seed, potting or aquatic) A mixture of materials consisting chiefly of loam, peat, sand and fertilizers. It is used as a medium for sowing seeds and potting plants.

Compound (leaf) A leaf divided into two or more subsidiary parts.

Concrete Sand, cement and aggregate, mixed with water to form a hard building material used under slabs and foundations.

Cone (flower) The central hard portion of some flowers to which petals are attached.

Container-grown (plant) A plant in a container as opposed to a bare-rooted one that is lifted from the open ground.

Cotyledon A seed leaf, usually the first to emerge above ground on germination.

Crown The basal part of a plant from which roots and shoots grow.

Crustacean A creature with a shell.

Cultivar A cultivated as distinct from a botanical variety.

Cutting A separated piece of stem, root or leaf taken in order to propagate a new plant.

Dead-head To remove the spent flowers or the unripe seed-pods from a plant.

Deciduous A plant that loses all its leaves annually at the end of the growing season.

Dibber A tool used to make holes in the soil in which to plant seedlings or cuttings.

Die back The death of branches or shoots, beginning at the tips and spreading back towards the stem.

Disc (flower) The central circular part of some flowers surrounded by stamens.

Division Propagation by means of dividing a single plant into smaller portions; also a way of thinning congested plants.

Dormant The resting period of a plant, usually in winter.

Dorsal fin Main fin rising up from the back of a fish.

Double (flower) A flower with a double row or multiple rows of petals.

Dressing A top dressing, like pea gravel, is applied to the surface of the soil.

Emergent A plant with stems and leaves above the water.

English bond (brick) This consists of three or

five courses of stretchers to one of headers.

Evergreen A plant that retains its leaves throughout the year.

Eye Used to describe a growth bud, particularly of waterlilies.

Flowers of sulphur A chemical in powder form which is used as a fungicide.

Foliar feeding A liquid fertilizer that is sprayed onto and absorbed through the leaves of a plant.

Frond The compound leaf of a fern.

Fry The young of various species of fish.

Fungicide A substance used for controlling diseases caused by fungi.

Gene A unit of heredity which determines characteristics.

Germination The development of a seed into a seedling.

Gill The respiratory organ of a fish.

Glaucous A bluish-white, bluish-green or bluish-grey waxy bloom.

Globular Shaped like a globe.

Growing season The period during which a plant is actively producing leaves and flowers.

Half-hardy A plant that is unable to survive the winter without protection but does not require greenhouse protection all the year round.

Harden off To acclimatize plants raised in warm conditions to cooler conditions.

Hardy A plant capable of surviving the winter in the open without protection.

Head (fountain) The vertical distance between the water level and the highest part of the discharge.

Header A brick laid across a wall so its end is flush with the surface.

Herbaceous Plants that are fleshy as opposed to woody.

Host A plant that harbours, or is capable of harbouring, a pest or disease.

Hybrid A plant produced by the cross fertilization of two species or variants of species.

Incurved (petals) Those that curve inwards at the top.

Inundation or immersion (plant) Complete water cover.

Inflorescence The part of a plant that bears the flower or flowers.

Iris The coloured centre of the eye.

Lance-shaped (leaf) Narrow leaves tapering to a point at each end.

Larva The active immature stage of some insects. The larvae of butterflies and moths are known as caterpillars.

Lateral A side growth that develops at an angle from the main stem.

Leaching The removal of soluble matter from material by water; minerals are leached from soil and free-lime from concrete.

Leaflet Any small leaf or leaf-like part.

Lesion Any injured or diseased tissue.

Lobe (leaf) A shape where the margin is indented at one or more points.

Margin The edge or border, especially of leaves and flowers; also the term given to the sunken marginal shelf around the edge of a pool, on which marginal plants or miniature waterlilies can be grown.

Mealy (plant) A sprinkling or covering of powder resembling meal.

Medium (growing) Soil or compost in which plants are grown.

Milt The sperm-bearing fluid of a fish.

Monocarpic Flowering and fruiting only once before dying.

Mortar A mixture of cement, sand and water, used as a bond for bricks and stones and for pointing and rendering.

Mutant A plant which has undergone genetic changes and is therefore a new creation.

Nacreous A shiny, pearly surface.

Native (plant) Originating in the country where they are grown; for example, British plants grown in Britain.

Ornamental A plant grown for its decorative qualities.

Overwinter To pass the winter, usually referring to the means by which a plant survives the winter.

Panicle A branched flowerhead, each branch having several individually stalked flowers.

Papery (petals) The term given to petals with a thin, paper-like texture.

Glossary 2

Pea gravel Fine gravel used as a top dressing for soil; also a material used for backfilling in construction.

Pectoral fin The pair of fins below the head of a fish.

Pendent A term describing part of a fish or plant that hangs down; for example, pendent barbels are dangling whisker-like appendages on fish.

Perennial A plant that lives for at least three seasons.

Pesticide A chemical used to kill pests; also, generally applied to chemicals used to control pests, diseases and weeds.

pH The degree of acidity or alkalinity. Below 7 on the pH scale is acid, above is alkaline.

Photosynthesis The process by which a green plant is able to make carbohydrates from water and carbon dioxide, using light as an energy source and chlorophyll as the catalyst.

Plantlet A plant produced naturally by the parent plant as a method of propagation.

Plumb line A string with a metal weight attached, used to determine verticality.

Pointing Finishing the joints in brickwork and stonework with mortar.

Portion Small clumps of the same plant, often the result of division.

Pricking out The transplanting of a seedling from a seed tray to a pot or another tray.

Propagation The production of a new plant from an existing one, either sexually by seed or asexually, for example, by cuttings.

Puddle (clay) A mixture of wet clay that is impervious to water.

Pupation The development of an insect larva into an adult.

Quarantine Period of isolation to prevent the spread of diseases.

Raceme An inflorescence in which the flowers are borne along the main stem, often with the oldest flowers at the base.

Render To cover a surface such as brickwork with mortar or cement.

Rhizome A creeping, usually horizontal stem that can act as a storage organ or produce buds that develop into new plants.

Rhomboidal (leaf) A shape with parallel adjacent sides of unequal length.

Rootstock The underground part of a plant from which roots and shoots are produced.

Rose (spray head) The attachment used to direct a fine spreading spray from the spout of a watering can.

Rosette A circular cluster of leaves growing from the base of a shoot.

Rough leaf (seedling) The first leaf produced that resembles the adult leaf.

Runner A trailing stem that grows along the surface, takes root and forms new growth at nodes or the tip.

Running bond (brick) This consists of stretcher courses with alternate rows staggered by half a brick.

Scavenger An animal which feeds on decaying organic matter.

Sealing compound A compound used to seal concrete to stop free-lime leaching into the water.

Seed head A faded flowerhead that has been successfully fertilized and contains seed.

Seedling A very young plant raised from seed.

Semi-evergreen Describes a plant intermediate between evergreen and deciduous. It bears some foliage throughout the year, but loses some leaves during winter.

Sepal One of the outermost, leaf-like structures of a flower.

Sessile A flower or leaf with no stalk which grows directly from the stem.

Sheath An enclosing or protective structure, such as a leaf base enclosing the stem of a plant.

Shuttering (concrete) The timber frame into which concrete is poured.

Single (flower) A flower with a single layer of petals.

Siphon A tube placed with one end in a container or pool of water and the other end outside at a lower level; fluid runs out of the container or pool under the influence of gravity.

Spadix The term given to a racemose inflorescence which has small sessile flowers borne on a fleshy stem, the whole being enclosed in a spathe.

Spathe A large bract which encloses an inflorescence.

Spawn The mass of eggs deposited by fish, amphibians or molluscs.

Species A group of closely related organisms within a genus.

Spike (flower) An inflorescence consisting of a raceme of sessile flowers.

Stamen The male reproductive organ of a flower, consisting of a stalk bearing an anther in which pollen is produced.

Stigma The terminal part of the ovary, where pollen is deposited.

Strap-like (leaf) A tongue-shaped leaf.

Stretcher A brick that is laid horizontally with its length parallel to the wall.

Stippling A pattern created by dots or specks.

Stripping (fish) The process of controlled fertilization.

Subsoil The layer of soil below the topsoil which is lighter in colour, lacks organic matter and is low in nutrients.

Sump A pool or container into which water drains, often housing a pump.

Swim bladder A temporary disorder affecting the balance of fish when they experience extreme temperature changes.

Syn. Abbreviation for synonym.

Tadpoles The aquatic larvae of frogs and toads.

Tamp To pack down firmly; concrete must be tamped down to expel trapped air.

Tassled (flower) The tuft of stamens at the tip of an inflorescence.

Tender A plant unable to withstand the prevailing weather conditions.

Thin To reduce the number of seedlings.

Topsoil The upper layer of dark fertile soil in which plants grow.

Toothed Small indentations occurring on the margin of a leaf or flower.

Trifoliate A plant with three leaves.

Truss (flower) A cluster of flowers growing at the end of a single stalk.

Turion A fleshy, overwintered bud attached to the creeping stems of water plants.

Umbel A flat-topped or domed flowerhead in which the flowers are borne on stalks arising from the top of the main stem.

Variegated Leaves with coloured markings.

Variety A distinct variant of a species, either a cultivated form (a cultivar) or occurring naturally.

Vent (fish) The external opening of the urinary or genital system.

Ventral fin Another name for the pelvic fin, the fin on the underside of the fish.

Viviparous Of plants, those that produce bulbils or young plants; of seeds, those that germinate before separating from the parent plant.

Watering in To water around the stem of a newly transplanted plant to settle soil around the roots.

Waterproofing compound A compound added to mortar or concrete to make it watertight.

Water table The level in the soil below which the soil is saturated by ground water.

Whorl Three or more flowers, buds, leaves or shoots arising from the same place.

Winter bud *see* Turion.

The pool ecosystem

The pool ecosystem consists of water, gases, mineral nutrients, plants and livestock. These interacting components are either producers or consumers. If the oxygen and nutrient balance is correct, the water will be clear and plants and fish will prosper, but if an imbalance occurs then the system will not operate successfully.

Plants are producers: in the presence of sunlight they build up complex substances from carbon dioxide and water and they produce oxygen, a process known as photosynthesis. Fish and other livestock such as tadpoles, insects and snails are consumers: they take in the oxygen and produce carbon dioxide. A pool must be well oxygenated and this is mainly done by submerged plants; the presence of moving water will also increase the oxygen level.

In order to function properly, a pool must have a careful balance of sunlight, mineral salts and surface cover plants to prevent the growth of water-discolouring algae (see page 182). Algae live off nutrients in the water and increase, rapidly turning the water green and cloudy; their growth is encouraged by sunlight. To keep this to a minimum, the water must be shaded from sunlight by surface cover plants, while other plants, floating aquatics and submerged plants in particular, must be introduced to use the mineral salts which algae feed upon.

The correct balance of a micro-organism community not only helps to achieve clean water but also provides the basis of a complex food chain which supports many larger animals. Having fed on organic debris, bacteria, fungi, snails and worms are themselves a source of food for water beetles and dragonfly larvae. In turn, these creatures provide food for fish and frogs. It is better to have several small fish than a few large ones, as the bigger fish will consume almost all the small creatures in the pool. The type of fish as well as the size is important: native fish are less likely to disturb the food chain than hybrid Koi carp, for example, as native fish will survive unaided in the pool environment, while Koi will require supplementary feeding.

The ecological balance of a pool may be severely affected by the pH (acidity or alkalinity) of the water (see pages 112 and 184). The availability of plant nutrients and the breeding capacity of the micro-organisms can be reduced by extreme acid or alkaline conditions. In the closed environment of an ornamental pool, it is therefore vital to ensure that extremes of pH levels do not occur. Where the level of acidity or alkalinity in the water is high, the adjustment to a more neutral environment must be made very gradually, as any sudden changes will endanger fish life.

The design and construction of a pool is an important consideration for its future success. Shallow pools will heat up much more quickly than deeper pools and this will encourage algal growth. Deep water zones in a pool will remain cool in summer and frost-free in winter, enabling micro-organisms to survive temperature extremes.

Pool maintenance will have a direct bearing on the ecological balance of a pool. The pool should not be cleaned out too often (see page 178), as cleaning disturbs the pool community; this will have to be re-established once the pool is re-filled.

ZONES OF HARDINESS

The most important aspect of climate for the water gardener to consider is temperature, because some of the more tender plants and fish may not survive harsh conditions. Broad climatic divisions are a useful basis for judging the general viability of specific plants or fish.

The map of hardiness shown here defines zones of consistent average annual minimum temperatures. The zones of hardiness given in this book relate to the range of tolerance which can be expected of individual plants and fish; information on specific plants and fish is given in the relevant directories. For example, all the waterlilies listed in zones 5-9 are hardy, but some of the more tender cultivars are only hardy in zone 10, although some of these can be grown under favourable conditions in containers or indoors. Similarly, the majority of goldfish, shubunkins and carp are hardy in zones 7-10, but the more tender varieties like orandas are only hardy in zones 9-10.

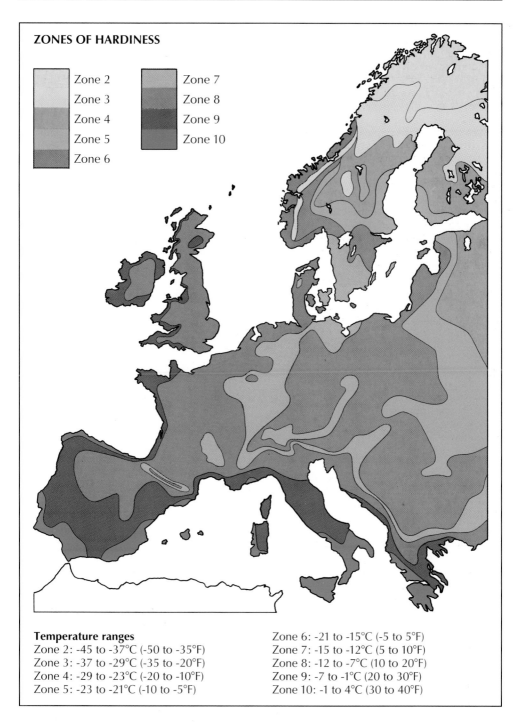

ZONES OF HARDINESS

Zone 2
Zone 3
Zone 4
Zone 5
Zone 6

Zone 7
Zone 8
Zone 9
Zone 10

Temperature ranges
Zone 2: -45 to -37°C (-50 to -35°F)
Zone 3: -37 to -29°C (-35 to -20°F)
Zone 4: -29 to -23°C (-20 to -10°F)
Zone 5: -23 to -21°C (-10 to -5°F)

Zone 6: -21 to -15°C (-5 to 5°F)
Zone 7: -15 to -12°C (5 to 10°F)
Zone 8: -12 to -7°C (10 to 20°F)
Zone 9: -7 to -1°C (20 to 30°F)
Zone 10: -1 to 4°C (30 to 40°F)

Areas and volumes

Areas
The surface area of a pool must be calculated to work out the fish stocking rate (see page 156) and how many submerged plants are required for algae-free water (see page 182).

Apply the relevant formula shown below to your own pool dimensions.

Square or rectangular pools
Multiply the length (l) of the pool by the width (w) to calculate the surface area.

Circular pools
Apply the following formula which involves using pi (3.14), a constant used in mathematics representing the ratio of the circumference to the diameter of a circle.

Square the radius (r) of the pool and multiply this by 3.14 for the surface area.

Irregular pools
For simple shapes, multiply the maximum width of the pool by the maximum length.

For more complex shapes, divide the pool into two or three sections (a, b, c), and calculate the area of each. Add the resulting figures together for the total surface area.

Streams
Multiply the maximum width (w) of the stream by the length (l) to calculate the surface area.

Waterfalls
Divide a waterfall up into its horizontal and vertical components, and calculate the area of each. Add the resulting figures together for the total surface area.

Volumes
In order to work out which pump to use for your water feature, you will need to know the volume, or water capacity, of the pool (see pages 14 and 66). You will also need to know the volume of your pool to calculate how much algicide to use. Apply the relevant formula to your pool and multiply the resulting figure by 6.25 for the capacity in gallons.

Alternatively, working in metres, calculate the volume according to the given formula and multiply this by 1,000. The resulting figure will be the capacity in litres.

Square or rectangular pools
Multiply the length (l) of the pool by the width (w), and multiply this by the depth (d) to obtain the cubic volume.

Circular pools
Square the diameter (di) of the pool and multiply this figure by the depth (d) to obtain the cubic volume.

Irregular pools
For simple irregular pools, take the maximum length and multiply it by the maximum width, and multiply this by the maximum depth to obtain the cubic volume.

For more complex pools, divide the area up into two or three sections and, using the relevant formula, calculate the volume of each section. Add the resulting figures together to obtain the volume of the pool.

Streams
Multiply the length (l) by the maximum width (w) of the stream, and multiply this figure by the maximum depth (d) to obtain the cubic volume of the stream.

Waterfalls
If the waterfall consists of pools set one above the other, calculate the volume of each pool and add the results together for the total cubic volume. If a single fall, treat it as you would a long stream.

RATE OF FLOW

Most cascade units require an output of at least 250 gallons (946 litres) per hour to provide a thin sheet of water and 300 gallons (1136 litres) per hour to provide a deep, continuous flow.

To calculate the rate of flow, run water through a hosepipe into a large container for one minute, with the tap adjusted for a fast or slow flow according to the desired effect. Measure the amount collected in pints and divide this by 8 to obtain the capacity in gallons. Multiply this by 60 to calculate the gallons per hour. Alternatively, measure the amount in litres, and multiply this by 60 for litres per hour.

AREAS AND VOLUMES

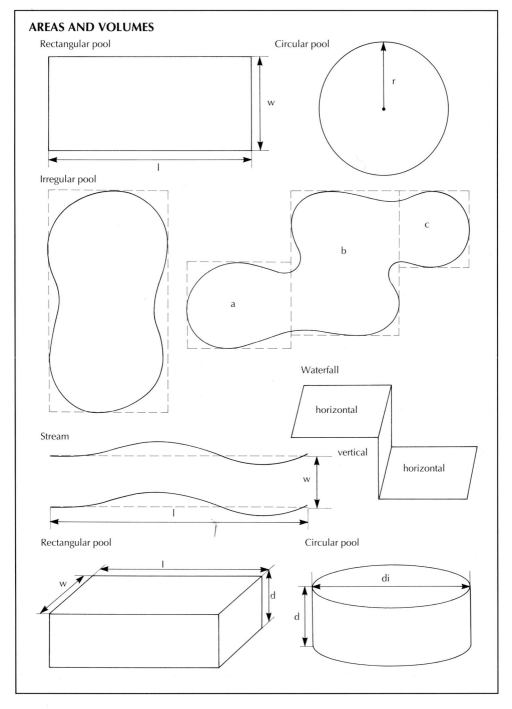

Rectangular pool

Circular pool

Irregular pool

Waterfall

Stream

Rectangular pool

Circular pool

Tools and equipment 1

Not all the following tools or pieces of equipment will be needed for every water feature; this is a comprehensive list that covers a range of needs.

Aquarium (a) It is useful to have an aquarium in which to house fish on a temporary basis while the pool is being cleaned; tender fish can also be overwintered in one.

Balls: rubber and tennis These are useful for absorbing the pressure exerted by ice in pools in freezing conditions.

Bicycle tyre repair kit Bicycle tyre repair kits can be used to repair tears and punctures in butyl rubber liners.

Blanketweed remover Although not essential, this is an excellent tool for removing large quantities of blanketweed.

Bucket A plastic or metal bucket is used for bailing out water; it can also be used to accommodate fish on a temporary basis.

Filter A filter removes debris from the water and, in some cases, also destroys bacteria. It is a necessary piece of equipment for a pool which is heavily stocked with fish.

Fork A garden fork is useful for removing heavily congested clumps of plants, but it should be used with caution if the pool is constructed with a liner as the prongs are capable of puncturing it.

Gloves (b) Strong gardening gloves or waterproof rubber gloves are necessary for any heavy manual work, such as laying concrete.

Hammer A hammer is needed for knocking in pegs and stakes when marking out a pool, and for woodwork, including making shuttering.

Hand fork (c) **and trowel** (d) Use either a hand fork or a trowel for planting aquatics.

Hose (e) A hosepipe is essential for filling and topping up the pool. A length of hose can be used as a siphon, and flexible hosepipe can be used to mark the outline of an irregularly shaped pool.

Knife A strong pocket knife is useful for trimming the edge of a liner. It can also be used for taking cuttings, dividing plants and pruning.

Mug Use a mug for catching small fish.

Net (f) A hand net is useful for catching fish and removing uneaten fish food, algae and other debris from the pool.

Planting baskets In the pool, water plants are grown in specially manufactured baskets.

These have lattice-work sides which permit the free exchange of gases and nutrients.

Pool heater In cold weather, a pool heater can be installed to prevent water freezing.

Pump A pump is needed to run a moving water feature. It can also be used to pump water out of the pool and to operate a filter.

Rake: iron Use an iron rake when preparing a smooth surface for pool construction.

Rake: lawn A lawn rake is useful for removing rampant floating plants or blanketweed.

Saw (g) A saw is needed for woodwork.

Scrubbing brush A coarse-bristled domestic scrubbing brush is very useful for cleaning out the pool.

Secateurs (h) Use a sharp pair of secateurs for taking cuttings, dividing and pruning plants.

Set square A set square is essential for measuring angles accurately.

Shovel A shovel is the best tool for mixing concrete and moving large amounts of soil. It should be sturdy, preferably made of stainless steel, and the correct height for the user.

Spade A strong, sharp spade is necessary for excavations.

Spirit Level (i) A spirit level is an essential tool for checking the accuracy of construction work. It is often used in conjunction with a straight-edged plank straddling a levelled surface or two levelled points.

Tape measure A metal builder's tape measure is used for marking out the pool area and measuring depths.

Trowel: bricklayer's (j) Use this large pointed trowel for laying mortar beds and spreading mortar on bricks.

Trowel: plasterer's (k) Use this flat trowel for smoothing off concrete for an even finish.

Trowel: pointing (l) Use this small pointed trowel for pointing brick structures.

Waders or wellington boots Wear waders or wellington boots when entering the pool.

Watering can (m) A standard garden watering can with a fine-rose attachment can be used to dampen freshly laid concrete until it sets. Choose one which has a long spout to make it easier to reach the centre of the pool. A watering can which has a fine-rose attachment is also needed for watering-in.

Wheelbarrow (n) A wheelbarrow is useful for transporting earth and bags of cement to and from the site.

TOOLS

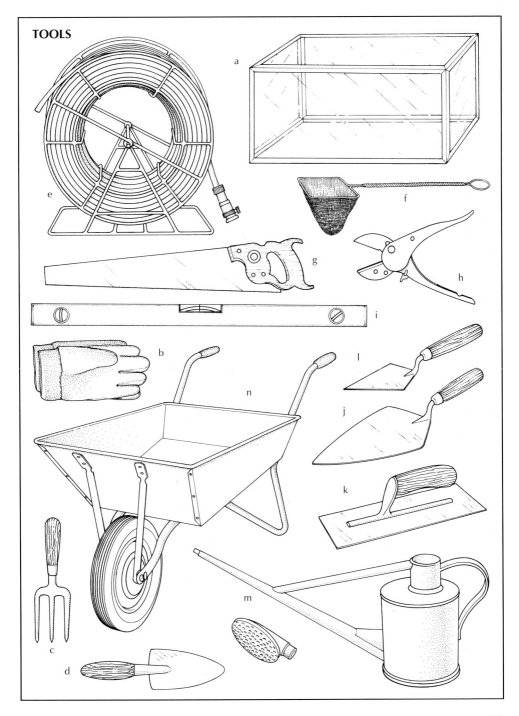

Tools and equipment 2

Pumps (see pages 10 and 66)
All pumps work in the same way: an electric motor draws the water in through an input unit. This has a filter attached to it to filter out any leaves, twigs and other debris. The output unit forces water out under pressure, the flow being adjusted by a flow-adjuster screw, and the whole unit is attached to a delivery hose or fountain assembly unit. With the addition of a T-piece, the pump will operate more than one feature. There are two types of pumps.

Submersible pumps
These are the most popular type of pump for the domestic pool and they will operate most fountains and gentle streams and waterfalls. They have the advantages of being silent and easy to install: place the pump on a level surface on the pool floor with the delivery hose and cable leading out of the pool, hidden by stones and plants.

Surface pumps
These are used to power fountains with high heads of water and streams and waterfalls with a large output. Surface pumps operate from a separate brick chamber built next to the pool. The pump chamber should be built at the same time as the pool itself, preferably in a position below the water level of the pool. If the chamber is above the water level, a foot valve and strainer must be used on the suction tube to retain the prime, which keeps the water pushing through. If the chamber is below the pool's water level, only a strainer is needed as the prime is maintained by gravity. The pump must not be housed where the vertical distance from the water level exceeds the suction lift of the pump. Make sure the pump chamber is dry and well ventilated. Build a single-layered running bond brick structure (see page 60) that will just accommodate the pump, incorporating an air brick in the top course for ventilation; use a paving slab for the roof.

Pool filters
There are two main types of pool filter: mechanical and biological. Mechanical filters are used in conjunction with pumps to clean the water, and they sit on the pool floor. Biological filters are used to clean and enrich the water, and they operate from outside the pool. In temperate climates, it is necessary to keep filters working throughout warm winters if algae still proliferate (see page 182).

For the gardener with an ecologically well-balanced pool, a filter may not be necessary; it should certainly not be considered as a substitute for a properly planted pool, but biological filtration is necessary in pools that are heavily stocked with fish. If you feel that fish-keeping may become an important part of your water gardening activity, select a simple biological filter which has the facility for modular additions. This will enable a modest system for an average garden pool to be adapted into a substantial and functional filter in pools stocked heavily with fish.

Mechanical filters
Mechanical filters are the simplest type of pool filters. They resemble a deep seed tray, and consist of two trays, one inside the other. The inner tray contains a foam filter which is covered with gravel or charcoal; the pump is attached to the outer tray. The water is drawn in through the gravel or charcoal and the foam, where it deposits any debris such as sticks, stones and algae, before being discharged through the pump unit. The inner tray must be cleaned every few days. A separate algal tray can be incorporated; this must also be cleaned regularly.

SAFETY

WATER AND ELECTRICITY DO NOT MIX: ALWAYS USE WATERPROOF ARMOURED CABLE AND A WATERPROOF CONNECTOR.

Carefully follow the manufacturer's instructions. All electrical equipment must be operated in conjunction with a circuit breaker to protect you from any electric shocks. This device cuts off the electrical supply within 30 milliseconds should problems occur.

Most pumps work directly from the mains 240 volt electricity supply. The armoured cable must be laid in a 1-2ft (30-60cm) trench to protect it from being cut or damaged.

The tube filter is another simple mechanical device. This consists of a perforated tube with a wrap-around jacket of coarse filter material, which is secured with velcro strips. When attached to the pump, the water passes through the filter and deposits algae and debris in the wrap. This should be removed and cleaned or replaced every few days so it does not get clogged up.

Biological filters

Biological filters convert harmful nitrites, the result of fish waste and rotting fish matter, into useful nitrates, as well as cleaning the water of algae and debris. Water passes through the filter medium, which contains beneficial bacteria; this changes the organic waste into useful nutrients.

Biological filters operate from outside the pool. They are rather large, ungainly-looking devices which are difficult to disguise and so should be sited with care.

Pool heaters (see page 176)

Install a pool heater in a pool containing fish if there is any chance of the pool freezing over. Pool heaters work directly off the mains 240 volt electrical supply; simply plug them in, making sure that both the cable and connector are waterproof.

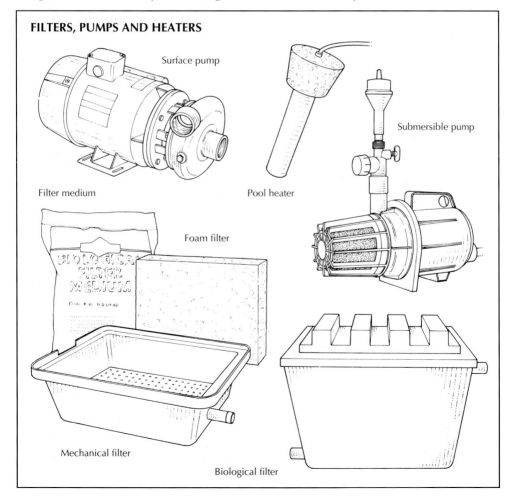

FILTERS, PUMPS AND HEATERS

Surface pump

Submersible pump

Filter medium

Pool heater

Foam filter

Mechanical filter

Biological filter

Lighting

Water can be greatly enhanced by lighting and there is a range of lights that can be used both inside and outside the pool to highlight various features.

The simplest form of lighting is the spotlight, which illuminates a specific area with a single beam. In many ways, this is the most effective method of lighting a water feature. It is possible to purchase units consisting of two or three lights fixed together, ideal for larger fountains or waterfalls. A simple white light is best and most complementary; although various different coloured lenses are available, these must be used carefully to be sympathetic to the rest of the garden.

Lights can be placed anywhere in or around the pool. Spectacular effects can be achieved with underwater lighting; a single spotlight placed in the water, set at an angle pointing upwards, will pick out a fountain or waterfall. Positioned around the edge of the feature pointing straight ahead, the same light will illuminate the water, including any fish and plants. The approach depends on the desired effect, be it subtle illumination or bright highlighting. Some spotlights are designed to float on the surface, and these can be weighed down and used as underwater units for a more mysterious light.

If you have fish in your pool, take care not to leave underwater spotlights on for long periods as fish do not like bright light.

A water garden can also be lit from outside by spotlights that are designed to stick into the

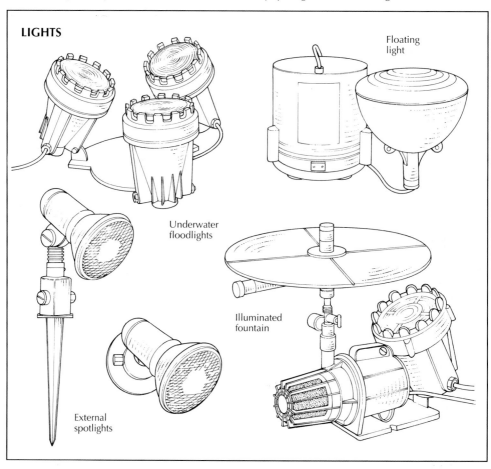

LIGHTS

Floating light

Underwater floodlights

External spotlights

Illuminated fountain

ground. If these are placed behind the feature, pointing straight ahead, they will illuminate marginal plants and the surrounding area, leaving the water as an inky black silhouette. Alternatively, direct the light onto a fountain or waterfall and it will highlight the feature, making the running water sparkle and leaving the surrounding water in darkness.

A floodlight can be installed, but this is a much less subtle form of lighting which illuminates large areas rather than highlighting specific features. They are, however, useful as blanket cover for security reasons.

Illuminated fountains (see page 80)
In addition to lighting units, illuminated fountains, which have lights built into them, are available. These provide spectacular displays at night, and during daylight hours the fountains can be used independently of the light source.

Illuminated fountains are sold in kit form. The basic unit is supplied with a submersible pump for the fountain, with a spotlight encased in a sealed underwater lamp-holder to provide the light. For more than one colour, choose a kit with a colour-changing unit. This consists of a revolving disk comprising red, blue, amber and green plastic segments, that runs off the pump. The speed can be selected to achieve the desired rate of colour change. The density of colour depends upon the jet; a column fountain or plume of water will give the best results.

SAFETY

WATER AND ELECTRICITY DO NOT MIX. Only install specially designed outdoor and underwater lights; never use an inside light outside. When installing the light, follow the instructions carefully.

Armoured cable must be used. Do not drape the cable over shrubs and hedges; bury it approximately 3ft (90cm) underground. Garden lights operate through a transformer on a 12 or 24 volt system; these low voltage systems are very safe. All underwater lights have waterproof adaptors, connectors, switches and junction boxes and are sealed into their holders with non-corrosive materials. Use each light in conjunction with a circuit-breaker, which cuts the electricity off within 30 milliseconds should a problem occur.

Burying the cable

1 Dig a trench for the cable a minimum of 3ft (90cm) deep and 6-8in (15-20cm) wide.

2 Place the cable inside a length of plastic conduit in the trench, and cover it with a row of roof tiles.

3 Stick a piece of bright warning tape along the length of the tiles and fill the trench with soil.

Siting

A pool is a complete miniature underwater world where plants and livestock depend upon one another for their existence, so conditions must be provided to enable each to develop to its full potential. This is partly achieved by the shape and internal structure of the pool, and partly by the position of the pool within the garden because some sites should be avoided.

Sunlight and shade

In order to prosper, the majority of popular aquatics, including waterlilies, need sunlight. Only site pools where they will receive full sun in summer, when plants are in active growth. It is not so important with bog gardens; there are several shade-tolerant bog plants available so bog areas can be partially shaded if you wish.

When assessing the degree of light that a site will receive, take into account nearby trees. This is best done in summer when the trees are in full leaf; in winter you will have to guess the shade potential of deciduous trees in order to assess the site.

The shade cast by buildings should also be taken into account. In winter, when the sun is low in the sky, more shade will be cast by trees and buildings than in summer, when the sun is high. Do not site a water feature on a site that is in heavy shade during the summer.

Sheltered sites

Site a pool in a sheltered position if possible. Open, wind-swept areas should be avoided as the wind may over-turn and damage container-grown marginal plants, and blow the spray of a fountain out of the pool. Furthermore, water evaporation will be greater in a windy site. An exposed area will also be cooler than a sheltered one, and the pool is more likely to freeze.

Before siting your pool in a sheltered spot, however, check the area is not in a frost pocket. These often occur in low-lying areas which trap cold air; such sites should be avoided and an alternative chosen.

Water table

The position of the water table should influence your choice of site. If it is just beneath the surface of the soil then some drainage

---

TREES TO AVOID

Certain trees should not grow in the vicinity of a pool.

While having strong associations with water, weeping willows should not be planted near a garden pool. Their rotting leaves produce chemicals which may cause the death of fish, and their vigorous roots will disturb the pool structure.

Plums and cherries (*Prunus*) should also be avoided as they are overwintering hosts of waterlily aphids that harm waterlilies and succulent marginal aquatics (see page 114). Other trees to avoid include the horse chestnut (*Aesculus*), the laburnum, which has poisonous seeds, and evergreens such as rhododendron and yew (*Taxus*). Poplars (*Populus*) should not be grown; they are vigorous and thirsty trees and their roots will spread great distances in search of water.

---

system will have to be installed in order to relieve the pressure on the fabric of the pool exerted by the water in the ground outside the pool. Without drainage provisions, the build-up of pressure may cause a liner to billow out and a pre-formed pool to be dislodged.

To check the depth of the water table, dig a trench or hole in the proposed site in wet weather; February is a good time to do this as the ground is more likely to be saturated. If the water table is less than 2 feet (60cm) below the pool floor, either install a drainage system or choose another site.

Water-logged, low-lying areas that are susceptible to winter or summer flooding should also be avoided.

Sloping sites

Although gentle slopes are easy to level, steeper gradients may need retaining walls to maintain the water feature satisfactorily.

Trees

A pool should not be sited under or within 15ft (5.5m) of any trees. This is partly because of the problem of falling leaves in autumn, partly due to spreading roots, which may damage the pool's foundations, and partly because plants in the pool will not thrive in excessive shade. The leaves of certain trees also contain chemicals which can harm fish.

Water and electricity
The proximity of a water supply to the garden pool is important. Not only will the pool need filling once it has been constructed and after subsequent cleanings, but it will need regular additions of water during the summer months due to evaporation.

Either install an outside tap near the pool if one does not exist already, or make sure you have easy access to an indoor tap so you can run a hose between this and the pool. The latter is less convenient, especially during summer, when the pool will need topping up almost daily. A rainwater butt is also useful, but should be within easy reach for siphoning the water into the pool.

Similarly, electricity should be close at hand in order to run pumps, filters, pool heaters and lighting.

Drains, water pipes and electricity cables
Do not excavate in the immediate vicinity of drains, water pipes or electricity cables. They are easily damaged and accidents may occur.

Access
Access to the pool is a further consideration; paths should be constructed if they do not already exist. As well as being practical, paths can also help unite the pool with the rest of the garden, particularly if accompanied by a well-planted border.

Expansion
It may seem premature to consider expansion of a pool at the planning stage, but many gardeners add to their existing water feature within a few years. A long-term view to potential expansion may influence your choice of site in the first place, enabling you to work within your existing garden design, rather than having to adapt your garden to fit the expanding feature later on.

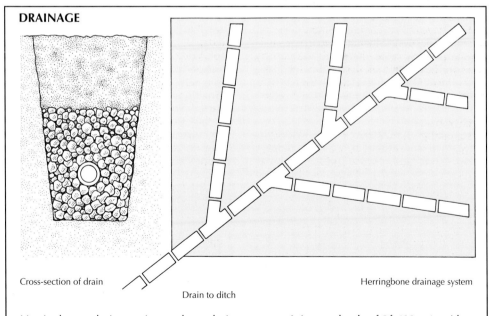

DRAINAGE

Cross-section of drain

Drain to ditch

Herringbone drainage system

Herringbone drainage is used to drain water away from the site of a pool to remove the pressure exerted by the water table. Bury the 3in (8cm)-diameter drains at a minimum depth of 2ft (60cm), with a fall of between 1:80 and 1:100. The pipes should feed into a 4in (10cm)-diameter main drain laid at a depth of 2½ft (75cm).

Pool designs 1

Even a modest plot can accommodate a water feature of some kind, such as a tub or planter in which a pygmy waterlily is grown; moving water can be introduced on a miniature scale in the form of a pebble fountain. The more room you have, the more you can experiment with larger pools, streams and waterfalls.

Whatever water feature you choose, it must blend in with the rest of the garden: a formal pool may look ill at ease in an informal setting; similarly, an informal pool will often look out of place in a formal design.

Water in the garden

Water can be used in the garden in many ways. A formal pool or fountain placed in a prominent position can be used as a focal point, whereas a wildlife pool or bog garden sited in a corner will merge into the surroundings. Water can also be used to tie up various parts of the garden: a stream or channel will create a horizontal link and a waterfall will connect different levels.

Water has long been used to give the illusion of space; even small bodies of water can make a garden seem much larger, reflecting the sky and nearby trees. A pool with few plants will have a mirror-like surface which can be used to reflect a statue or plants.

Other illusions can be created with still water: a large formal pool with an eye-catching fountain will make the garden seem smaller, whereas a finger of water which disappears behind a group of shrubs will make the garden appear larger. A long, narrow stream or channel running the length of the garden will make the garden seem longer; set across the garden the same feature will make the garden look wider.

POOLS

Pools can be formal or informal; Oriental-style and wildlife pools are popular options.

Formal pools

Formal water features are mostly installed for decorative purposes, and they usually form the centre-piece of an area. For the greatest effect, planting should be kept to a minimum, with perhaps a few choice waterlilies or one or two isolated groups of plants. Introduce brightly coloured ornamental fish.

Siting and design

Formal pools are associated with straight lines, definite curves and symmetry: circles, ovals, squares, rectangles and other geometric shapes are all suitable. The shape of the pool should blend well with other shapes in the garden; make sure the sides of a straight-sided pool are parallel with lines of nearby walls or borders, for example.

If the garden is made up of a series of swirls and curves, design a sweeping pool which will echo these shapes; where there are rectangular lawns and borders, for example, the pool should take a similar form. Alternatively, use contrasting shapes within a design: a circular pool can be used to complement a surrounding framework of squares.

The materials used should be consistent with other materials in the vicinity, and the surrounding coping or paving should tie in neatly with the design. For example, regular square paving slabs around a rectangular or square pool will enhance its formal rectangular shape, whereas crazy paving used in the same situation would be visually out of place because of its informality.

Raised structures

For the most part, raised pools and channels are formal, and they are often used to mask difficult features. They are good devices for linking different levels, and in a formal setting they can act as a focal point, often with a fountain as a centre-piece.

Siting and design

Raised pools can make attractive features on terraces and patios and they should be built of the same material as the paving or walls. Raised pools can also be useful for masking sloping sites, especially when set beside a formal feature, such as a flight of steps.

The ambitious gardener will not just create square or circular structures, but create triangular or L-shaped pools. The pools do not have to be used on their own: a series of raised pools can be built, either interlocking or as separate units. As with other formal features, use a material which matches any surrounding structures.

As a practical feature for the less able, a raised pool should be arranged so that there is wheelchair access from all sides.

Oriental pools

An Oriental-style water feature can consist of a trickling and tumbling body of water leading from one part of the garden to another, often disappearing temporarily and suddenly reappearing elsewhere; or it can be a simple, placid, reflecting pool, perhaps ornamented with a few carefully placed rocks, stones or statues and maybe a bridge as well. Use only Oriental-looking plants.

Siting and design

An Oriental pool can be set in a large landscape, ideally hidden away and surrounded by flat plains of rocks. If the pool is primarily for the enjoyment of fish, it should be plain and stark, with only a seat or two on the bank beside it. As a less formal feature, an Oriental pool can be shallow with a small cobbled beach and groups of rocks, with plants arranged around the margins. In a small garden, an Oriental pool may be positioned next to the house so that it will reflect the features of the building; the pool itself can be designed in such a way as to echo the lines and angles of the adjacent building.

Informal pools

An informal pool is usually intended to appear natural; it should be well planted and blend in with the garden. A wide range of fish, including native species, can be introduced.

Siting and design

The surface design of an informal pool can be any shape, but straight lines and sharp angles should be avoided, with sweeping arcs and curves used instead.

While a formal feature tends to stand alone, an informal one should be well integrated into its surroundings, perhaps linked to a bog area, a rock garden or even a large border. Consider the surrounding landscape and create a shape that will fit in well.

Bog gardens

A bog garden is often linked to an informal water feature and helps to integrate the pool or stream with the rest of the garden. Here, plants that will tolerate damp conditions but not standing water can be grown.

Siting and design

It is possible to site a bog garden in partial shade as a range of shade-tolerant bog plants is available, but it is preferable to position it so that at least half of the bog area receives full sun so a wider and more exciting selection of plants can be grown.

A bog garden may be made in any shape, although, generally speaking, formal arrangements should be avoided and bold, sinuous lines used instead.

Wildlife pools

The creation of wildlife pools is becoming increasingly popular. The aim should be to recreate the natural environment as accurately as possible, thereby providing a variety of habitats for aquatic and semi-aquatic wildlife. The planting should merge into the surrounding landscape to make the feature look as natural as possible; use native plants.

Siting and design

The design of a wildlife pool should be at ease with the rest of the garden. It is only possible to have wildlife pools in informal settings, as they do not fit in with manicured lawns or formal stonework. If your garden is formal and well tended, position the wildlife pool in a separate area and mask it with a hedge or a shrub border so it is hidden.

Wildlife pools are best sited so their inhabitants are disturbed as little as possible. If there is a natural water source in the garden it can be adapted to form a wildlife pool, as native plants cope well with unpredictable water levels. In such cases, the water feature will only need shaping to create the best conditions for insects, birds and small mammals which may already be present.

All wildlife pools should be irregular and curved rather than angular, and they should have a shallow beach area made of pebbles and gravel for easy access, where birds and animals can drink and bathe.

MOVING WATER FEATURES

Moving water, in the form of fountains, streams, channels and waterfalls, can be formal or informal, depending on the requirements of the garden owner.

Fountains

For the most part, fountains are used in formal situations, and only the most simple ones are appropriate for an informal feature.

Pool designs 2

Siting and design

There are two types of fountain, those that throw jets of water into the air in various configurations, and simple ones where water issues from a figure or sculpture. The placing of water jet fountains should be governed primarily by light: they are best viewed from the north so that sunlight passes behind them, creating an array of rainbow colours.

Wind is a problem for all but the smallest fountains, so only install a fountain if the pool is in a sheltered spot otherwise the spray may be blown out of the pool entirely.

Simple figures are best used in small gardens or confined areas; decorative and complicated ones should only be used in larger, formal settings. Position human figures as naturally as possible: for example, place a bathing maiden on the edge of the pool and a bearded Neptune in the middle. Objects like urns and shells can be used in informal settings, perhaps set off-centre among plants; circular pools are well suited to non-representational, abstract figures. In the garden, water spouts and wall fountains can be placed in the middle of a terrace or patio wall or, for an informal feature, in a hidden corner. They may also be used effectively in conservatories and sun rooms.

The position of fountains within the pool depends to a great extent on the shape of the pool or basin. In a semi-circular pool, the fountain should preferably be located in the centre towards the back; in a circular, square or rectangular pool, set the fountain in the middle of the water.

Streams and channels

A stream or channel draws the eye along its course; the more regular the design, the more formal the effect.

Siting and design

An artificial stream running through a garden must have a purpose; it must look as though it is coming from somewhere and leading somewhere. For an informal effect, create a twisting stream, running through foliage and round corners. An informal stream must be well integrated into the surrounding garden; either excavate the feature into the existing lie of the land or build up the landscape around it so that it looks natural.

Most channels are formal and straight and are used to link up various parts of the garden. Unlike streams, the success of a channel lies not in integration but definition: a channel should stand out as a structural feature. Both streams and channels need to be built on slopes, although only the smallest fall is needed to make water flow.

Waterfalls and cascades

Two types of waterfall are commonly constructed: those that rush and tumble, and more gentle ones which flow in a ribbon of water over a few rocks. Built as a series of concrete channels falling into one another, the effect will be symmetrical, elegant and formal; built as a series of interlinked pools surrounded by plants, the waterfall will look informal and natural.

Siting and design

The most important consideration when installing a cascade or waterfall is to make sure that the slope is sufficient to allow the water to flow naturally. As with artificial streams, informal waterfalls must look as though they are a part of the landscape.

For a dramatic effect, design a waterfall with a chute that will channel water rapidly from one pool to the next. This type of fall will create a focal point in the garden, whereas some of the more natural-looking, peaceful waterfalls can be less obtrusive if sited in a corner. A formal feature can be created using a series of raised pools, either set on different levels or built in diminishing sizes, so water is transferred from one down to the next.

Containers

A water garden can be established successfully in any watertight container. Tubs or half-barrels are the most popular, but sinks, planters or urns can also be used. These are best planted with a few prize waterlilies or lotus, although a sink can be turned into a miniature waterscape using a few stones.

Siting and design

Containers can be used to decorate terraces, patios and conservatories. The larger and more ornate the container, the more effective a centre-piece it will be. For a more informal look, arrange containers of different shapes and sizes in a group.

Indoor water features

Most indoor pools in conservatories or sun rooms are decorative, providing an opportunity to grow tender plants and display more exotic, less hardy fish. With careful planning, the feature can give year-round interest.

Siting and design

Indoor water features, either formal or informal, can take the form of raised or semi-sunken pools, wall fountains or containers, all of which should be sited in sunny positions. Corner pools are particularly attractive.

CAVITY DESIGN

Since plants grow and adapt to the amount of space they have, the underwater shape of the cavity will determine the overall look of the pool, not the surface outline. While some types of pool, for example, wildlife pools, benefit from special conformations, there are certain basic features common to most pools which you can adapt to suit your design.

Pools should have a minimum depth of 1½ft (45cm) in temperate areas, and 2ft (60cm) in cold areas with severe winters. This will satisfy the growing requirements of most popular waterlilies, and provide enough depth for fish to overwinter on the pool floor. The floor must be smooth and level for planting baskets or a pump to sit on, and draining the pool will be easier if a small dip is made in the floor to catch the remnants of water.

More formal pools are mostly constructed with straight sides, but informal designs often have a shelf around the edge for marginal plants. Most marginal plants grow in 8-12in (20-30cm) of water, so the shelf should allow for this depth, with a width of approximately 9in (23cm) in order to accommodate relatively large planting baskets. The surface of the shelf must be level so that the baskets sit firmly in place; this is particularly important if you wish to grow tall marginal plants.

The angle of the walls above the shelf will usually be determined by the design and method of construction. Most walls are relatively steep, between 60° and 90°; when a planting basket is in position on the shelf, the gap between the side of the basket and the wall should be no more than 1in (2.5cm). A more gentle slope may be necessary in areas of light soil, otherwise the walls may collapse. Concrete pools should never have perpendicular walls; they should batter outwards. The wall of the main pool cavity should be less steep, no more than 40°.

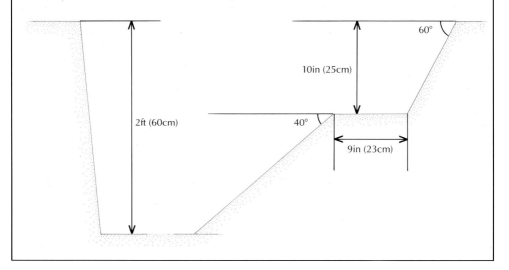

Methods and materials

There are several methods of pool construction using various different materials. The simplest way is to use a pre-formed shell, but you can also excavate the soil in accordance with your own specifications and use a liner or a layer of concrete to construct the pool.

Each material has its advantages and disadvantages: liners are easy to install and can be adapted to a variety of designs, but they are the least resistant to damage of all the materials; pre-formed units are much stronger but, by the very nature of their pre-formed shape, they are the least adaptable; and concrete, while being strong and permanent, is very difficult to lay successfully.

Liners

Liners offer the amateur gardener the greatest versatility: using a butyl rubber or PVC liner you can make your pond any shape or size, sunken or raised, to fit in with the most complex garden design. Liners are, however, relatively easy to damage by rough handling or accidental puncturing by garden forks.

Liners are available in a wide range of materials including butyl rubber, PVC and polythene. Polythene is the cheapest material but rubber and PVC, although more expensive, are worth the extra cost as they are more durable than polythene.

Butyl rubber is an extremely tough, long-lasting, flexible, heavy gauge material which, if damaged, can be satisfactorily repaired. For custom-made pools it is possible to have sheets welded to any shape or size, but these should be installed by a professional as they need accurate excavations which are difficult for the amateur to achieve.

PVC is less durable than butyl rubber and may crease, but the liners are still hard-wearing. They are available in a range of colours; black and stone can be recommended as they tend to blend in well with the surroundings. PVC liners are sometimes reinforced with a nylon web which provides a greater burst resistance than normal PVC. This does not mean that reinforced PVC is less likely to puncture than butyl rubber, the latter is still stronger.

Rubber and PVC liners are easy to install: simply stretch them over the excavation area, moulding them into the contours of the feature if necessary, and add water.

Polythene is a weak material that is easily damaged by exposure to ultraviolet light when the pool water evaporates in hot weather. Polythene liners are not so useful; they will not last for long periods and should not be used where permanent lining is required. However, polythene can be used successfully sandwiched between layers of soil (see page 52) and for bog gardens, as the soil will protect the liner from exposure to sunlight. Polythene liners may also be used for temporary pools in which to keep fish and plants while the main pool is being cleaned.

As polythene has little elasticity, it should be spread out in the sun for half an hour to improve its flexibility before being moulded into the pool and water added.

Pre-formed pools

Pre-formed pools are tough and long lasting and they provide a fairly quick, but not always easy, method of pool construction. They are available in a variety of curved and geometric shapes, but the more elaborate the design, the more difficult the installation. Some of the more irregular designs are provided with special planting baskets which fit into the various curves and shelves.

Pre-formed pools are usually made of fibreglass (glass reinforced with plastic resin); plastic and PVC ones are available, although these are not as hard-wearing and are more difficult to install. Fibreglass will withstand most wear and tear, although if damage does occur (by heavy footsteps, for example) it can be satisfactorily, but not easily, repaired. You should not, however, use a pre-formed pool if you wish to install stepping stones or heavy fountains.

The obvious disadvantages of pre-formed pools are their fixed shape and rigid nature. You are restricted to shapes commercially available, none of which may fit in with your design. Pre-formed pools also preclude the presence of an integrated bog garden; any bog area must be constructed with a liner as a separate entity.

Concrete

Concrete-laying is a skill that demands considerable knowledge and practice. If you are at all unsure of your ability to do a satisfactory job, employ a professional to do it for you instead. A well-constructed concrete pool, however, will last far longer than pools constructed from other materials, and it should need little or no repair work for many years. If repairs are needed, they can be done without too much difficulty. On the other hand, a badly made concrete pool will only last for a few years and will be a constant source of trouble; frost and ice will work on any initial weaknesses and cause flaking and cracking.

Concrete pools are best designed in simple shapes which are easy to construct, and any bog areas must be made with a liner as a separate feature.

SECTIONAL POOLS

Pre-formed modular pools are available and these can be mixed and matched in various configurations, providing a range of different shapes from which to choose. The point at which each section meets is uniform, but the overall shape can differ widely. The separate sections are fixed together and then a sealant is applied to make them watertight (see pages 32 and 68).

Pre-formed sectional pools often come with specially designed planting baskets which fit their curves exactly.

CONSTRUCTION MATERIALS

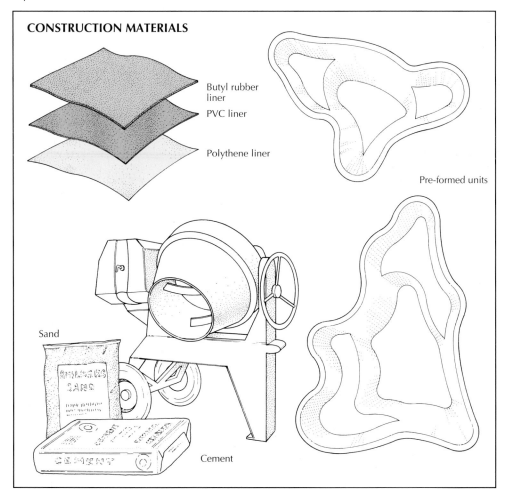

Butyl rubber liner

PVC liner

Polythene liner

Pre-formed units

Sand

Cement

Marking out/excavating 1

Incorporate a bog garden into the design at the planning stage, along with any functional accessories such as external biological filters and surface pumps. Once you have decided on the siting and design of your water feature, and the method of construction, mark out the appropriate shape on the chosen site.

Tools and equipment
You will need: a tape measure, a ball of string, a number of pegs (use short pieces of cane or stake), a sharp stake or pointed cane, a spirit level and a length of hosepipe.

Circles
Take a length of string, the same length as the desired radius of the pool, and attach a peg at one end and a piece of pointed cane or a stake at the other. Knock the peg into the ground at the centre of the proposed pool and stretch the string taut. Walk around the peg, making a circle on the ground with the cane.

Ovals
Calculate the length of the oval at its longest point and insert one peg at each end and one in the middle. Make sure they are all aligned.

Measure two-thirds of the length between the central peg and each end peg, and mark the two intermediate points with more pegs.

Stretch a piece of string around one of the end pegs and the intermediate peg furthest away from it, and place the loop around the intermediate pegs. Using a short length of pointed cane or a stake, take up the slack and move towards the outside of the pool until the string is taut. Walk a full circuit around the pool, keeping the string taut, and mark an oval in the ground with the stick as you go.

Right-angled triangles
Regardless of the pool dimensions, mark out a 3ft (90cm) long baseline, from which the re-maining outline of the pool is derived. To do this, place two pegs 3ft (90cm) apart at one end of the chosen site, and tie a piece of string between them. If applicable to your design, make sure this is parallel to or perpendicular with any nearby wall, path or border by measuring from the straight edge of the existing structure to each peg: the two measurements should be the same.

Create a right angle. Tie a second piece of string 4ft (1.2m) long to one of the baseline

Circles

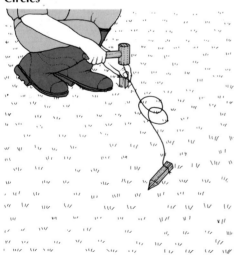

1 Attach a peg to one end of the string and a sharp cane or stake to the other. Knock the peg into the ground.

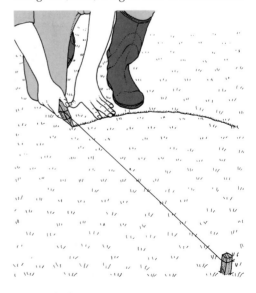

2 Stretch the string taut and walk in a circle around the centre point, marking the ground as you go.

Ovals

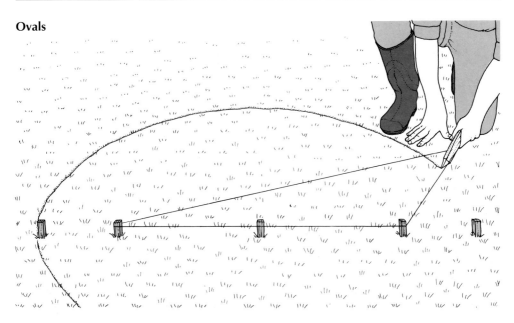

Mark out the longest axis of the oval with a peg at each end and one in the middle. Insert two intermediate pegs between the middle peg and each end peg.

Loop the piece of string around the two intermediate pegs. Using a sharp cane or stake, pull the string taut and walk around the pegs, marking the ground as you go.

Right-angled triangles

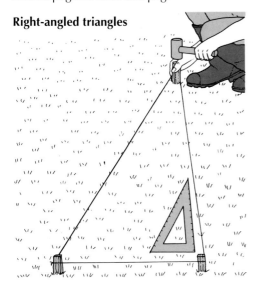

Using string and pegs, mark out a triangle using the 3-4-5 system. Check the right angle with a set square.

Other triangles

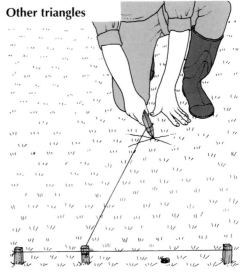

Using the marker line, mark two arcs in the ground. The point at which the two arcs cross is the third point of the triangle.

Marking out/excavating 2

pegs and tie the other end to a peg placed at an approximate right angle, 4ft (1.6m) away.

Go to the opposite end of the baseline and attach a third length of string 5ft (1.5m) long to the peg. Holding the string, walk towards the far end of the second line to form a triangle and, after repositioning the top peg so that both pieces of string are taut, insert it in the ground; the base angle of this triangle should be 90°. Relate the triangulation to your own pool measurements by either lengthening or shortening the sides as appropriate. Using a pointed cane or stake, mark out the outline on the ground.

Other triangles

Using pegs and string, mark out a base line the same length as one side of the proposed triangle. Take a piece of string two-thirds the length of the base line and tie a peg to one end and a pointed stake to the other; this is the marker line.

Insert the peg of the marker line one-third of the way along the base line and, with the string taut, mark an arc where the next point of the triangle should lie. Repeat this process

with the marker line inserted two-thirds of the way along the base line; the point at which the two arcs cross should form the third point of the triangle.

Squares or rectangles

A square or rectangle comprises two right-angled triangles. Follow the instructions for right-angled triangles, repeating the process to form the square or rectangle.

Irregular shapes

Position the irregular pre-formed unit on site and prop it up approximately 3in (8cm) above the ground on piles of bricks or stakes. Transfer the shape of the outer edge of the pool to the ground by placing a spirit level vertically between the rim of the unit and the ground. Mark the points with a stick, remove the unit and join the points.

If using a liner or concrete, map out the most important measurements (the maximum and minimum lengths and widths) on the ground, and wind a length of hosepipe between each peg. Mark the irregular outline in the ground.

Irregular pre-formed pools

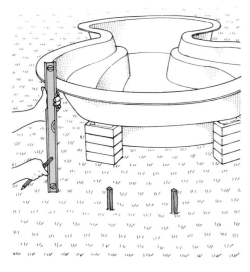

Prop the shell up on bricks or stakes and mark around its perimeter on the ground, using a spirit level as a guide.

Other irregular shapes

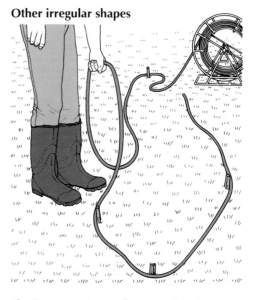

If using concrete or a liner, outline the shape of the pool with pegs and wind a length of hosepipe between them.

Once the design has been marked out to the correct dimensions, excavate the site.

The excavation must be done very carefully and accurately as it is extremely important that the hole is completely level. Adapt the following techniques to your chosen water feature design.

Tools and equipment
You will need: a tape measure, a number of 12in (30cm) pegs, a spirit level and a small plank of wood. For the excavation, use a spade or a mechanical digger.

Levelling the pool edge
If the site is level, start at any part of the outline and hammer a peg into the ground to a depth of 4in (10cm). This first peg, the datum peg, is an important reference point from which all the levels are measured. Continue around the outline of the pool, knocking pegs into the ground approximately 1ft (30cm) apart. Make sure all the tops of the pegs are level by placing a plank on adjacent pegs and putting the spirit level on it: the bubble on the spirit level should rest exactly between the

two central lines. Continue this operation until the complete outline has been marked out with level, evenly spaced pegs.

Digging the hole
You can either dig by hand or use a mechanical digger. Keep the topsoil separate from the subsoil; the topsoil may be used for building artificial mounds (see page 74) or to landscape around the pool, while the poorer subsoil should be discarded.

Diggers A very large pond will obviously be easier to excavate with a machine, providing there is access to the site. A digger reduces the time and effort involved as well as conveniently loading a trailer or skip to take the soil away. It does tend to make more peripheral mess, however.

Hand-digging For accurate excavations in small gardens it is better to dig by hand. If your soil is particularly fine and you are installing a pre-formed pool, keep the soil for backfilling (see page 32), placing it on a large heavy plastic sheet until it is needed. Do the same if you are going to use the soil elsewhere in the garden.

Excavating

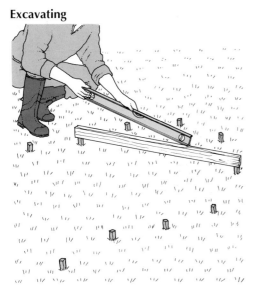

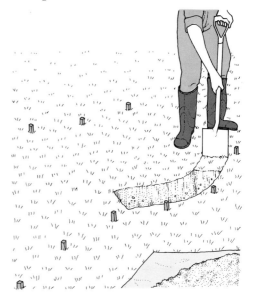

1 Mark the outline with pegs. Using a spirit level and a plank of wood, check that each peg is level, even if the ground is not.

2 Dig a trench inside the outline of pegs. Excavate in even layers, sloping the walls slightly inward as you dig down.

Marking out/excavating 3

With a spade, dig a trench inside the outline of the pegs. Remove all the soil to the same depth across the whole pool, measuring from the tops of the pegs to the ground for a level surface. If excavating a rectangular hole for a pre-formed pool, dig down in large chunks rather than even layers.

Marginal shelving

Continue digging down in even layers until you reach the depth of the shelf, if your design includes one. Measure from the top of the pegs downwards to determine where the shelf should be or, provided the ground is level, place a plank across the top of the excavation and use a tape measure to measure down to the surface. Take care not to cut beyond the correct depth as the shelf must be solid and will not remain stable if the soil is loosened too much during spadework. In order to check that the shelf is level, knock a few more pegs into it at random intervals, disturbing the soil as little as possible, and check them with the spirit level. Slope the walls slightly inwards as you dig, so the angle between the wall and shelf is obtuse.

Once you have dug down to the shelf and checked that it is level, measure out from the wall to the required width of the marginal shelf. Mark this area with an inner circle of pegs which will indicate where to dig down to the base of the pool.

Pool floor

Dig out the soil in even layers, measuring from the top of the original pegs down to the required depth of the pond, or measuring down from a plank spanning the excavation. Knock some pegs into the floor and use a spirit level to check it is level. Incorporate a small dip in the pool floor to catch the remnants of water when the pool is being emptied. Make sure the walls from the shelf to the floor are less steep than those from the shelf upwards.

Pre-formed pools

Excavate a rectangular hole approximately 6in (15cm) bigger than the unit and 3in (8cm) deeper. Alternatively, dig down to the depth of the marginal shelf and lightly rake the surface. Position the shell in the excavation and press it down into the earth so that it leaves an imprint when removed. This imprint will indicate the floor area. Excavate down to the correct depth, keeping to the size and shape of the imprint.

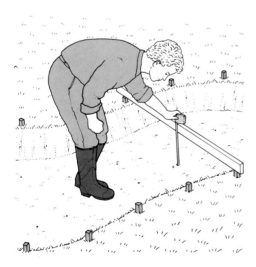

3 Span the excavation with a plank of wood and measure down to the ground to determine the depth of the marginal shelf.

4 Working your way around the pool, measure the width of the marginal shelf and mark the outline with an inner circle of pegs.

EXCAVATING SLOPING GROUND

To level a site, start at the lowest level and hammer a peg 4in (10cm) into the ground. Working your way up the slope, hammer in more pegs, all level with the first one. As you dig down, measure from the top of each peg to the required depth for a flat surface, checking it with a spirit level.

You may need to build a retaining wall above the pool to keep the soil in place. If you are incorporating the pool into a slope so that it lies half way between the lowest and highest points, you may need to build a retaining wall below the pool as well as above it. A standard brick wall (see English bond page 60) will look more formal than one built of irregularly shaped stones.

To level a very steep slope, soil can be introduced to extend the surface area of the site. This is most likely to be done in waterfall construction. Re-create the profile you have excavated with the same soil to make a flat surface.

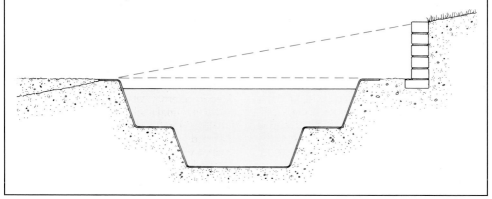

5 Following the inner circle of pegs, dig down in even layers, sloping the walls inward, until the floor is reached.

6 To check the pool is the required depth, span the excavation with a plank of wood and measure down to the pool floor.

Pre-formed pools 1

Fibreglass shells are much easier to manage than thin plastic or PVC shells, which are more flexible and quick to distort during the installation process.

Do not introduce plants until the pool is full of water (see page 100).

Design
The only part of a pre-formed unit that is going to be seen is the surface. Select a pool that has a flat bottom so that a planting basket or pump will sit level, and check it is deep enough to accommodate the plants and fish desired (see plant and fish directories).

If you have chosen a pool with a margin, it must be wide enough to support a planting basket; some pools have narrow ledges meant for thin strips of soil and these are not to be recommended as, once planted, the ledges need constant attention.

Tools and materials
For the installation you will need: a pair of gardening gloves, a spirit level and a small plank of wood, a trowel, a hosepipe, some builder's sand, a few bricks or stones and backfilling material. If you are paving the edge of the pool you will need: a shovel, a plasterer's trowel, a pointing trowel and a board to work from, mortar (see page 34) and stones or paving slabs.

Marking out and excavating
Mark out and excavate a rectangle or contoured hole that is approximately 6in (15cm) bigger than the shell and 1in (2.5cm) deeper. Check the excavation is level.

Underlining
Make sure that the surface of the excavation is smooth and free of stones. Tamp the soil down very firmly with your feet and spread 1in (2.5cm) of damp builder's sand on the floor. This acts as a cushion for the shell and will stop it moving about so much during the backfilling process.

Fibreglass shells: installation
Position the shell centrally in the hole with the base on the sand. Build up the shallow areas not touching the floor with bricks or stones so that the bottom of the unit is well supported. Firm the shell down and, using a spirit level on a plank of wood spanning the pool, check it is level from side to side and end to end, either adding or taking away material until the shell is level.

Fill the shell with approximately 4in (10cm) of water and check the level again; pre-formed units are often flexible and the level may change with the addition of water. In such cases, make any adjustments necessary to realign the shell.

Backfilling
If the soil from the excavation is fine enough to flow around the contours of the pool, it can be used for backfilling. Alternatively, use fine gravel – pea gravel is ideal – or dry builder's sand instead.

Using a trowel, a shovel or your hand, add a layer of material approximately 6in (15cm) deep by systematically working your way round the pool, pushing the material down into the cavity between the shell and the wall of the excavation, adding the material as you go. It is essential to consolidate each layer so that the shell is firmly held in place, as any

---

SECTIONAL POOLS (see pages 24 and 68)

Following the manufacturer's instructions, assemble the pool by screwing the units together and sealing the joins with the sealant provided in the kit. Measure the maximum length and width of the whole structure, add 6in (15cm) to each measurement, and excavate a hole accordingly, making it 4in (10cm) deeper than the maximum depth of the structure.

Place a 4in (10cm) layer of damp builder's sand on the floor of the excavation. Accurately measure where each joint will fall and place a length of wood with a 4in (10cm) sq cross-section along each mark. Press these down till they rest on the earth floor and remove them so you have an imprint of each one.

Lower the structure into the hole: the joints should fit neatly into the spaces left by the lengths of wood. To stabilize the pool while backfilling around it, add 4in (10cm) of water.

Pre-formed pool installation

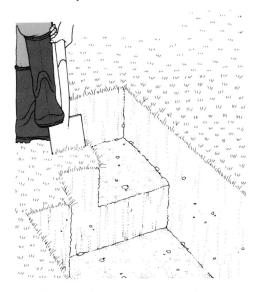

1 Mark out and excavate a rectangle or a contoured hole that will easily embrace the pre-formed unit.

2 Remove any sharp stones or roots and tamp the soil down with your feet by treading the earth with regular footsteps.

3 Lay a layer of damp sand on the floor of the excavation. This will act as a cushion for the unit.

4 Position the unit in the excavation, building up any areas not touching the ground with bricks and stones.

Pre-formed pools 2

movement will alter the water level. Each time you have completed a circuit, check the pool is level from side to side and end to end.

Continue backfilling until you reach the height of the marginal shelf. If you have used gravel or sand, fill the remainder with soil so plants can be grown up to the edge of the pool to disguise the unit.

Thin plastic and PVC shells
Add water to thin plastic and PVC shells as you backfill otherwise the unit will buckle and twist. With a hosepipe, regulate the flow of water so that the water level is the same as the backfilling level, checking the shell is level at regular intervals. If one level overtakes the other the pool will distort and must be emptied and removed, along with the backfilling material, and the whole process must be started again.

Edging
Edge the pool with stones or plants, or a mixture of the two.
Stones Select sufficient flat stones or paving slabs to edge the pool. Lay a mortar bed 1in (2.5cm) thick, the same width as the slabs. Set

each stone or slab in position, about ¼in (0.5cm) apart; the stones should overhang the pool by 2in (5cm). Firm them slightly, at the same time checking they are level with a spirit level. Point the cracks between the stones with mortar using a pointing trowel and smooth the surface. To finish, clean the stones with a wet cloth; the mortar should take several days to set and the paved edges must be covered with plastic if it rains.
Planting Plant around the edge of the pool in the soil layer of the backfilling. This area will be no more moist than the rest of the garden and garden plants rather than aquatics should be grown.

MORTAR

Mix together five parts builder's sand and one part cement, measured with a shovel or bucket, and add a waterproofing compound according to the instructions. Add enough water to make a stiff but wet consistency: place the shovel in the mixture and withdraw it in a series of jerks; if it retains peaks then the mortar is ready to use.

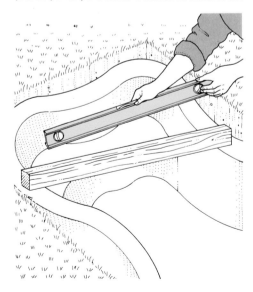

5 Once installed, check the unit is level by spanning it with a plank of wood bearing a spirit level.

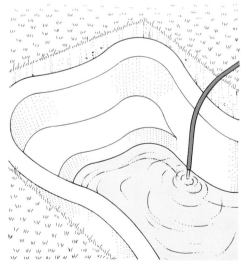

6 Using a hosepipe, fill the unit with approximately 4in (10cm) of water before backfilling around the unit.

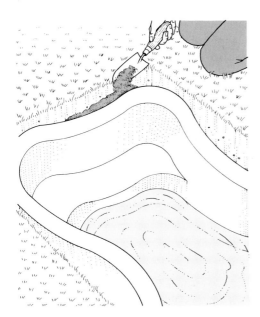

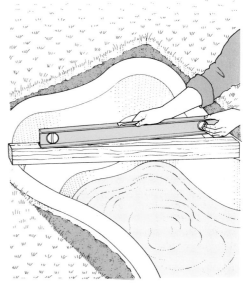

7 Backfill the unit in place. Work your way around the pool, feeding in a small quantity of material with a trowel or with your hand as you go.

8 After each full circuit, check the unit is level using a plank of wood and a spirit level. Backfill the top layer with soil if the edge is to be planted.

Edging

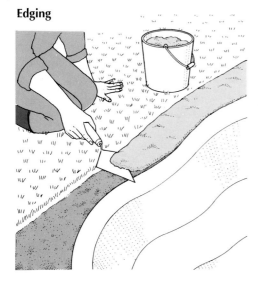

1 Once the unit is firmly installed, lay a bed of mortar approximately 1in (2.5cm) thick using a bricklayer's trowel.

2 Position each piece of paving so that it overhangs the edge of the pool, and point the cracks between each one.

Pool liners 1

Select the type of liner best suited to the proposed feature, and then calculate the quantity of liner needed.

Calculating the amount of liner

The following formula can be used to calculate how much liner or underlining you will need for your pool.

Square and rectangular pools Double the maximum depth of the pool and add this figure to the length. Double the maximum depth of the pool and add this figure to the width. Multiply the resulting figures for the total area of liner needed.

Circular pools Use a square of liner folded into a circular pool based on the following formula: double the maximum depth and multiply this by the diameter; square the resulting figure for the total area of liner needed.

Irregular pools Treat simple shapes as regular squares, rectangles or circles accordingly, and use the relevant formula. For complicated shapes, divide the pool into two or three sections and apply the relevant formula

to each section. Add the totals for the area of liner needed.

Streams Double the maximum depth of the stream and add the figure to the length. Double the maximum depth again and add the figure to the width. Multiply the resulting figures for the total area of liner needed.

Waterfalls Measure the length of each fall and add an extra 2-3in (5-8cm) to the figure; this will allow for an overlap. Calculate the area of each fall and add these figures together to get the total fall area.

Calculate the area of liner required by each pool and add the figures together. Add the resulting figure to the total fall area for the area of liner needed.

Design

Keep the pool design to sweeping arcs and curves rather than angular shapes so as to minimize the number of folds and wrinkles in the liner when it is installed. Make the marginal shelf a little wider than for other construction methods to reduce soil slippage.

Liner installation

1 Mark out the pool and dig down in even layers, incorporating a marginal shelf if desired. Span the excavation with a plank and measure down to the depth of the floor.

2 Remove any sharp stones, sticks or roots from the excavation that may otherwise puncture the liner. Using an iron rake, smooth the surface.

Tools and materials

For the installation you will need: gardening gloves, an iron rake, a plasterer's trowel, bricklayer's sand, fleece, geo-textile or polyester matting and some heavy stones. If you are paving around the edge of the pool, you will need: a shovel, a plasterer's trowel, a pointing trowel, a board to work from, mortar (see page 34) and stones or paving slabs.

Marking out and excavating

Mark out and excavate the area; the excavation must be level and exactly the same shape as the finished pool but 1in (2.5cm) longer, wider and deeper.

Underlining

Clear the site of sharp stones, twigs and other debris that might damage the liner once it is subjected to the pressure and weight of water. Rake the excavation smooth.

Line the pool with fleece, geo-textile or polyester matting, all available at most good garden centres. Calculate the amount needed as you would for a normal liner, and spread it in the hole, moulding it into the shape of the pool as neatly as possible. If more than one strip is used, there must be a minimum overlap of 6in (15cm) to ensure adequate cover if the underlining is moved when the liner is being installed.

Alternatively, plaster a 1in (2.5cm) layer of damp bricklayer's sand over the inside of the excavation with a plasterer's trowel or by hand. It is easier to achieve a smooth underlining using sand, but damp sand will not adhere to very steep sides, and fleece, geo-textile or polyester matting must be used on such surfaces instead. Old carpet can also be used, although this often creates lumps which will show through the liner. Do not use damp newspaper because it will deteriorate quickly in wet conditions.

Installing the liner

Butyl rubber/PVC Spread the liner across the excavation, making sure it is centred. This can be very difficult with irregular pools and

3 Line the pool with fleece, geo-textile or polyester matting. Spread it over the excavation and carefully mould it into the contours of the hole.

4 Alternatively, using a plasterer's trowel, plaster the excavation with a 1in (2.5cm) layer of damp sand, making sure it adheres well to the walls.

Pool liners 2

only trial and error will determine the right position. For very large pools, spread the liner out on a surface other than grass (in hot conditions the grass will turn yellow within half an hour) and roll the liner up from both sides to create two rolls meeting in the middle of the piece. Place the double roll across the middle of the excavation and unroll one side at a time until it is spread out in a central position across the excavation.

Weigh the edges of the liner down with stones or paving slabs and, using a hosepipe, slowly add water. As the weight of the water pulls the liner down, gradually lift the stones to release the liner to accommodate the water, and at the same time smooth out any wrinkles into a few bold pleats. When the pool is full of water, the butyl rubber liner will have moulded itself to fit the exact contours of the excavation.

Polythene Spread the polythene out in the sun for half an hour (on a surface other than grass) to improve its flexibility. Once it has softened, lay the polythene over the excavation, making sure it is centred.

Beginning in the centre, gently mould the polythene liner to the shape of the excavation with your hands. Allow sufficient ''give'' at the corners to prevent the material from stretching too much and splitting with the weight of water. Smooth out as many wrinkles as possible, easing all the trapped air towards major folds for a neat finish.

Gradually introduce the water, smoothing out the wrinkles as the pool fills.

Edging

Edge the pool with turf, stones or plants, as required. Work out how much liner to leave for edging purposes – about 6-15in (10-38cm) for turf or stones and twice this amount where the margins are to be planted – and neatly cut off the excess liner.

For all methods, bury the edge of the liner under at least 3in (8cm) of soil. If planting up to the edge of the pool, excavate down around the edge of the pool to a depth of approximately 6in (15cm), anchor the liner with bricks and bury it. The point at which the soil and liner meet must always be above the

5 Lay the piece of liner over the excavation, making sure it is centred. Anchor the liner with large stones placed around the edge of the pool.

6 Fill the pool with water from a hosepipe. The liner will stretch into the shape of the excavation as it fills; gradually lift the stones to release the liner.

maximum water level to prevent the soil from muddying the water and the water soaking away into the surrounding soil.

Turf Turf provides a natural finish. Make sure the soil around the pool is firm and lay the turf up to the pool edge. All grass cuttings must be collected before they fall into the water, as they will rot down and cause water discoloration. Do not use any fertilizer or weed-killer on your lawn as this may run off into the pool, harming plants and fish.

Stone Paving stones provide a more formal effect than turf. Use either paving stones or regular, matching stones set in 1in (2.5cm) bed of mortar; the stones should overhang the pond by about 2in (5cm).

Plants Plants soften the edge of the pool and may be grown among carefully placed rocks to obtain a more natural effect. Use garden plants that complement the pool planting rather than water plants as the soil at the pool edge will be no more moist than elsewhere in the garden. Position the plants so that they will integrate the water feature into the surrounding landscape.

Edging

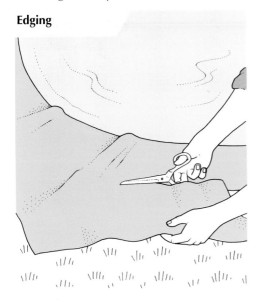

1 Using a pair of sharp scissors, neatly trim the liner, leaving a margin of approximately 6in (15cm) for turf or stone edging and twice that amount for planting.

TURF EDGING

In areas of heavy soil, turf can be laid around the edge of the pool. Pack the pieces closely together so that they abut the edge of the pool.

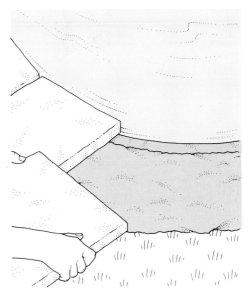

2 Bury the edge of the liner in up to 6in (15cm) of soil. Pave around the pool with paving slabs laid on a bed of mortar; the paving should slightly overhang the pool.

Using concrete

Well-laid concrete pools are solid and permanent, important factors to consider if you wish to install a heavy fountain ornament. However, concrete can deteriorate within a few years if it is not correctly prepared and laid; the concrete must also be allowed to set slowly to ensure a watertight finish (see page 42). Pools constructed on heavy clay soil are particularly prone to leakage as the clay shrinks during hot weather, causing the concrete to fracture. Once laid, all concrete must be sealed before water, fish and plants are added, to prevent leaching of free-lime.

Concrete can either be purchased ready-mixed or it can be mixed on site.

Ready-mixed concrete Ready-mixed concrete is of a known and uniform consistency. It is important to know in advance how much concrete you will need to order the right quantity; spare concrete is of no use unless it can be used straight away.

Home-mixed concrete You can make your own concrete provided you are able to mix and lay it within a 24 hour period. If the first batch is allowed to dry out before the next batch is laid, the pool is likely to leak.

Concrete is best mixed as near the site as possible, on a board or a hard surface. For large quantities it is worth hiring a mixer.

Tools and materials

You will need: waterproof gardening gloves, a bucket and shovel, builder's sand, cement, 3/4in (1.5cm) gravel and water, a waterproofing agent and colour (optional).

Mixing the concrete

With a bucket or shovel, measure out one part cement, two parts builder's sand and four parts gravel.

Mix the dry materials together until they are a uniform greyish colour and add a waterproofing compound according to the manufacturer's instructions. If you are mixing some coloured concrete for the final layer, mix in colour pigment. Mix the dry materials with water for the right consistency.

Colouring

Concrete can be coloured with waterproof paint or it can be tinted with colour pigments mixed in at the dry-mix stage: red oxide gives a terracotta-coloured finish, chromium oxide provides a deep green finish and cobalt blue and manganese black give blue and black finishes respectively. Incorporate the pigment in any proportion up to 10% by weight of the overall weight of the dry cement; the higher the percentage of pigment, the more intense the colour.

Special cements can also be used as an alternative to normal cement: snowcrete and fine Derbyshire spa both produce an attractive white finish.

Waterproofing

Correctly prepared and laid concrete is waterproof but the addition of a waterproofing compound should ensure a watertight finish. Either incorporate a waterproofing powder into the concrete mix at the dry-mix stage or instruct the supplier to do so.

Plastic waterproof paints can also be used and these too will seal the concrete. Although the paint will give the concrete a watertight finish, it is only available in rather bright

---

CONCRETE CONSISTENCY

Add enough water to make a stiff but wet mixture. In order to test the consistency, place the shovel in the mixture and withdraw it in a series of jerks. If the ridges remain stiff and firm then the concrete is ready to use.

HOW MUCH CONCRETE?

Square, rectangular and circular pools Calculate the area of each surface to be covered (see page 10) and multiply this by the depth of concrete needed. Add all the figures for the total quantity of prepared concrete required; for example: 1 (floor area × depth of concrete) + 2 (lower walls area × depth of concrete) + 3 (shelves area × depth of concrete) + 4 (upper walls area × depth of concrete) – see diagram below.

Irregular pools Draw a scaled-down version of the floor and margin of your pool on graph paper, so that each square represents a given size, for example, 1 sq ft (30 sq cm). Mark each square according to how much of it is filled; where the shape of the pool only partially fills a square, calculate the proportion as a quarter, half or three-quarters filled; these proportions are sufficiently accurate for the calculation. Add the figures to calculate the surface area of the floor and margin.

For the walls, measure the circumference of the whole pool and the circumference of the floor. Multiply the depth of the pool above the marginal shelf by the circumference of the whole pool; multiply the depth of the pool below the marginal shelf to the pool floor by the circumference of the base area. Add the resulting figures to calculate the surface area of the walls.

For the total quantity of concrete, add the surface areas of the pool floor, margin and walls, and multiply the resulting figure by the depth of concrete required.

Streams Calculate the surface area of the stream and multiply this by the depth of concrete required.

Waterfalls Divide the waterfall into its horizontal and vertical faces. Calculate the surface area of each face, add all the figures together, and multiply the resulting figure by the depth of concrete required for the total quantity needed.

Rectangular and square pools

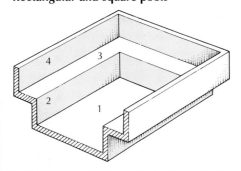

Irregular pools

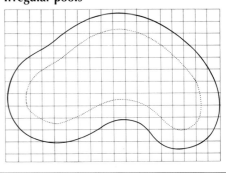

colours and the end result is a shiny, plastic finish similar to a pre-formed unit. Once the concrete is completely dry, paint the surface of the pool with paint primer. When this is dry, after about 24 hours, apply the waterproof paint in a thick, even coat. This will take three to four days to dry out, after which time the pool can be filled with water.

Sealing

If the concrete is not sealed before water is added, free-lime will leach from the concrete into the water, harming fish and turning the water cloudy. A sealant will lock in the lime and seal the concrete by a process known as internal glazing; this will not change the appearance of the concrete, but having been treated, the pool is safe for fish.

Purchase a proprietary sealant and mix the white granules with water according to the instructions. Paint the mixture onto the dry concrete inside the pool in an even layer. The pool can be filled with water when the sealant is dry, after about 24 hours.

Concrete pools 1

It is possible to make concrete pools without using shuttering.

Design
The pool must be simple in shape, with the maximum angle of the sides no more than 45°, otherwise the concrete will not stick.

Tools and materials
You will need: waterproof gardening gloves, a board from which to work, a watering can with a fine rose, a shovel, a plasterer's trowel, a spirit level, heavy gauge builder's polythene, concrete (see page 40), wire mesh with a mesh size of 2in (5cm) (chicken wire is ideal), sacking, bricklayer's sand or hardcore (for areas of heavy clay) and sealant or waterproof paint (optional).

Marking out and excavating
Mark out and excavate a hole that has the exact contours of the finished pool but is 6in (15cm) larger and deeper; check the excavation is level. On areas of heavy clay soil, excavate to a depth of 9in (23cm).

Underlining
Remove any sharp stones or roots from the excavated area and firmly tamp the surface down. In areas with heavy clay soil, lay a 3in (8cm) layer of damp bricklayer's sand over the excavation; the floor can be of well-rammed hardcore. The sand and hardcore will reduce the chance of fractures appearing when the clay shrinks in very hot weather.

Line the excavation with a layer of heavy gauge builder's polythene. Calculate how much is needed (see page 10) and mould it into the shape of the excavation.

Laying the concrete
Working from a board, start at one end of the pool and lay a 4in (10cm) layer of concrete; use a plasterer's trowel for the walls and apply the concrete from the bottom upwards.

Smooth the surface and check it is level by gently placing a spirit level on the floor.

Mesh wire
Press a layer of wire mesh into the wet concrete; if you are using more than one piece, make sure there is an overlap of 4in (10cm).

Lay a further 2in (5cm) layer of concrete over the mesh, incorporating a colour pigment if you wish. Trowel the surface smooth.

Setting regime
It is very important to leave the concrete to set in the correct way. If it sets too quickly, hairline cracks will appear over the whole structure and in icy conditions these will gradually develop into larger cracks.

To protect the wet concrete from rapid moisture loss, cover the surface with damp hessian sacking. Keep the sacking moist and do not remove it until the concrete has set, after about one or two weeks, depending on the weather. The resulting surface will be hard and glossy-looking.

Alternatively, water the concrete. Using a watering can with a fine rose, sprinkle the concrete with water regularly to keep it damp. This may need to be three times a day in very hot weather; do not over-water.

Sealant and waterproof paint (see page 40)
Once the concrete is completely dry, paint on a sealant or waterproof paint.

Laying a concrete pool

1 Mark out and excavate the site, remove any sharp stones or roots and tamp the surface down. In areas of heavy clay, lay a foundation of hardcore or sand.

2 Underline the excavation with a sheet of plastic, moulding it to fit the contours of the pool. Smooth out as many folds and wrinkles as possible.

3 Working from a board on the floor of the excavation, start at one end of the pool and lay a uniform layer of concrete over the inside, smoothing it for an even finish.

4 Cover the excavation with a layer of wire mesh, pressing it a little way into the wet concrete, and lay a final layer of concrete over the pool.

5 Cover the surface of the concrete with damp hessian sacking. Water the sacks regularly to keep them moist and remove them once the concrete has set.

Concrete pools 2

Wooden shuttering is often used to form a mould in which to pour the concrete. This method of casting concrete demands considerable knowledge and a high degree of practical skill; the resulting pool will only be watertight if the concrete is of exactly the right consistency and tamped down thoroughly and evenly on casting.

Design
Shuttering is mainly used for pools with steeply angled sides.

Shuttering
The shutter boards must be very well constructed, with internal and external bracing; a marginal shelf will need separate shuttering.

The shuttering must be prepared well in advance of the concreting process.

Tools and materials
You will need: a tape measure, a saw and a hammer, 3in (8cm) round-headed nails, a set square, a plank of wood and a spirit level, planed timber at least 1in (2.5cm) thick and 4-6in (10-15cm) wide or several lengths of marine ply, a number of upright posts a minimum of 3 x 2in (8 x 5cm) thick on which to nail them, two lengths of stout timber about ½ x 3in (1.25 x 8cm) wide and 12in (30cm) longer than the pool and some wooden pegs.

Square and rectangular pools
The following measurements are required for

SHUTTERING

Make the shuttering by nailing strong, thick, planed lengths of timber to upright posts. The boards must be straight and the surface smooth; make sure the timbers are tightly fitted together with no cracks in between them. Use plenty of nails to secure the timber to the posts; the shuttering must be strong enough to bear the considerable weight of the concrete without buckling out of shape.

If your design includes a marginal shelf, make a separate set of shuttering the height of the shelf. Joint the two sets together using stout timber and strong nails.

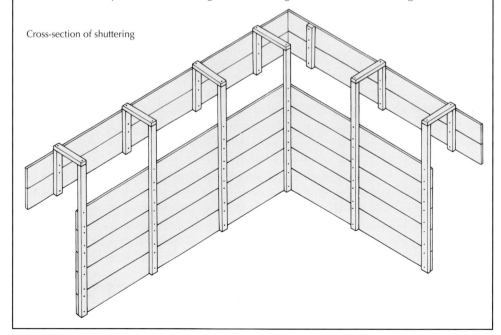

Cross-section of shuttering

a 6in (15cm) layer of concrete with a 1in (2.5cm) sand underlining on the pool floor and the marginal shelf.

Subtract 12in (30cm) from the length and width of the pool and cut the timber to these measurements. Measure the height of the pool, subtract 7in (18cm) and cut the posts to this length.

Place the posts 2ft (60cm) apart and nail the timber to the posts to construct a solid, firm, smooth panel with no cracks in it. This is the shuttering board.

If your design includes a marginal shelf, build the main shuttering to the height of the shelf plus an extra 7in (18cm), but do not alter the length of the upright posts. Make the marginal shuttering the height of the shelf minus 7in (18cm).

When you have finished you should have four panels corresponding to the four sides of the pool, and, if applicable, four marginal panels. Firmly nail the panels together, checking each angle with a set square, and make sure the shuttering is level by spanning it with a board and spirit level.

If incorporating a marginal shelf, join the main shuttering to the marginal shuttering by nailing a length of wood the width of the shelf across the top of both structures.

In order to hang the shuttering in place, span the whole structure from one end to the other with two or three lengths of strong timber. Nail in wooden pegs at each end of the timber, and nail the timber onto the shuttering with a 6in (15cm) overhang each side. If you leave the nails slightly raised they will be easier to take out once you have finished.

Circular pools

You will need to construct curved shuttering for a circular pool.

Follow the instructions for square or rectangular pools, but use marine ply instead of timber to construct the structure. This is a very flexible material which will bend and curve to fit contours.

Take a length of marine ply and bend it to fit the sweep of the pool. Nail a strong piece of timber across the end of the curved panel to keep it in place.

Using shuttering

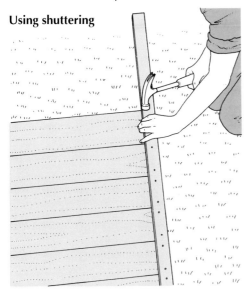

1 Starting at the bottom of the post and working upwards, nail lengths of timber one on top of the other to the uprights to form a smooth wooden panel.

2 Before installing the shuttering, lay a concrete floor lined with wire mesh and insert metal rods in the wet concrete along the edge of the floor.

Concrete pools 3

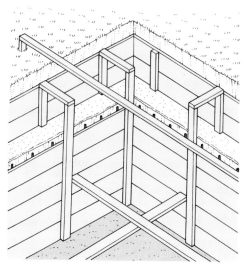

3 Water the shuttering or paint it with limewash before installing it. This will stop the concrete sticking, making it easier to remove the shuttering.

4 Position the structure in the excavation and firmly push the pegs of the supporting timber into the ground. Brace the shuttering inside with strong timbers.

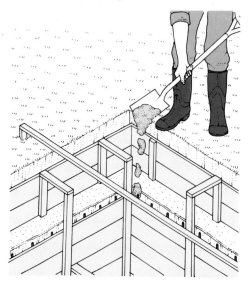

5 Pour a 2in (5cm) layer of concrete into the cavity between the walls and the shuttering; make sure the shuttering is still damp or coated with limewash.

6 Using a stout stick, tamp the concrete down to drive out the air. Continue adding the concrete in layers, tamping as you go, until the walls are complete.

Once the shuttering has been prepared, the concreting can commence.

Tools and materials
You will need: waterproof gardening gloves, a shovel, a plasterer's trowel, a watering can with a fine rose, hessian sacks, builder's sand and concrete, wire mesh with a 2in (5cm) mesh size, 1/2in (1.25cm) diameter reinforced metal rods, water or limewash, sealant or waterproof paint.

Marking out and excavating
Mark out and excavate a hole 6in (15cm) larger and 7in (18cm) deeper (9in (23cm) deeper in areas of heavy clay) than the finished pool but of the same shape and contours. Check the excavation is level.

Underlining
Remove all sharp stones and roots so the surface area is smooth, and tamp the soil down firmly. Place a 1in (2.5cm) layer of builder's sand on the floor of the excavation and smooth it down. In areas of heavy clay, lay a 3in (8m) layer of sand or hardcore.

7 For the marginal shelf, lay a concrete floor lined with wire mesh and push metal rods in around the edges. Lay the concrete in layers, tamping down each one.

Laying the floor
Lay a 4in (10cm) layer of concrete over the floor, smooth it down and cover it with a piece of wire mesh. Lay a further 2in (5cm) layer of concrete over the wire mesh and smooth the surface.

Reinforcing the walls
Push metal rods the same height as the pool into the wet concrete around the edge of the main pool at 6in (15cm) intervals. Alternatively, line the walls with pieces of wire mesh; each piece must overlap the next by a minimum of 4in (10cm).

Positioning the shuttering
Using a watering can with a fine rose, soak the shuttering in water or apply a coat of limewash; this will help prevent the concrete from sticking to the wood.

Position the shuttering in the pool cavity, with the pegs of the timber supports firmly in the ground on either side of the pool; it should hang just above the level of the concrete on the main floor. Firmly brace the structure inside with two or three strong timbers wedged lengthways and widthways so that it will withstand the pressure of the concrete.

Constructing the walls
Shovel a 2in (5cm) layer of concrete into the cavity between the walls and the shuttering and tamp it down thoroughly, using a stout piece of wood, to get rid of the air pockets. Repeat this process until the top of the shuttering or the marginal shelf is reached.

Lay a 4in (15cm) layer of concrete on the floor of the shelf and cover it with wire mesh. Either push metal rods every 6in (15cm) into the concrete around the walls or line the walls with wire mesh, and lay a 2in (5cm) layer of concrete over the mesh floor. Concrete the marginal walls, following the same tamping method previously described.

Leave the concrete to set according to the setting regime on page 42; the shuttering can be removed after three or four days.

Sealant and waterproof paint (see page 40)
Once it is dry, paint the inside of the pond with either sealant or waterproof paint to stop free-lime leaching into the pool water.

Clay-puddled pools 1

It is possible to construct an earth-bottomed pool or bog garden (see page 54) by puddling the excavation with clay and covering the pool floor and margins with soil. This can be planted in the manner of a wildlife pool (see page 104) or plants can be grown in planting baskets, but on no account should plants be grown in the puddling as their roots will penetrate the clay and the pool will then leak.

Clay puddling is not very practical and needs regular maintenance. Pools must be frequently topped up with water as the puddle ceases to be watertight if it dries out. Any exposed areas above the water level must be watered to keep the clay supple and stop it shrinking; use a watering can with a fine rose. The puddle is also susceptible to damage from worms unless it is properly treated with soot or ash before the pool is puddled.

Design

A puddled pool can be any shape and can include a marginal shelf. The walls should be at an angle of approximately 45°; if steeper, the clay will not adhere to the surface.

Tools and materials

You will need: thick rubber gloves, a plasterer's trowel, a board from which to work, a watering can with a fine rose, soot or ash, clay and damp hessian sacks.

Clay

A good quality clay with a high degree of plasticity must be used for puddling, and local clays like London clay and Cambridge boulder clay can be recommended. Test the clay by rolling it in your hands; it should be moist and malleable, not dry and crumbly.

As well as natural clays, there are two types of processed clay available: sodium and calcium clays, known collectively as bentonite clay. These clays are difficult to handle and should only be used for pools over 6 x 8ft (1.8 x 2.4m), with a minimum depth of 4ft (1.2m). This is because a chemical harmful to fish leaches from the clay into the pool water, and the smaller and shallower the pool, the higher the chemical concentration.

Sodium and calcium clays are available as powders which swell into an impermeable

Clay puddling

1 Mark out and excavate the pool. Remove any sharp stones or roots that may otherwise puncture the clay. Tamp the surface down.

2 Dampen the excavation with water using a watering can with a fine rose. Do not use too much water or it will form muddy puddles in the soil.

gel when mixed with water. Sodium clay swells approximately fifteen times its volume, and calcium clay eight times. If it dries out, sodium clay will re-swell if water is added, but calcium clay will not. To minimize chemical leaching, cover the marginal shelf, the floor and the walls of the pool with soil while the clay is still wet.

Up to a third of the clay, as measured by volume, is air which will disperse when water is added. To calculate the amount of clay needed for puddling a 6in (15cm) layer, follow the instructions for concrete on page 40 and multiply the resulting figure by one third to account for the air present. This should give you the correct quantity.

Marking out and excavating

Mark out and excavate the site to the desired shape and design, taking into account the 6in (15cm) layer of clay and, if applicable, the 4in (10cm) layer of soil on the pool floor and marginal shelf. Remove all sharp sticks and stones and tamp the surface down with the back of a spade or a piece of wood.

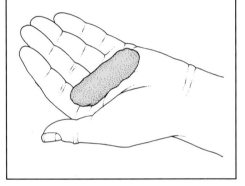

TESTING CLAY

To test the clay, take a handful and remove any stones, twigs and other debris. Roll the clay in the palm of your hand to form an elongated clay "worm".

If the clay is suitable for puddling it will be pliable, damp and hold together well. However, if the clay is dry, it will crumble and should not be used because it will not be watertight.

3 Before the water dries, carefully sprinkle the area with a light, even covering of soot or ash to stop worms penetrating the puddling. This is best done with a shovel.

4 Fill a bucket with clay and place a board on the floor of the pool. Starting at one end of the excavation, plaster the walls with puddle in a smooth, uniform layer.

Clay-puddled pools 2

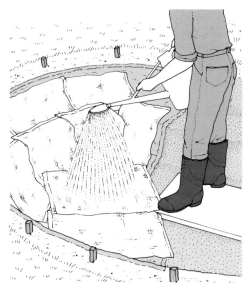

5 Work your way along the excavation and lay three layers of puddle, each approximately 2in (5cm) thick; there should be 6in (15cm) of puddle covering the excavation.

6 Do not let the puddle dry out otherwise it will crack; keep it moist with damp sacking or water the surface regularly with a fine-rosed watering can.

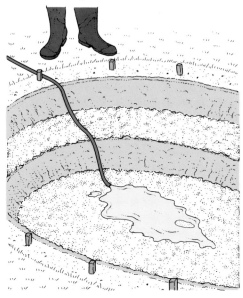

7 Cover the pool floor and marginal shelf with a 4in (10cm) layer of soil while the clay is still damp.

8 Fill the pool with water trickled from a hosepipe. The pool must always be kept full; top it up regularly.

Underlining
Dampen the excavation with water and sprinkle the area with a layer of soot or ash, enough to lightly cover the soil. This will prevent earthworms from pushing up through the puddle, causing leaks.

Puddling
Add enough water to the clay to make it moist and sticky but not wet. Place a board inside the pool from which to work and, wearing a pair of thick rubber gloves, use your hands to plaster a 2in (5cm) layer of clay puddle over the inside of the pool. Start at one end of the pool and puddle the wall from the bottom upwards before puddling a section of floor, and continue in this manner until the whole excavation is covered, gradually moving the board across the floor to the other end of the pool until the entire surface is covered.

Repeat the puddling process in 2in (5cm) layers until the puddle is 6in (15cm) deep. Do not let the clay dry out: each finished layer must be covered with wet sacking or watered with a fine-rosed watering can until the next layer is applied. Keep the unused clay damp in a similar way.

Introducing soil and water
Cover the wet clay on the floor and marginal shelf with 4in (10cm) of soil and fill the pool with water immediately, before the puddle can dry. To avoid disturbing the soil, trickle water into the pool from a hosepipe.

Once the pool is planted, scatter a 1/2in (1.25cm) dressing of clean pea gravel over the marginal shelf.

If using planting baskets, do not lay any soil but fill the pool with water before introducing the baskets.

Plants to avoid
Vigorous species such as *Phragmites australis*, *Sparganium erectum* (syn. *S. ramosum*), *Typha angustifolia* and *T. latifolia* should be avoided. They all have strong, spreading root systems which are capable of quickly growing through the soil and puncturing even the best puddled pools, causing the water to slowly leak out.

NATURAL POOLS

On areas of heavy clay it is possible to make a pool in the existing soil.

Excavate the pool to the finished shape and size, with or without a marginal shelf. Remove all sharp stones and roots and tamp the soil down with the back of a spade or a piece of wood. To compact the soil further, tread the surface until it is hard and smooth. Unless you are planting in baskets, lay a 4in (10cm) layer of soil on the pool floor and marginal shelf. Slowly fill the pool with water trickled from a hosepipe. Dress the marginal shelf with 1/2in (1.25cm) of pea gravel once it is planted.

Wildlife pools

Although similar to an ornamental pool, a wildlife pool incorporates certain construction and design features that will greatly assist the wildlife population and create a more natural looking feature. It is also planted with plants, many of them native, which attract wildlife (see page 140).

Among the most satisfactory wildlife pools are those made with a layer of polythene or builder's plastic sandwiched between two layers of soil, although clay puddling can also be used (see page 48).

Design

Design a simple shape which includes a peninsula or inlet; this will provide a secluded nesting site and encourage wildlife.

At least one third of the pool edge should be gently sloping at an angle of approximately 20°; this area can be made into a beach to allow wildlife easy access. The rest of the pool should have a shelf for marginal plants and steep sides of approximately 75°.

The pool should also have a central area over 3ft (90cm) deep; this will help stabilize the overall water temperature, providing a more stable environment. In large pools, build a small island in the middle of the pond to act as a refuge for wildlife; incorporate a bog garden if you wish (see page 54).

Tools and materials

You will need: a plasterer's trowel, gardening gloves, bricklayer's sand, fleece, geo-textile, polyester matting or old carpet and a mixture of large and small pebbles and pea gravel.

Marking out and excavating

Use a length of hosepipe to outline the pool. Excavate the site, making the hole 4in (10cm) larger than the proposed pool.

Underlining

Remove any sharp stones or sticks and line the excavation with a 1in (2.5cm) layer of damp bricklayer's sand, fleece, geo-textile or polyester matting (see page 36). Make sure the surface is smooth.

Installing the liner

Calculate the amount of polythene or plastic needed (see page 10). Place it over the surface of the excavation and smooth out the wrinkles into a few large folds.

Once the lining material is correctly installed, bury the edges in 3in (8cm) of soil.

Introducing the soil

Cover the floor and margins with a 4in (10cm) layer of soil. Fill the pool with water, carefully trickling it into the pond using a hosepipe so as to disturb the soil as little as possible.

Once planted, cover the surface of the marginal shelf with a 1/2in (1.25cm) dressing of clean pea gravel.

The beach area

Position large pebbles around the edge of the sloping area to form the boundaries of the beach and, using smaller pebbles and gravel, build a ramp leading from the pool edge to the pool floor.

Edging

Arrange stones and soil around the edge of the pool to form pockets in which to grow appropriate plants.

Constructing a wildlife pool

1 Having marked out and excavated the site, lay the underlining. Next, cover the excavation with a sheet of plastic, moulding it into the contours of the pool.

BUILDING AN ISLAND

Any pool over 20ft (6m) sq is large enough to accommodate a small island, which should cover approximately one eighth of the surface area of the pool. Construct the island while the pool is empty, using soil-filled hessian sacks.

Arrange the sacks around the perimeter of the island to form a ring, and fill the middle with soil or gravel. Continue building in layers until the desired height is reached, using good-quality heavy soil to fill in the last 6in (15cm) of the ring.

2 Smooth out any wrinkles in the plastic and, using a shovel, lay a 4in (10cm) layer of soil on the pool floor and marginal shelf, and a little way up the gently sloping sides.

3 Make a stony beach on the sloping ground. Arrange large stones around the outside of the beach as edging, and fill the area with small pebbles and gravel.

Bog gardens 1

A bog garden may be constructed as an integral part of a water feature or it may form a separate unit which abuts the pool area. In both cases, the pool and bog garden should be considered as part of the same scheme and therefore should be designed and constructed at the same time, although this is not essential if the bog garden is a separate but complementary feature.

An integrated bog area will draw a substantial amount of water from the pond, which must be topped up regularly. If the water level falls below the level of the soil, the bog will dry out. Separate bog gardens require regular watering by hand or with a hosepipe to keep the soil saturated, otherwise the plants will quickly die.

Design

A bog area can be any shape but it must have a minimum depth of 1-1½ ft (30-45cm) otherwise it will dry out too quickly. To avoid looking out of scale and drying out towards the back, it should be no bigger than the surface area of the pool.

Tools and materials

You will need: waterproof gardening gloves, a plasterer's trowel, bricklayer's sand, fleece, geo-textile, polyester matting or old carpet, soil, gravel, some stones and a piece of fine mesh plastic netting.

Butyl rubber is the best material to use for constructing a bog garden that is integral to a pool, but puddled clay can also be used. As a separate feature, however, the bog area can be lined with a plastic or PVC liner or a pre-formed unit.

Marking out and excavating

For an integral pool and bog garden, mark out the site so that the two features are about 3-4in (8-10cm) apart and excavate. The interconnecting wall must be 3in (8cm) lower than the pool edge.

Underlining

Remove any stones or other sharp objects and line the excavation with a 1in (2.5cm) layer of bricklayer's sand, fleece, geo-textile, polyester matting or old carpet.

Making a bog garden

1 Make sure both excavations are free of sharp stones or roots that may otherwise puncture the liner, and lay an underlining of the chosen material.

2 Carefully place the liner over the pool and bog area, making sure it is centred over the two excavations. This may involve two or three attempts.

EXCAVATING

When constructing an integrated bog garden, the pool and bog area must be situated alongside each other so that water can flow from the pool into the bog.

Excavate the two features to the required depth. Take care not to damage the interconnecting wall, which must be lower than the edge of the pool.

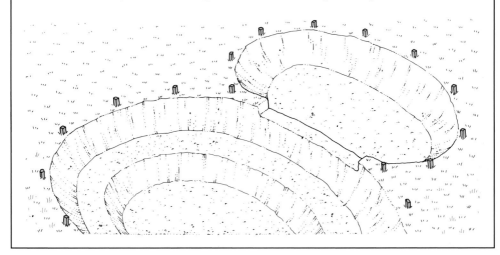

3 Using a hosepipe, fill the pool with water to just below the level of the interconnecting wall. As the pool fills, lift the stones up to free the liner.

4 Cover the floor of the bog garden with a layer of gravel for drainage, and fill the area with soil to just below the top of the interconnecting wall.

Bog gardens 2

ARTIFICIAL STREAMS

A natural stream that is constantly flowing will always retain a damp bankside area, but an artificial stream will need a bog area to be constructed to achieve the same effect. To calculate the amount of liner needed, use twice the amount needed for the stream alone (see page 10).

When excavating the stream, dig an additional shallow area along its length, approximately 9in (23cm) deep; the interconnecting wall must be approximately 2in (5cm) lower than the stream edge.

Line the stream and bog area and bury the edges of the liner in 3in (8cm) of soil. Using soil-filled hessian sacks, build a barrier along the interconnecting wall, and fill the bog area with soil. Choose spreading marginal plants to disguise the barrier.

5 Build a barrier of rocks and stones along the interconnecting wall; larger stones are better than smaller ones, which may fall into the pool.

6 Once the barrier is complete, carefully place a layer of fine mesh plastic netting along the back of the barrier, on the side of the bog garden.

Installing the liner

Lay the liner over both features and anchor it in place with stones. Fill the pool with water to the height of the interconnecting wall, releasing the liner from under the stones as the pool fills. Lay a 1-1½in (2.5-2.75cm) layer of gravel on the floor of the bog area to help drainage, and fill the bog with soil (see page 98) to the level of the interconnecting wall.

Puddled clay

For a puddled clay bog garden, follow the instructions on page 48. Puddle the pool and fill it with water to just below the level of the interconnecting wall, watering the exposed puddle until the pool is topped up. Puddle the bog area in the same way and fill it with soil.

Creating the bog

The pool and bog area must be separated by a barrier that allows water to pass through into the bog but prevents soil from washing back and entering the pool.

Build a barrier out of rocks and stones between the pool and the bog, firming each one down. Place a layer of fine mesh plastic netting behind the barrier, on the side of the bog garden. Fill the bog area with soil to the top of the barrier, and raise the level of the pool so that the water trickles over the barrier into the bog garden. Edge the pool (see page 38) and lay turf or plant around the bog feature.

Separate bog gardens

A bog garden can be a separate feature abutting a pool. This is usually the case if the pool is already installed and the bog area is an afterthought, or if the pool is built using a pre-formed unit. It is also possible to have a bog area on its own, in isolation from any water.

In such cases, any type of liner or pre-formed unit can be used to construct the bog garden although a liner is more versatile.

Mark out and excavate the area and install a liner or pre-formed shell as you would a pool. Cover the floor of the feature with a 1-1½in (30-45cm) layer of gravel to help drainage, and fill the bog area with soil.

In order to maintain the bog effect, the soil must be kept moist at all times.

7 Shovel more soil into the bog area, packing it behind the barrier. Once the bog garden is full, the soil should be the same level as the surrounding ground.

8 Top up the pool with water. When the pool is full, water will seep through the barrier into the bog garden, keeping the soil moist. The bog area can now be planted.

Raised/indoor pools 1

Most raised pools consist of brick or wooden free-standing frameworks lined with liners or pre-formed shells. Pre-formed concrete sections are also available (see page 86).

Raised pools can be circular or geometric in shape, ideal for patios or terraces. They can equally well be built indoors as decorative features of conservatories and sun rooms.

Design
The shape and size of pool will depend on personal choice and the type of materials available. If using a pre-formed shell, build the framework about 6in (15cm) wider and longer than the shell and 1in (2.5cm) higher, to allow for backfilling and a cushioning layer of sand on the floor of the excavation.

Timber structures
Timber is used for straight-sided and angular raised pools.

Tools and materials
You will need: a spade, a set square, a spirit level, a number of railway sleepers or timber lengths (use either sawn or rough wood,

depending on the design) with a minimum cross-section of 4 x 6in (10 x 15cm), and some screws or dowels.

Preparing the ground and marking out
Level the pool area and mark out the pool, allowing for the width of the timber.

Building the frame
Cut the timber to the dimensions of the pool. Carefully notch the lengths together with halving joints: at one end of the piece of wood mark off a rectangle using a set square. Cut the rectangle out to a depth of half the height of the timber. Do the same for the interlocking piece, cutting out a corresponding notch. When in position, the two should form a neat joint. Adapt the shape and angle of the joints for pools that do not have right angles.

With a set square, ensure that the corners of the structure are square or of equal angles and fasten them using dowels or screws. Make sure each timber is level before the next one is positioned. Place the layers of timber on top of one another so that the joints are staggered, until the required height is reached.

Building a raised wooden structure

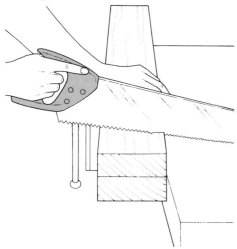

1 Join the lengths of wood together using halving joints. At the end of each piece of wood, cut out a rectangle half the height of the piece of wood.

2 Make sure the ground is level and build the first layer of the frame. Fit two interlocking pieces of timber together to form a neat, close-fitting joint.

FIXING THE LINER

Underline the raised structure by carefully folding the material into the corners and smoothing it down. Tack the underlining in place using small nails. Place the liner in the raised structure, pleating the folds into each corner. Once the liner is smooth, secure it by trapping it under the top layer of timber.

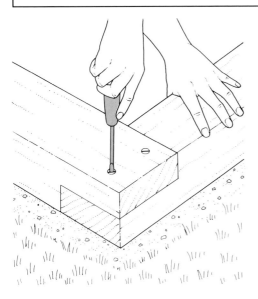

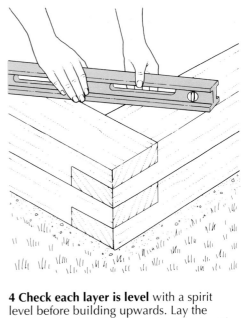

3 Firmly fasten the corners in place with screws or dowels, having first checked with a set square that the corners are square or of equal angles.

4 Check each layer is level with a spirit level before building upwards. Lay the timber so that the joints are staggered until the framework is the correct height.

Raised/indoor pools 2

Brick structures

Square, rectangular, hexagonal and circular raised pools can be made from bricks.

Tools and materials

You will need: a pair of gardening gloves, a tape measure, a set square, a spirit level and a small plank of wood, a plasterer's trowel, a pointing trowel, a piece of string, mortar (see page 34), facing bricks and either coping or paving stones.

Marking out and excavating

When marking out the site allow an extra 9-10in (23-25cm) all round to accommodate the width of a double row of bricks.

Excavate the foundation to a depth of 6in (15cm) and check that it is level, otherwise the brick structure will be uneven.

Laying the floor

Lay a 6in (15cm) layer of concrete (see page 40) and check that it is level by gently placing a spirit level on the surface. Follow the setting regime (see page 42); it should take between one and two weeks to set.

Building the structure

For the brick raised pool, mix the mortar and build a raised structure using English bond, if necessary trimming the corner bricks with a cold chisel for the correct angle. For circular structures, use a double row of curved bricks laid in a running bond.

Corners

Stretch a length of string between each corner so you have a straight line.

Using a plasterer's trowel, begin in one corner and spread a ½in (1.25cm) layer of mortar on the floor and on the ends of each brick and construct a corner. With a spirit level and set square, check the bricks are level and square and construct the other corners. Check that the whole structure is square by measuring the diagonals: they should be exactly the same length.

Walls

Lay the rest of the bricks; there must be a ½in (1.25cm) layer of mortar between each brick face for a secure bond. Always check that each brick is level before going on to the

ENGLISH AND RUNNING BOND

A brick laid lengthways is called a stretcher and a brick laid widthways is called a header.

English bond consists of stretcher and header courses, three or five courses of stretcher to one of header. Running bond consists of stretcher courses with alternate rows staggered by half a brick; it is not as strong as English bond and for this reason it is often laid in a double row.

Use a single row of bricks laid in English bond for straight structures; curved structures should be built with a double row of running bond.

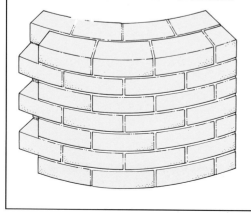

Building a raised brick structure

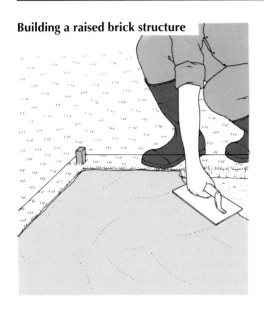

1 Mark out the site and excavate. Using a plasterer's trowel, lay a smooth concrete floor. Check it is level by resting a spirit level on the wet concrete.

2 Having marked out the periphery with string, lay a strip of mortar on the concrete floor and butter the end of each brick with more mortar.

3 Build the corners first, trimming bricks if necessary, and check each corner is square or of an equal angle. Use English brick bond for the walls.

4 Check each course is level before building the next. Place a spirit level along the wall; if it is not level, tap the brick down with the shaft of the trowel.

Raised/indoor pools 3

next and, after about three or four layers, point what you have built. This is done by smoothing off the mortar surface and, using a small pointing trowel, filling in the gaps between the bricks with more mortar for a neat finish. It should take a minimum of 48 hours for the walling to set; it must be covered with a plastic sheet if it rains.

Capping
There are a number of ways to finish off a raised structure. Either cap the top with bricks laid in a row on their edges, or use coping stones or paving slabs. If the raised structure is to accommodate a liner, do not cap the structure until the liner is in place because the liner must be secure under the capping.

Rendering
Brick structures can be made waterproof by rendering. Once dry, plaster the inside of the raised pool with a ½in (1.25cm) layer of waterproof mortar (see page 34). Follow the setting regime, and finish off by sealing the inside with a coat of sealant or plastic waterproof paint (see page 40).

Liners
Both timber and brick structures can be lined with PVC or butyl rubber liners.

Tools and materials
Depending on your method of construction you will need: a hammer and small round-headed nails, wooden battens 2 x 1in (5 x 2.5cm) and underlining material such as fleece, geo-textile or polyester matting; old carpet can also be used.

Installing the liner
Line the structure with fleece, geo-textile, polyester matting or old carpet, held in position by industrial adhesive or coping stones; the lining of wooden structures can be tacked in place with small round-headed nails instead of adhesive.

Calculate how much liner you will need (see page 10) and place it inside the structure, pleating the folds of excess liner into each corner. Add water and smooth the creases as the pool fills.

Secure the liner in place by trapping it under the top layer of timber or coping stones.

5 Using a pointing trowel, point the brickwork by filling the gaps in between each brick with mortar and smoothing it off for an even finish.

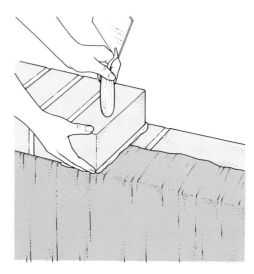

6 Cap the structure with bricks laid on their edges, coping stones or pieces of paving. If using a liner, install it first and trap the edges under the capping.

Pre-formed shells

Pre-formed shells can be used to line brick or timber structures. Choose a black or dark grey unit as this will show less than a bright blue one. The shell must be a minimum of 6in (15cm) smaller than the raised structure and approximately 1in (2.5cm) shorter. Like pool units, they will need backfilling in place.

Tools and materials

You will need: gardening gloves, a spirit level, a trowel, builder's sand, some bricks or stones, backfilling material such as fine soil, dry builder's sand or pea gravel, and paving stones and mortar (optional).

Installing the shell

Lay a 1in (2.5cm) layer of damp builder's sand on the pool floor. Position the shell centrally inside the structure, making sure that it is level. Prop up any parts which do not touch the floor with bricks or stones. Fill the shell with 4in (10cm) of water and then backfill (see page 32); use soil towards the top if planting. For a formal finish, edge the pool with paving or brick set in mortar (see page 34).

PRE-FORMED UNITS

Lay an edge of paving set in a bed of mortar; alternatively, for a softer look, backfill the last layer of the cavity around the unit with soil and plant round the edges.

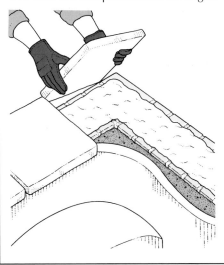

7 Alternatively, render the brick structure with a thin layer of waterproof mortar plastered on with a plasterer's trowel. Smooth the surface.

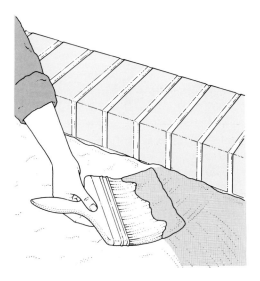

8 Coat the rendered brick structure with a layer of sealant. Apply this with a large paint brush in even strokes; waterproof paint can also be used.

Containers

Tubs, barrels and sinks can be successfully adapted to make miniature water features suitable for terraces and patios, either on their own or arranged together in a group. They can also be placed indoors, in conservatories and sun rooms.

Tubs and half barrels
It is easy to make an attractive pool out of a tub or half barrel.

Tubs and barrels must be thoroughly cleaned before use; do not use old wooden containers without lining them first as they are often impregnated with oil, tar or other noxious materials that will pollute the water. Any new tubs that have been treated with wood preservative must also be lined.

Tools and materials
You will need: gardening gloves, a scrubbing brush, a blow torch, butyl rubber or PVC liner, 2 x 1in (5 x 2.5cm) dark wooden battens or dark-coloured flexible carpet edging and some screws.

Cleaning the tub
Thoroughly clean the tub using a scrubbing brush and clean water. Add a pinch of potassium permanganate (remember to wear rubber gloves) but never use detergent as it may seep into the wood and harm plants and fish.

Charring
Plain wood barrels and tubs can be preserved by charring. Turn the tub on its side and run a blow torch over the interior to produce a hard, blackened surface. This should be resistant to decay. Do not put the tub in a hot, dry atmosphere when empty as the wood will shrink and split.

Lining the tub
Use black liner as this will hardly show. First calculate how much liner you will need (see page 10) and then place it in the tub, making several bold, neat folds rather than numerous small ones.

Add water to within about 3in (8cm) of the top of the container and fold the edge of the liner over and inside itself, next to the barrel. Using small pieces of batten placed every 4in (10cm), firmly screw the liner to the tub or cask so that it is fixed just above the water level. Alternatively, use dark-coloured carpet edging in the same way.

Sinks
Provided they are watertight, old glazed sinks make excellent small water gardens; the exterior can be coated for a stone-like appearance. This must be done in cool weather otherwise the coating rapidly dries, shrinks and falls off.

Tools and materials
You will need: waterproof gardening gloves, a scrubbing brush, a small pointing trowel, moss peat, sand, cement, PVA (polyvinyl acetate) adhesive, mud, liquid seaweed fertilizer or milk and cow dung (optional).

Cleaning
Thoroughly clean the inside and outside of the sink with a scrubbing brush and allow it to dry. Make sure any soap is rinsed out.

Mixing the coating
Mix two parts of moss peat, one part sand and one part cement in their dry states. Add enough water to make a stiff but workable mixture that will adhere to the sink's walls.

Coating the walls
Liberally spread PVA adhesive over a portion of the sink to serve as a bonding agent, and after 10-15 minutes the glue will become tacky. Using a small pointing trowel, coat the

---

MINIATURE WATERSCAPE
Using chunks of rock and small plants, construct a miniature waterscape in a sink. Millstone grit, slate and granite are appropriate, but do not use limestone or sandstone as they will crumble.

Coat the sink to give it a stone-like appearance, if desired, and leave it to dry. Arrange the rocks in the sink so that they are piled above the proposed water level, and fill the gaps between each rock with aquatic planting compost. Plant the pockets and carefully fill the sink with water (see page 104).

exterior of the sink with a ½in (1.25cm) layer of the peat, sand and cement mixture. Continue the coating 3in (8cm) down the inside walls. Smooth the surface or roughen it for a more natural effect. Once dry, the coating is tough and water resistant.

The coating will take up to two weeks to dry, depending on the weather. Once dry, paint it with mud, liquid seaweed fertilizer or a stiff mixture of milk and cow manure to encourage the rapid development of moss and algae for a weathered look.

Tubs and half barrels

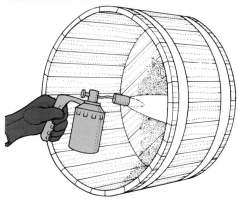

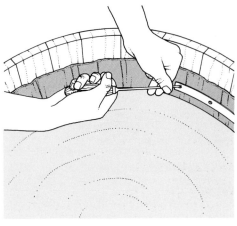

1 Clean the tub or half barrel with water and, once dry, carefully char the inside with a blow torch.

2 Once lined, fill the container with water and secure the edge of the liner with battens or carpet edging.

Sinks

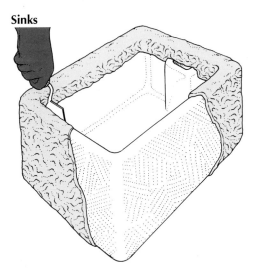

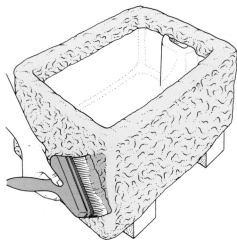

1 Having cleaned the sink, apply a layer of adhesive and, when this is tacky, coat the sink with a layer of the peat, sand and cement mixture.

2 Once the coating is dry, paint the surface with mud, liquid seaweed fertilizer or milk and cow manure; this will encourage the growth of moss and algae.

Introduction

Running water adds much to a garden and there are a variety of moving water features which the amateur gardener can construct successfully, the main ones being streams, waterfalls and fountains.

Methods and materials
Streams and waterfalls may be constructed using a liner, pre-formed units or concrete. The easiest method is to use pre-formed units because liners and concrete need very accurate excavations which can be rather time-consuming and difficult to achieve.

Fountains can be placed in any type of pool, but heavy stone fountain heads should only be used in concrete pools that will support their weight. Do not consider installing such a fountain in fibreglass pre-formed shells as the units are likely to crack.

Pumps (see page 14)
Fountains and artificial waterfalls and streams all require a water pump to provide running water. Pumps are available in a range of designs. Different jets will produce different fountains, anything from a bell fountain to a geyser; replace the fountain nozzle with a delivery hose, and the pump can be used for a waterfall or stream.

Calculate the volume of water in the feature and the desired rate of flow (see page 10) and decide how the water is to be delivered to produce the desired effect. For streams and waterfalls, take the delivery hose out of the water and run it up beside the feature to its source. Disguise the hose with a few carefully positioned rocks and plants, and build the pump outlet into a natural-looking arrangement of stones to create the effect of a spring feeding the feature.

Siting and marking out
It is often difficult to site streams and waterfalls as they must blend in with the surrounding landscape. They also need to be constructed with appropriate falls to provide a natural effect.

Use sand to mark out the outline of the feature on the chosen site, amending it as required, until you feel it is correctly positioned. Do this by walking slowly around the area while trickling sand from a bag.

If the proposed stream or waterfall is to be part of a larger scheme, mark out all the features to check that the overall look and scale are right before excavating. As streams and waterfalls are situated on a gradient, a range of heights has to be considered rather than a flat excavation.

Natural springs
Natural water sources are not common, but any springs present in the garden may be made into a water feature. Either leave the spring to bubble to the surface and plant around the source or, if the spring appears some way up a slope, create a header pool and stream, or a waterfall if the surrounding terrain is suitable.

Springs are not predictable sources of water and the quantity of water they deliver will change with different seasons. Only grow plants around them that will tolerate extreme weather conditions.

Natural streams and waterfalls
No artificial construction can match the appearance of a natural stream or waterfall, although man-made features may still be attractive in a garden setting. Natural streams and waterfalls vary considerably in character: some are fast-moving and deep while others are shallow and slow-moving, with stony or pebbly bottoms. Such features should be left undisturbed, apart from planting appropriate waterside plants and perhaps providing some stepping stones if required. Changes that alter the flow of the stream or waterfall, however, may affect the volume of water that arrives downstream and are not permitted without reference to and permission from the local water authority.

Water flow
One of the greatest problems with some natural streams and waterfalls is the unpredictable nature of their flow. They can be reliable and consistent sources of water during spring, but the water level can drop in summer, and streams and waterfalls often burst their banks during winter, especially after a thaw. Planting on the margins should not include delicate plants that cannot withstand such variations in water flow.

Erosion

Erosion may be a problem with natural streams and waterfalls. This is a continuous process and is most evident on bends, where the current is strongest, which may undermine the banks until they eventually collapse. Sheet erosion of the top soil may also occur along the length of streams. If erosion is a serious problem, large boulders or stones may be used to divert the fast water flow, or wood, treated with a preservative other than creosote, can be used to construct an artificial barrier to protect the bank.

If erosion is not a serious problem, simply grow plants along the margins of the stream or waterfall and on the outside of any bend. The roots will bind the soil so the bank will be less susceptible to erosion.

PREVENTING EROSION

Treated wood is the easiest material to work with and the most acceptable in a natural setting, but do not use creosote as this is harmful to plants.

You will need: a number of strong stakes about 1½ft (45cm) longer than the stream is deep, and some rough planks of wood. An alternative method uses treated larch poles approximately 2ft (60cm) longer than the stream is deep.

Drive the stakes about 1ft (30cm) into the ground along the edge of the stream every 2-3ft (60-90cm), following the line of the bank as closely as possible. Place the rough planks behind them, between the stakes and the bank. This will protect the bank from further erosion. It is easy to disguise the structure by banking up the soil behind the barrier and planting up to the edge. Choose some vigorous-growing plants that will disguise the planks.

Alternatively, drive a number of larch poles into the bank close together to a depth of approximately 18in (45cm) to form a barrier. Trim the tops of the poles to the required level.

1 Drive some stakes into the edge of the stream, closely following the line of the bank. The stakes should be driven in to a depth of 1ft (30cm).

2 Place the rough planks between the stakes and the stream bank to form a solid barrier. Disguise the planks with built-up soil and plants.

Streams 1

Pre-formed units

Streams can be constructed using pre-formed units which are installed in a natural or artificial slope (see page 74).

Pre-formed stream lengths are relatively easy to install but they are difficult to blend in with the surroundings because of their hard outlines and artificial look. Pre-formed units also preclude the use of stepping stones and heavy ornamental stone fountains.

Pre-formed stream lengths are short; for a longer stream, use more than one unit, one set into the other to avoid water leakage. Streams can also be linked together with a series of specially designed pre-formed pools for a more varied look.

The source

An artificial stream should look as though it has a natural water source. A bubbling spring is suitable and easy to construct. Bury the end of the delivery hose in a container full of stones – a small dustbin or bucket is ideal – and sink the container into the ground, merging it into the surroundings with rocks and plants. Alternatively, construct a header pool at the top of the stream with the delivery hose running into it; the hose should be hidden by rocks and plants. Ensure that the outlet of the delivery hose is above the level of water in the header pool or the water will be siphoned out when the pump is switched off.

Design

The slope of a stream should be between 10 and 30°. Water may run straight from the source to a main pool, from where it is recirculated by a pump, or the stream may be designed to flow through a series of shallow waterfalls or small pools. In such cases, the stream unit must lie flat between the pools so that the water runs smoothly along it. Narrowing part of the stream will make the water look as though it is flowing faster at this point; only do this once or twice in the design or it will appear unnatural.

Tools and materials

You will need: waterproof gardening gloves, a plasterer's trowel, a small plank of wood and a spirit level, bricklayer's sand, and fine, stone-free soil for backfilling.

Installing the units

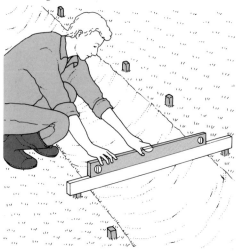

1 Mark out and excavate the stream to the correct dimensions. Span the excavation with a plank of wood and a spirit level to check it is level.

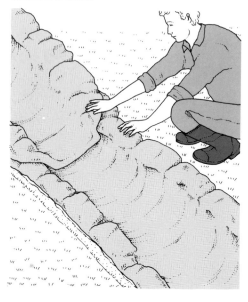

2 Having laid a thick layer of sand, install the units and firm them down. If using more than one, make sure each unit overlaps the one below.

Marking out and excavating

Mark out and excavate a site for the pre-formed stream lengths and any pool units included in your design; each excavation must be the same shape as the pre-formed units but 6in (15cm) longer and wider and 3in (8cm) deeper. If using more than one unit, each one must abut or overlap the one below, depending on the design of the feature. Using a spirit level and a plank of wood, check the excavation is level from side to side.

Underlining

Remove any sharp stones and roots and plaster a 3in (8cm) layer of damp bricklayer's sand onto the floor and sides of the excavation, moulding it into the exact shape.

Installing the units

Starting at the bottom of the feature, position each unit and push it into the sand, checking it is level. Once the units are firmly embedded, backfill the remaining space around them with fine soil, packing it down well. Check the final level of each unit.

The stream bed and margins

Disguise the pre-formed units with carefully positioned stones and pebbles so that the feature looks as natural as possible. Additional stones can be placed on the stream bed to alter the rate of flow (see page 70).

SECTIONAL STREAMS

Sectional pre-formed stream units have special height-adjuster panels that are useful for sloping sites. Each 5ft (1.5m) of stream length can be bridged by a fall of approximately 1ft (30cm) so that when the pump is switched off, the water level is maintained in the individual stream components. These are sealed off from one another by the bridging panels and thus only surplus water runs away into the lower units, leaving each one full of water for a more natural look.

For construction and installation details, follow the method on page 32 for pre-formed sectional pools.

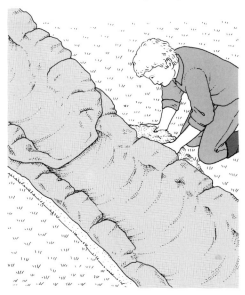

3 Once you have checked the units are level, backfill the excavation with fine soil, packing it down well. Check each unit is level after backfilling.

4 Position the delivery hose in the header pool or at the top of the stream and wedge it in place with stones, disguising it as much as possible.

Streams 2

Liners
Using a liner you are free to create any design, incorporating any number of pools or waterfalls. Use butyl rubber or PVC.

Tools and materials
You will need: waterproof gardening gloves, a plasterer's trowel and bricklayer's sand or underlining material (see page 36).

Marking out and excavating
The success of using a liner depends upon accurate spade work. Excavate the pools and stream to the size and shape required, allowing an extra 1in (2.5cm) all round. For a series of pools and streams, excavate the site so that the pools are deeper at the back, with lips that overlap into the adjacent stream. The stream lengths should also have these lips. The stream units should either lie flat between the pools or be at a slight angle, deeper at the end that receives the water.

Underlining
Remove stones and sharp objects and, using your hands or a plasterer's trowel, line the excavation with a 1in (2.5cm) layer of damp bricklayer's sand or some underlining material.

Installing the liner

1 Mark out and excavate the stream, making sure it is level. Remove any sharp sticks and stones; lay a sand underlining.

Installing the liner
Calculate the amount of liner needed (see page 10); for designs which include a number of pools and streams, use a separate piece of liner for each section of the feature, and allow for vertical overlaps of 6in (15cm).

Spread the liner over the excavation; if using more than one piece, the 6in (15cm) overlap must run in the same direction as the water. Mould the liner into the shape of the excavations and smooth it down.

Bury the edges of the liner under at least 3in (8cm) of soil; the point where soil and liner meet must be above the maximum water level, otherwise the soil will muddy the water and the water will soak away into the surrounding soil.

The stream bed and margins
To avoid puncturing the liner, only use smooth, rounded stones. Position these on the stream bed and along the margins, and grow plants along the bank. Plants can also be grown in hessian bags containing soil, either placed in the water at the edge of the stream or along the banks. If the bags are in the water, grow bog or marginal plants, depending on the water level.

2 Spread the liner over the stream excavation and smooth it down so it fits neatly into the contours of the stream.

THE STREAM BED

Place large stones or pebbles on the stream bed and the pool floors to make the feature look as natural as possible.

Water flow can be modified by using carefully positioned rocks; placed mid-stream they will create the effect of fast-flowing water, while one or two flat stones on the stream bed will have the opposite effect of appearing to slow the water down. Stones may also be positioned in a semi-circle near the bank to provide a calm area in which several types of aquatic plants will grow more successfully than if they were in mid-stream.

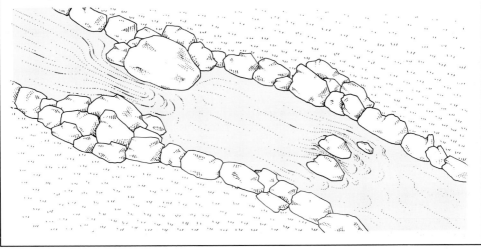

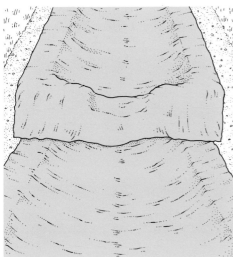

3 If you are using more than one piece of liner, make sure there is a good overlap running in the direction of the water flow.

4 Bury the edge of the liner in at least 3in (8cm) of soil and arrange stones along the stream margin.

Streams 3

Concrete

It is much easier to make a concrete stream than a concrete pool; a stream is shaped and sculptured in an irregular, natural way, while a pool is laid in even, smooth layers. A well-built concrete stream will weather and blend into the surroundings. Concrete waterfalls can also be constructed in a similar manner (see page 78).

Design

The sides of the stream should be at an angle of no more than 45° otherwise the concrete will not adhere. If pools are incorporated into the design, these must be deeper at the back and have lips which overlap the adjacent stream. The more gradual and shallow the lip, the smoother the fall. The stream lengths between each pool must be level or, if angled, deeper at the point at which they receive water. These should also have overlapping lips where necessary.

Tools and materials

See page 42 for concrete pool construction.

Marking out and excavating

Mark out the site and excavate to the same shape and contours as the finished stream, making allowance for a 3in (8cm) layer of concrete. The top of the excavation must be level from side to side. In areas of heavy clay, excavate 2-3in (5-8cm) deeper.

Underlining

Calculate the amount of polythene needed (see page 10), and line the excavation with it, smoothing out air pockets and creases as much as possible.

In areas of heavy clay, lay a 2-3in (5-8cm) layer of sand.

Laying the concrete

Starting with a patch of floor and a portion of wall, work in small sections, moving from one end of the feature to the other. Concrete the walls from the bottom upwards.

Using a shovel to move the main bulk and a plasterer's trowel for the smoothing, spread the waterproof concrete in a 3in (8cm) layer over the whole structure, carefully following the contours of the excavation.

The stream bed and margins

Once the concrete mixture has stiffened, after two or three hours, build up the edges of the stream and any pools with large stones or small rocks, embedding them a little way into the semi-wet concrete. Scatter the pool and stream floors with smaller stones and gravel, firmly pushing them into the concrete so they do not get washed away and the feature looks as natural as possible.

Push small rocks into the concrete along the overlapping lips of each feature. As a general rule, a barrier of rocks with a gap in the middle will give the effect of fast-moving water, while different-sized stones or rocks arranged across the pool to form a gentle dip in the middle will create a softer effect. Flat stones set at the same level will produce a smooth curtain of water.

Build up the margins of the stream with rocks and plants for a natural look.

Setting regime and sealing

The concrete must be allowed to set slowly; once dry, seal the areas visible between the rocks with a sealant (see pages 40 and 42).

Laying concrete

1 Using a plasterer's trowel, lay the concrete over the plastic underlining in a smooth, even layer. Follow the contours of the excavation carefully.

CONCRETE CHANNELS

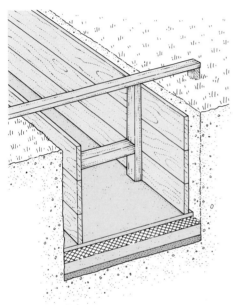

Concrete channels can be constructed using wooden shuttering. If the area is extensive, lay the concrete in several different sections using a new set of shuttering, and fill the gaps between each section with a proprietary expansion compound.

Excavate a channel 6in (15cm) wider and 4in (18cm) deeper than the finished feature, and construct a set of shuttering to the required dimensions (see page 44). Spread a 1in (2.5cm) layer of builder's sand on the floor of the excavation. Lay a 2in (5cm) layer of concrete over the sand. Press wire mesh into the wet concrete and lay a further 1in (2.5cm) of concrete.

Install the shuttering, having soaked it in water or limewash. Working your way round the channel, pour a 2in (5cm) layer of concrete into the cavity between the shuttering and the excavation walls and tamp it down. Repeat this until the top of the shuttering is reached.

The concrete must be kept moist as it sets and then be sealed (see pages 40 and 42).

2 Arrange rocks and stones along the edges of the stream, pressing them firmly into the wet concrete. This will make the feature look more natural.

3 Press more rocks and stones in the bed to form a lip over which the water will run. The shape of the stones and how they are arranged will determine the water flow.

Cascades and waterfalls 1

Waterfalls can be created using pools connected by channels or overlapping lips. They can also be built into a stream to form a series of cascades.

Waterfalls and cascades can be made with liners, concrete or pre-formed units. Pre-formed units are popular as they are easier to install than liners or concrete, but they are more difficult to disguise and blend in with the surroundings. The gardener is also restricted to the shapes on offer.

Pre-formed units
Pre-formed cascade units are available in a variety of finishes, from textured rock to grit and pebbledash. They are either manufactured as an all-in-one series of pools and falls, or as individual pools in a variety of designs, positioned according to the desired effect to create a cascade or waterfall.

Design
Waterfalls can cover any distance, falling at a range of heights: the steeper the fall, the more dramatic the effect. For a vertical fall, the top pool should overlap the bottom pool by 2-3in (5-8cm) to ensure the water falls freely without touching the wall behind.

For a sufficient quantity of water to build up to make an effective display, a waterfall must start from a header pool. The lip of the pool will dictate the angle and style of the waterfall. A lip with a narrow gap set at an acute angle will give a compact, fast flow of water, while a shallow lip which gradually dips will give a smooth, gentle flow.

Tools and materials
You will need: waterproof gardening gloves, a plasterer's trowel, a small plank of wood and a spirit level, bricklayer's sand and stone-free, fine soil for backfilling.

Marking out and excavating
Mark out the site and excavate to the same shape and contours as the finished feature, but 6in (15cm) longer and wider and 3in (8cm) deeper. Check the excavation is level.

Underlining
Remove any sharp stones or roots. Line the bottom and sides of the excavation with 3in (8cm) of damp bricklayer's sand, moulding it into the shape of the excavation.

Installing the units
Starting at the bottom of the waterfall and working upwards, place the units in the sand, either abutting one another or with a 1-3in (2.5-8cm) overlap.

Bed them down firmly and backfill with soil, packing it tightly around each unit so that they are firmly embedded.

The waterfall bed and margins
Place matching stones or rocks along the margins, arranged so that the strata run in the same direction to resemble a rocky outcrop. Fill the gaps with soil and grow suitable plants along the edge of the waterfall. Large stones can also be placed inside the pools; these must be heavy enough to withstand the pressure of the water flow.

The waterfall effect is enhanced by the lip-stones: a piece of slate will create a smooth, wide sheet of water known as a mirror flow; larger stones placed at random will create a lively, irregular flow resembling rapids.

Installing the units

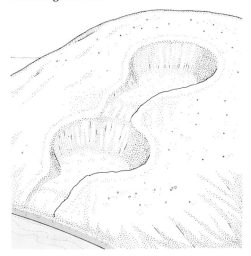

1 Mark out the waterfall and carefully excavate the site. Having checked the excavations are level, line each one with a thick layer of sand.

ARTIFICIAL SLOPES AND MOUNDS

If a natural slope does not exist, carefully contoured slopes and mounds can be built using well-consolidated, heavy soil – subsoil from a previous excavation is ideal. Wet soil should be left to dry out for a day or two before it is used.

Mould a profile to fit the surrounding landscape and firm the surface with the back of a spade. For the best results, construct the mound two months prior to building the water feature to allow the soil to settle so soil slippage does not occur.

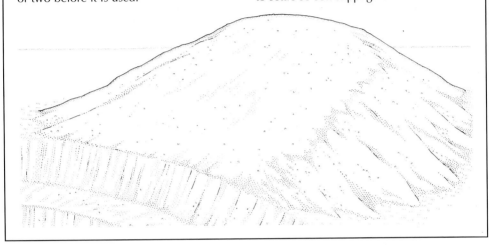

2 Install the lowest unit, firmly embedding it into the sand. Check the unit is level and backfill around it with fine soil, firming it down well.

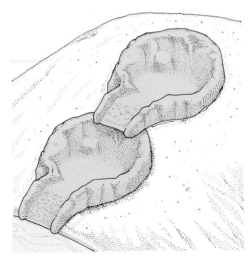

3 Place the second unit in the excavation above, positioning it so that the lip overlaps the edge of the pool below. This will prevent water leakage.

Cascades and waterfalls 2

4 Press the unit down into the sand and check that it is level. Backfill around the pre-formed waterfall shell with soil, packing it down well.

5 Place large, heavy rocks along the lip of the waterfall to create the impression of a rapid water flow. For a smooth flow, use a flat piece of slate.

Building rockwork

1 Having installed the main pool, build a wall rising above it using stones and rocks bonded with waterproof mortar. Leave the mortar to set.

2 After a minimum of two days, the mortar will have set enough to continue construction. Backfill the cavity behind the rockwork with soil.

THE WATERFALL BED AND MARGIN

Fill the gaps in the rockwork and margins of the pools and waterfalls with soil and plants to blend the feature into the landscape. Small rocks and stones can also be placed in the pools, around the edges and along the lips (see page 74).

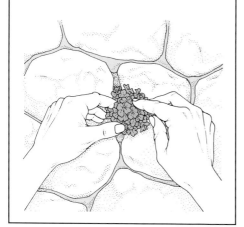

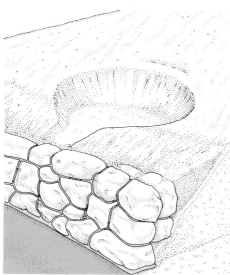

3 Excavate the pool above. Position the unit and mark the level of the rim on the back wall. Remove the unit and build the next wall rising up from the mark.

Waterfalls and cascades can be constructed using pre-formed pools built into a series of rockwork terraces. Although time-consuming, the end result is particularly natural looking.

Tools and materials

You will need: waterproof gardening gloves, a shovel, a plasterer's trowel, a small plank of wood and spirit level, bricklayer's sand, waterproof mortar (see page 34), regular rocks and stones and fine, stone-free soil for backfilling.

Marking out and excavating

Position the pool units on site. Mark out their positions with a trickle of sand. Starting with the bottom pool, excavate the site so that it is 6in (15cm) larger and 3in (8cm) deeper than the unit. Place the rockwork for the first pool and then excavate the pool above. Continue this process until the feature is complete.

Rockwork

Plaster a 3in (8cm) layer of damp sand on the floor and walls of the pool excavation and settle the unit in place. Using a sharp stick, score the soil where the top of the unit lies at the back of the excavation. Remove the unit and build a wall of rockwork above the unit, rising up from this point.

Using a shovel and a plasterer's trowel, build the first course of the rockwork on a ½in (1.25cm) bed of mortar, making sure there is a ½in (1.25cm) layer of mortar between each stone. When constructing the rockwork, press the stones together firmly so that as little mortar is visible as possible. Leave occasional gaps in the wall for planting, and continue building until the required level is reached, cutting into the soil wall behind if necessary. The rockwork can be steep or gently receding. It does not have to follow the contours of the slope and can be freestanding. Once the mortar has set, backfill with soil.

Installing the units

Once the wall is complete, position the unit and firmly press it into the sand. Check it is level. Backfill the area around it with soil and pack the surface down. Fill in the crack between the unit and the rockface with waterproof mortar. Continue upwards, building rock faces and installing units.

Cascades and waterfalls 3

Liners

Using a liner for a waterfall provides the opportunity to construct almost any configuration. The waterfall can consist of a series of pools, each one overlapping the one below or, for a more gentle effect, placed some distance apart with the water slipping down the connecting face. Accurate spadework is required to produce the correct shape; use a PVC or butyl rubber liner, not plastic.

Tools and materials

You will need: gardening gloves, a plasterer's trowel, a spirit level and a small plank of wood, geo-textile, fleece or polyester matting.

Marking out and excavating

Starting at the bottom with the main pool and working upwards, excavate the site to the exact shape and contours of the finished feature. Shave the soil away carefully; the more compact the soil, the easier it is to achieve accurate spadework. Any pools must be deeper at the back, with lips at the front over which the water can fall. If the water is to flow down the connecting walls from one pool to the next, the walls must be excavated to form a gently-curving niche to stop the water splashing out of the waterfall. Contour the lip of each excavation very carefully to provide the type of fall required and check the excavation is level.

Underlining

Remove any stones and other sharp objects that may puncture the liner, and line the excavation with a layer of geo-textile, fleece or polyester matting; this should cover the connecting walls as well.

Installing the liner

Calculate the amount of liner needed (see page 10); if the design is complicated, use several pieces rather than one, making allowance for 6in (15cm) overlaps.

Starting with the main pool and moving upwards, spread the liner over the excavation and mould it into the contours, smoothing out the wrinkles into a few bold pleats. Continue in this way until the fall is lined; any overlaps must run in the same direction as the water.

Bury the edges of the liner under at least 3in (8cm) of soil. The point at which the liner and the soil meet must be above the maximum water level otherwise the soil will muddy the water and the water will soak away into the surrounding soil.

The waterfall bed and margins

Follow the instructions on page 76 for pre-formed units. Select rocks and stones with flat surfaces and fit them snugly against the vertical faces of the waterfall; be very careful not to use sharp or angular rocks or stones which may puncture the liner. Place stones in the pools and along the lips.

USING CONCRETE

Cascades and waterfalls can also be constructed using concrete, in a similar manner to streams.

Follow the instructions for concrete streams (see page 72), adapting the excavation to suit the needs of your particular waterfall design. Arrange the stones and rocks for the desired effect so the fall looks as natural as possible.

Installing the liner

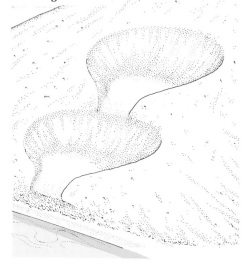

1 Working from the bottom of the slope upwards, excavate the site. Each pool should be deeper at the back, with a lip over which the water can fall.

2 Remove sharp stones and roots that might otherwise puncture the liner. Once the excavation is smooth, line it with underlining material.

3 If using several pieces of liner, fit the bottom piece first. Mould the liner into the contours of the pool. Pay special attention to the lip; it must be smooth.

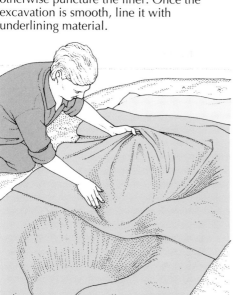

4 Install the second piece of liner in the pool above. This piece must have a generous overlap lying in the same direction as the water flow.

5 Having lined the waterfall, arrange rocks and stones around the edge of each pool. Place smooth stones along the lip of the pools to disguise the liner.

Fountains 1

There is a wide range of fountains available, from small, simple sprays, which do little more than provide the sound of moving water, to elaborate sculptures, where carefully created plumes of water provide a centre-piece in a design. Fountains are powered by submersible or surface pumps (see pages 10, 14 and 66). The more powerful the pump, the higher and wider the spray and the quicker the sequence of changing spray patterns.

All fountains work on the same principle: the fountain head, or jet unit, is connected to a pump which drives the water up and through the head, creating a fountain of water. Jets are available with different numbers and arrangements of holes, allowing you to select the most appropriate spray pattern. The height of the water jet can be adjusted to suit any design.

There is also a range of automatically changing spray patterns which are operated by a simple device fixed to the pump outlet. The fountain works in a sequence, with one spray pattern continuously following another.

Positioning

When choosing the position of a fountain, it is important to bear in mind spray drift, which can be considerable on windy days. Make sure the catchment pool is large enough to accommodate the spread of the fountain; it should be at least twice the diameter of the projected spread of the spray. The pump instructions will give the height and spread of the fountain.

Installing simple fountains

Two or more features with outflows in different parts of the pool can be operated with the same pump by using a T-junction.

Submersible pump Attach the jet unit to the delivery hose and place the pump on a piece of paving on the pool floor. If the pool is made with a liner, place the paving on a double layer of geo-textile, fleece or polyester matting to prevent any punctures. The fountain jet must sit 2-3in (5-8cm) above the maximum water level; place the pump on some paving or bricks if necessary. The outlet is then less likely to become clogged up with debris than if the pump is placed directly on the floor.

Surface pump Connect the delivery hose to the fountain jet and place the pump in its chamber. If the chamber is some distance from the fountain itself, a fountain assembly unit is needed to link them.

Simple fountains

Place the pump in the pool, on a piece of paving if necessary, to bring it up to the required height.

Ornamental fountains

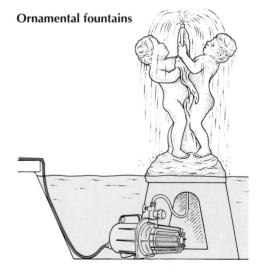

Connect the pump to the fountain jet. If the fountain plinth is hollow, hide the pump inside it.

Installing an ornamental fountain

For a more decorative fountain, an ornamental figure, such as a cherub or fish, can be installed, on a plinth if necessary. Stone figures are more attractive than concrete or artificial stone figures, but they are rather expensive. Abstract designs made of metal or perspex can also be used. Heavy fountains should only be considered for concrete pools.

Ornamental fountains are designed to hold a jet and delivery hose. Simply push the hose up inside the fountain so that it connects with the jet, which is already in place, and connect the other end of the hose to the pump.

PLANTS AND FOUNTAINS

Although fountains look and sound attractive, they preclude the cultivation of various aquatic plants nearby. Water-lilies in particular dislike any kind of water movement and will not tolerate the spray of fountains or the turbulence created by pumps. Most marginal plants will tolerate some degree of moving water and the majority of submerged plants can also be grown, but deep-water and floating aquatics require still water.

FOUNTAIN SPRAYS

Make sure the fountain head will create the right effect for the water feature.

Bell: a fountain that produces a sculptural, almost semi-circular sphere of water that falls in a bell shape from a central pipe.

Bubble: this head makes a natural-looking, low fountain of water that bubbles up gently as though issuing from a spring.

Column: two or three columns of white water shoot up in a neat and stylized manner; good for a modern design.

Geyser: the geyser fountain forces water up into the air, sometimes to great heights, to give a natural-looking rush of foaming white water and a gushing sound.

Plume: seething and foaming plumes produced by this head create an architectural feature, best operated from a simple but substantial pool.

Tier: a traditional fountain that produces continuous tiered circles of water gently falling in a pyramidal-shaped display.

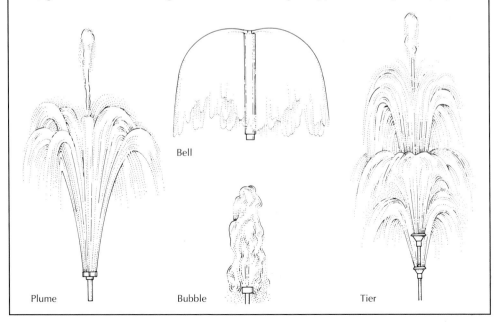

Plume

Bell

Bubble

Tier

Fountains 2

FOUNTAINS

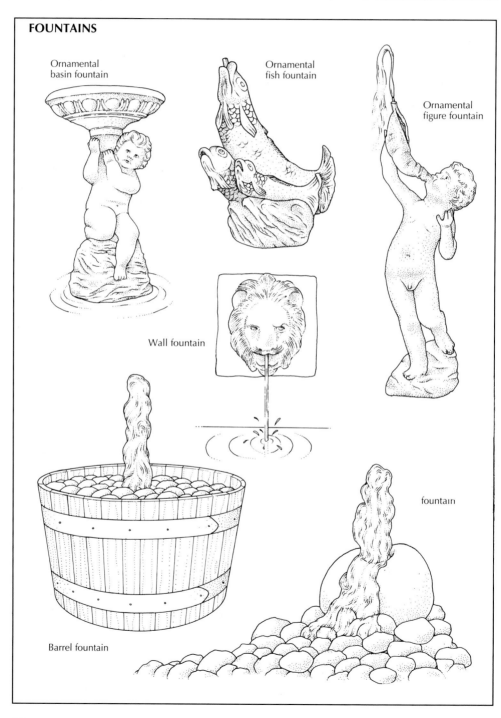

Ornamental
basin fountain

Ornamental
fish fountain

Ornamental
figure fountain

Wall fountain

fountain

Barrel fountain

Other fountains

Small moving water features are ideal for decorating terraces and patios or sun rooms and conservatories. Such features are operated by submersible pumps; the electricity cable that runs the pump can be concealed under paving slabs or any other surface or it can be hidden in a nearby border.

Millstone fountain

Millstones can be used to create very attractive and safe water features. When the pump is switched on, a small fountain of water emerges from the centre of the stone and washes over the edge, through the cobblestones surrounding the millstone, and back into the lined excavation or dustbin beneath. Use a bell fountain, a simple bubble fountain or a small geyser.

Genuine old millstones are heavy to handle so, as an alternative, you may prefer to use one made from fibreglass with a rough sandstone finish instead. Once these are in place and have developed a covering of moss and algae, they look remarkably like the real thing.

Tools and materials

You will need: gardening gloves, a spade, a tape-measure, a spirit level, a piece of string, a millstone, PVC or butyl rubber liner or a plastic dustbin, 1in (2.5cm) diameter metal reinforcing rods or reinforced wire mesh, concrete blocks (optional), a small piece of paving stone and some cobblestones.

Marking out and excavating

For a lined excavation, mark out and dig a circular hole (see page 10) 3ft (90cm) deep and 1in (2.5cm) larger than the diameter of the millstone. If using a plastic dustbin, excavate a hole to accommodate it so the lip of the dustbin is flush with the ground.

Dig a margin around the excavation for the cobblestones; it should be about 4in (10cm) deep and 6in (15cm) wide. Check the excavation is level.

If using a real millstone, excavate the area under the margin and sink a circle of concrete building blocks into the ground around the feature. This will support the considerable weight of the stone and prevent it from moving or sinking at an angle.

Millstone fountain

1 Dig a circular hole with a wide margin around it. Either line the excavation with a piece of butyl rubber liner or install a plastic dustbin in the hole.

2 Having installed the pump, place the wire mesh over the excavation. Feed the delivery hose, attached to a piece of string, through the mesh.

Fountains 3

Underlining
Calculate the amount of liner needed (see page 10) and mould it into the excavation, smoothing it into three or four big folds for a neat finish. Fold the liner over the margin.

Alternatively, lower the dustbin into the ground and line the margin.

Installing the pump
Fasten a strong piece of string around the delivery hose. Position a piece of paving on a double layer of geo-textile, fleece or polyester matting in the middle of the excavation and place the pump on the stone. Pull the hose up and onto the ground using the string.

Support frame
Whether the millstone is real or man-made, it will need a support frame on which to sit. This can be made of reinforced metal rods or a piece of reinforced wire mesh.

Cut the rods to fit the diameter of the excavation (including the margin), and place them 4in (10cm) apart over the top of the hole, like a grill. If you are using wire mesh, cut a circle the same size as the margin and place it over the hole. For real millstones, rest the rods or wire mesh on the concrete building blocks sunk into the ground under the margin.

Make sure the delivery hose belonging to the pump is threaded through the centre of the support frame.

Positioning the stone
Once the support frame is in position, lower the millstone onto it, threading the string and delivery hose through the hole. Attach the hose to the fountain jet; the jet should be large enough to sit firmly in the hole of the millstone without slipping through.

The margin
Cover the margin with a layer of cobblestones, hiding the liner and pump cable. Fill the lined excavation or dustbin with water and top up as necessary.

Pebble fountain
A pebble fountain is similar to a millstone fountain but it has a layer of pebbles rather than a millstone covering the support frame. The water bubbles up through the pebbles

3 Position the millstone on the wire mesh so that it sits centrally over the excavation, feeding the piece of string and delivery hose through the hole in the millstone.

4 Once the millstone is installed and the jet unit is correctly positioned, cover the margins with cobblestones so that they cover the pump cable and the mesh.

like a spring; use a simple bubble fountain, a bell fountain or a small geyser.

Follow the instructions for constructing a millstone fountain, with a support frame of fine mesh reinforcing netting. Cover this with a 4in (10cm) layer of cobbles, and build them up around the jet.

Barrel fountain
It is possible to construct a simple but effective fountain in a tub or half barrel using cobblestones and a low jet fountain. The water will flow over the cobblestones before falling into the barrel.

Tools and materials
You will need: gardening gloves, a tape measure, a saw, a tub or half barrel, some pieces of timber with a cross-section of about 1in (2.5cm) sq that have been treated with preservative, and cobblestones.

Preparing the barrel
Be sure that the barrel is clean and free from pollutants and seal it by charring or lining it (see page 64).

Installing the pump
Place the pump on a piece of paving on the bottom of the barrel, and mark the side of the barrel 2in (5cm) above the maximum height of the body of the pump. If the barrel is lined, place the paving on a double layer of geo-textile, fleece or polyester matting.

Support frame
Measure the diameter of the barrel where you have just marked it and, using pieces of timber, make a support structure of wooden bars that will wedge into the tub to form a level surface. Cut the timber to the required length, and lay these 1in (2.5cm) apart at the marked level, like a grill. Position the supply hose and fountain jet in the middle of the support frame while it is being constructed so that the jet is wedged in place. Feed the pump cable through a notch in the top of the barrel so it is less obtrusive.

Cobblestones
Cover the support with a 4in (2.5cm) layer of cobblestones, building them up around the jet, and fill the barrel with water.

Barrel fountain

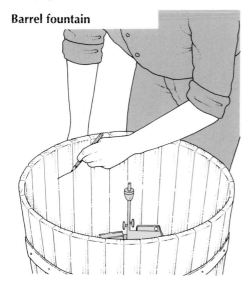

1 Clean the barrel and either char the inside or line it. Having installed the pump, draw a line around the inside of the barrel 2in (5cm) above the body of the pump.

2 Wedge pieces of wood inside the barrel like a grill, at the height of the mark. Feed the delivery hose through the grill and cover it with cobblestones.

Fountains 4

Wall fountains

Wall fountains, suitable for patios, sun rooms and conservatories, are available in a number of designs, including simple spouts and ornate gargoyles. They may flow into raised or sunken basal pools, bowls or dishes.

Spouts and gargoyles

Create a fountain using a spout or gargoyle. The traditional gargoyle or mask is usually a wild-looking human face or a mythical beast that spouts water from its mouth into a basin or pool below. Ferocious-looking masks look particularly effective when placed in shady corners, while masks with friendlier expressions are perhaps more appropriate for patios. They are available in real or imitation stone, lead, terracotta, fibreglass and plastic.

Basal pools, bowls and dishes

The ideal basal pool for a wall fountain is a raised pool with a large enough surface area to accommodate the fountain spray. A raised pool built with a cavity wall will support coping wide enough to sit on, adding considerably to the enjoyment of the wall fountain. Sunken or semi-sunken pools built adjacent to the wall with formally edged surrounds are also suitable.

Either build a pool using any of the given construction methods (see pages 32-64), or buy a ready made basal pool instead. These are usually pre-formed raised structures made of concrete which are easy to install. For semi-circular or curved pools, pre-formed concrete sections and matching coping stones can be used.

Concrete containers like sinks and basins provide a useful alternative to purpose-built basal pools. However, while saving considerable work, the range of sizes available is very limited. Dishes and bowls can also be used for wall fountains, either individually or one above the other, to create a tiered effect.

The wall

A wall fountain will look best if it is attached to a cavity wall consisting of two parallel walls of bricks laid in running bond (see page 60). This will allow the delivery hose to be hidden in the wall. The two walls are held together approximately every six courses at staggered intervals by metal wall ties. If the existing wall is not a cavity wall, consider whether it is possible to take the delivery hose up the back of the wall, or disguise it with plants or a section of decorative drain pipe.

The basal pool

A concrete container or concrete sections can either be laid on a level surface or partially sunk into the ground.

A raised pool

Determine the position of the basal pool under the wall spout and prepare a firm, level base to accommodate paving slabs or other paving material. To do this, excavate a 2in (5cm) deep hole, at least 12in (30cm) wider than the size of the container.

Lay the paving stones on dabs of mortar placed under the four corners and the centre of each stone (see page 34). There should be a 1/2in (1.25cm) gap between each slab; use a small piece of wood as a spacer for accuracy. Check the paving is level and bury the electric cable under it.

Basal pools

1 First prepare the paving. Excavate the site and mark it out with string. Lay the paving stones on dabs of mortar, leaving a small gap between each slab.

Once the mortar has hardened, after a minimum of two days, point the gaps between each stone by brushing dry mortar into them. Water the pointing using a watering can with a fine rose.

After a further two days the pointing will have set and the basal pool can be installed. Position the pool close to the wall and check that it is level; any slight discrepancies should be corrected by wedging small pieces of stone under the pool. Point the gap around the container with waterproof mortar to seal it in place.

A sunken pool

Concrete containers and sections can also be partially sunk into the ground. Mark out the shape of the pool on the ground. If the floor has already been paved, lift all the slabs that have been marked as well as those covering the proposed site of the pool. It is important that you know where each slab came from. Using a stone-cutter, trim the paving stones as marked. If the area is unpaved, install the pool before paving.

Excavate to the required depth, making allowance for a 1-2in (2.5-5cm) layer of sand. Line the excavation with the sand and install the pool. Replace the trimmed paving stones or, if the area is unpaved, lay paving around the sunken pool, shaping it according to the shape of the pool.

Once installed, line the pool with a butyl rubber or PVC liner held in place by coping stones, or render the structure with waterproof mortar. Waterproof paint will also give a watertight finish.

Pumps

If the submersible pump is housed in the basal pool, the cable must be disguised by some carefully placed stones and plants. If the pump is housed in a sump near the pool, the flexible waterpipe linking the pool and the sump should be disguised in a similar way so that the connection is concealed.

Installing a sump

Before installing the basal pool, dig a hole adjacent to the main pool and sink a dustbin

2 Point the gaps between the paving by brushing dry mortar into the cracks. Water the pointing using a watering can with a fine rose attachment.

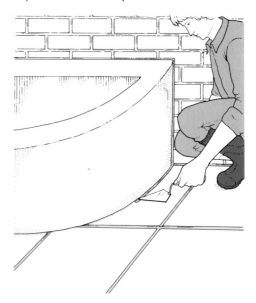

3 Once the pointing has set, position the basal pool next to the wall. Check that it is level and point the gap around the pool with waterproof mortar.

Fountains 5

into it. The dustbin must be deep enough to house the pump, covered with 12in (30cm) of water. Connect the sump to the pool with a well-disguised length of flexible waterpipe that feeds directly into the pool, or by attaching it to a drainage outlet in the pool floor.

Installing a drainage outlet

Although a little more complicated to install, a drainage outlet is better than a pipe hooked over the lip of the pool as it is not visible.

Many precast basal pools have depressions in the base that may be knocked out to provide drainage holes. Fit a domestic bath drain into the drainage hole, sealing it in position with waterproof mortar (see page 34). Once the mortar has set, after approximately two days, connect the drain to a flexible waterpipe leading to the adjacent pump chamber; the connection should be watertight.

If the pool is made with a pre-formed shell or a butyl rubber liner, use an outlet valve, available from most water garden specialists; this makes a watertight outlet in the pool floor through which the waterpipe can lead.

Installing the wall fountain

If installing a spout or gargoyle in a cavity wall, knock a small hole the size of the delivery hose through the first layer of brick at the point at which the delivery hose is to be connected to the spout or mask.

Dangle a plumb line from the hole and knock a second hole the same size as the first at the bottom of the line, just above the edge of the pool. Holding on to one end, feed a strong piece of string from the top hole inside the cavity and out through the base hole. Attach the supply hose to the string at the base of the wall and pull the hose up through the top hole.

Join the spout or gargoyle to the hose. Install a spout by wedging it in the hole with mortar; masks are attached to the wall using screws and wall plugs. Mark the position of the screws and drill the holes; insert the wall plugs and screw the mask to the wall.

If the wall does not have a cavity, attach the hose to the spout or gargoyle. A gargoyle should have a channel running down the back of it to accommodate the hose; if not,

Installing the fountain

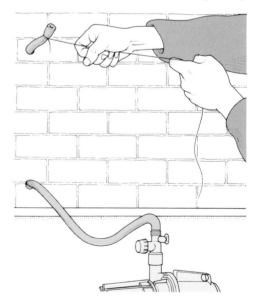

1 Drill a hole in the wall where the fountain will go. Dangle a plumb line from here and drill a second hole at the base of the wall, below the first hole.

2 Feed a piece of string in through the top hole and out through the bottom hole. Attach the delivery hose and pull the string through the top hole.

carefully chisel one out, or chisel a channel in the wall. Fix the spout and gargoyle in place and clip the hose to the wall with plumber's pipe fasteners.

With a little ingenuity, the hose can be disguised with plants; ivy provides a suitable cover and looks good with stone. Alternatively, choose a tall marginal plant and place the pot in front of the hose so the leaves hide it. For a more finished appearance, cut a decorative fluted drainpipe in half lengthways and mortar this to the wall over the hose.

PLANTING

Although waterlilies and deep water aquatics dislike running water, as do floating aquatics, marginal plants will tolerate moving water created by the flow of a fountain. The plants should be kept in their containers and placed on the pool floor around the edge of the pool, on bricks if necessary. Disguise the pots with a few carefully-placed stones.

PRE-FORMED WALL FOUNTAINS

There are pre-formed wall fountain units available that have pumps built into them. These are simple to install: hang the unit on the wall, fill it with water and plug the pump into the electricity supply.

Non-cavity walls

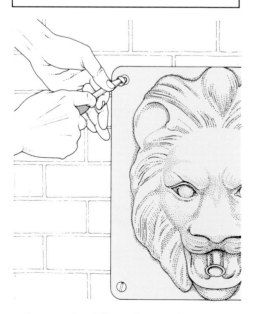

3 Connect the delivery hose to the spout or mask. Either mortar the spout in place or firmly attach the mask to the wall using wall plugs and screws.

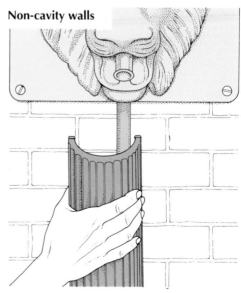

Chisel a channel in the wall or the back of the mask and attach the hose to the fountain jet. Clip the hose to the wall and hide it with a length of drainpipe.

Stepping stones

Stepping stones built across pools or streams are an invitation to cross the feature to discover what lies on the other side. The stones can be placed in a straight line or, for a more informal effect, they can be arranged in a zig-zag pattern.

For safety reasons, stepping stones should not be used in pools or streams that are over 1ft (30cm) deep. Furthermore, they are not suitable for water features constructed with pre-formed shells as the units may crack under the weight of the stone.

The stones must be installed when the pool or stream is empty. The surface of each stone should be at least 2in (5cm) above the surface of the water to avoid getting wet feet.

If the feature is made with a liner, the stepping stones should be planned in advance so that provision for their weight can be made. In such cases, lay a 4in (10cm) layer of concrete on the floor of the excavation and, once dry, cover this with a layer of geo-textile, polyester matting or fleece, before constructing the pool or stream. Otherwise lay each stone on a paving slab, firmly mortared in place.

Stone
Various kinds of stone may be used for stepping stones; select one which matches the rock or stonework of the feature. Paving stones and artificial stepping stones are available at most garden centres.

Millstone grit This is one of the best stones to use for stepping stones. It is hard-wearing and will tolerate water immersion year after year without deteriorating.
Sandstone Only use sandstone if it has properly weathered and developed a hard outer surface. Most sandstone, newly quarried material in particular, flakes badly if soaked in water and exposed to frost; the rich orange-red carstone is particularly soft. Weathered sandstone, although harder, may be slippery if you are wearing rubber-soled shoes or wellington boots.
Westmorland slate Westmorland slate can be used but it is rather slippery.
Limestone Do not use limestone as it is easily eroded and will flake. Limestone is also slippery and will leach lime into the water.

Stepping stones

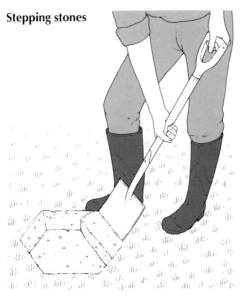

1 Home-made stepping stones are simple to make. First, using a spade, excavate a series of holes the same shape and size as the finished stones.

2 Line each hole with a layer of polythene; this will stop the wet concrete sticking to the earth. Pour the concrete into the holes and smooth the surfaces.

Home-made stepping stones

Stepping stones can be made out of concrete rather than natural stone.

In a spare part of the garden, dig holes the size and shape of the desired stepping stones and line them with polythene. This will stop the wet concrete sticking to the soil.

Mix three parts aggregate and one part cement with enough water to make a wet consistency and pour the mixture into the holes. Make sure that the surface of the concrete is level as this will be the surface of each stepping stone.

The concrete will take up to a week to dry; if it rains, cover the stepping stones with a piece of plastic. Once set, lift out the stepping stones, remove the polythene and brush off any soil. Paint them with a sealant (see page 40) to prevent the escape of free-lime.

Positioning the stones

Position the stepping stones in the feature, testing them for stride length before securing them. Mortar the stones in place (see page 34), checking each one is level. If the stream or pool is made with a liner, mortar a double layer of geo-textile, polyester matting or fleece to the liner and underside of each stone to protect the liner.

If necessary, build the stones up to the correct level with large pieces of paving slabs; these must be firmly mortared in place for the utmost safety.

SAFETY

Do not consider using stepping stones in water over 1ft (30cm) deep in case of accidents. It is very important that stepping stones are big enough to accommodate the whole foot, and that they are level. The steps should be placed at a sensible distance from each other so that crossing them is as safe as possible, and each one must be securely mortared in place. Keep the stones free of algae by regularly scrubbing them with a stiff scrubbing brush and water; do not use algicide as this may harm plants and fish.

3 Once set, lift each stone out of its mould and remove the polythene. Using a paintbrush, coat each one with a sealant and leave it to dry.

4 Mortar each stone in place. If necessary, set the stepping stones on a plinth made of pieces of paving mortared together to bring them to the right level.

Bridges

Building a bridge

1 Dig out a hole for each pier. The excavation must be approximately 2ft (60cm) deep and at least 6in (15cm) larger than the pier.

Simple crossing

A simple crossing over a narrow body of water, no more than 2½ft (75cm) wide, can be constructed using two piers spanned by a slab of stone. The ground on either side must be firm and level; the piers can either be raised or sunk into the ground.

Tools and materials

For the piers you will need: two large sections of rock, precast concrete posts or strong wooden posts approximately 1½ft (45cm) in length; for the bridge you will need: a large, thick slab of stone or slate, a railway sleeper, a solid plank with a minimum cross-section of 4in (10cm) or logs halved lengthways; concrete and mortar (see pages 40 and 34) or screws. All wood must be treated with a preservative other than creosote.

Excavating

Excavate down to solid subsoil, usually found at a depth of approximately 2ft (60cm) below ground level. Each excavation must be at least 6in (15cm) larger than the piers all round.

2 Install the piers in the excavations and check they are level. Concrete them in place, leaving the last few inches free for backfilling with soil.

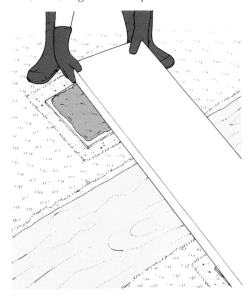

3 Span the water feature with the stone slab and fix it with mortar. Check the bridge is level across the water; if not, build up one end with more mortar.

Installing the piers

Position the piers; they can be raised above ground level or lie flush. Check that they are level and straight. Concrete each one firmly in place, leaving the top 4-6in (10-15cm) of the excavation to be backfilled with soil once the concrete has dried.

Constructing the walkway

Secure the slab of stone in place with a ½in (1.25cm) layer of mortar.

Alternatively, position the railway sleeper or plank and screw each end to the wooden posts; if using halved logs, each one must be firmly secured to the piers.

Safety rails

A handrail can be built out of timber or machined wood, according to the desired look; both should be treated with a preservative. Use 3-4ft (90cm-1.2m)-long circular or square posts which have a minimum cross-section of 4in (10cm).

Dig 18in (45cm) deep holes for each post, insert the posts and concrete them in place, leaving the top 4-6in (10-15cm) of the excavation free for backfilling with soil. Firmly screw each end of the handrail onto the posts at the correct height.

SAFETY

Whatever type of bridge you are constructing, it must be safe to use. Always make sure the piers are strong and firmly embedded into the ground, preferably set in concrete. If the walkway of the bridge is made of wood, the timber must be strong and thoroughly treated with a wood preservative; do not use creosote, however, as this is harmful to nearby plants. Avoid a slippery surface by covering the wood with fine mesh wire netting securely nailed in place. Keep stone walkways free of algae by scrubbing them with water.

If the water is particularly deep, or you have small children, it is vital to construct strong safety rails.

4 For the handrail, sink the posts into the ground next to the walkway. Concrete the uprights in place, making sure they are level across the feature.

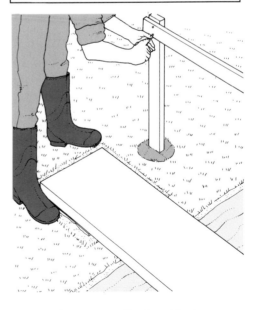

5 Once the posts are firmly set in the concrete, screw the handrail onto each post. Make sure the rail is well attached so there is no danger of it coming loose.

Statues and other accessories

Statues

Statues can add much to a water feature, especially formal pools. Traditional classical statuary is often more effective if presented in isolation so the reflective qualities of the pool can be enjoyed fully. Modern sculpture looks good reflected in an open sheet of water.

Some statues, however, look best in association with informal pools, half hidden among plants. Stone birds such as herons look attractive standing beside well-planted pools, emerging as if about to enter the water.

Urns and other containers may be arranged in geometric patterns around formal pools, either placed on the ground or raised up on plinths for a more imposing effect.

Oriental accessories

The Oriental style is easy to create using ready-made decorative accessories drawn largely from Japanese tradition. These are mostly available from good garden centres.

Water basins

Stone water basins are the most frequently used Oriental accessories. There are two basic types: the chozubachi – tall basin – and the tsukubai – low basin. The tall basin comes in many forms but the most traditional shape is that of a bridgepost: a cylindrical stone pillar up to 3ft (90cm) high and 1-1½ft (30-45cm) in diameter, with a shallow basin hollowed out of the top and a rectangular depression on one side, which represents the point at which the bridge railing would have been fastened. Almost any shaped tall basin can be used instead. The low basin, originally used for washing before the tea ceremony or entering a shrine, is set close to the ground, and takes the form of a simple, shallow bowl approximately 1ft (30cm) in diameter.

If you wish to include running water, hide the pump in a sump and drainage outlet as you would for a basal pool (see page 86).

Bamboo channels

Bamboo channels are traditional Japanese water accessories.

To make a bamboo channel, take two standard garden canes about 3ft (90cm) long and push them halfway into the ground next to a water basin so that they cross, forming an "x" shape. Tie them together at the point where they meet. This forms the stand.

For the channel, take a length of bamboo or a thick cane 1½-2ft (45-60cm) long and, using a sharp knife, carefully sharpen one end. Place the channel on the stand so that the sharp end is just overhanging the basin.

If you wish to connect the channel up to a pump, carefully place the end of the delivery hose inside the blunt end of the bamboo channel. The rest of the delivery hose can be disguised by well-placed stones or plants.

Ornaments

There are many stone ornaments including lanterns, small buildings, towers and buddhas which can be set by or in the pool.

Stepping stones and bridges

Stepping stones are used in and out of the water, to lead across a pool or gravel area. Bridges are also popular, from brightly coloured wooden arched structures to simple planks or slabs of stone set across a stream.

ORIENTAL-STYLE WATER GARDENS

The key elements of Oriental gardens are water, stone and greenery; flowers play a relatively minor role. The overall effect should be one of serenity and purity.

Oriental pools are placid and informal in shape, often leading off around a corner to another area of the garden. Some are quite shallow with pebble beaches and others are deep and reflective. Streams and waterfalls are installed because of the sound and water patterns they create; streams are usually wide, shallow and boulder-strewn, while waterfalls are gushing and tumbling. Waterfalls are a lively contrast to calm pools, and they add vertical planes to the predominantly horizontal ornamental garden.

Place smooth, rounded stones in the water and arrange sharp, rugged rocks to form outcrops on the ground. Position boulders around the edge of the pool, with a few isolated ones in the water, and build a pebble beach leading into the pool; scatter the pool edge with gravel.

STATUES AND OTHER ACCESSORIES

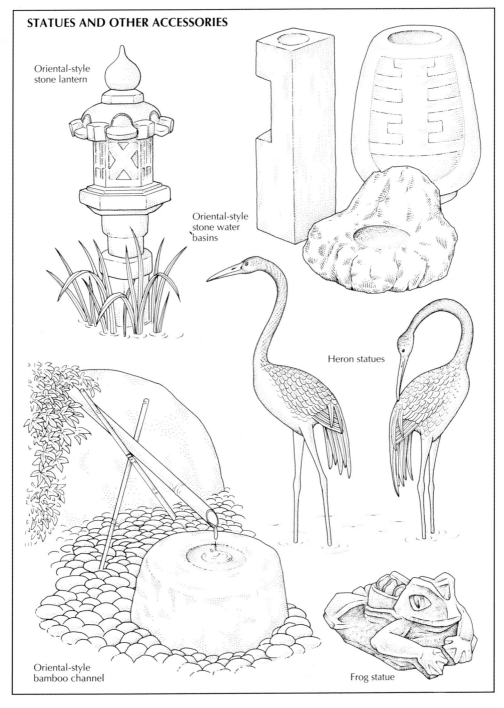

Oriental-style
stone lantern

Oriental-style
stone water
basins

Heron statues

Oriental-style
bamboo channel

Frog statue

Introduction

Aquatic plants can be divided into the following groups: waterlilies, deep-water aquatics, floating aquatics, submerged plants, marginal plants and bog plants (see plant directory).

In order to create a well-balanced, algae-free pool (see page 182), the pool must have enough surface cover to starve algae of the light they depend on for their existence. This is created by surface-leaved plants, the most important being waterlilies, as these are among the first plants to put out their leaves in spring. Deep-water aquatics and, to a lesser extent, floating aquatics also provide surface cover. The pool must also contain sufficient plants to starve the algae of the mineral salts they feed on. Competition for nutrients is provided by submerged and floating aquatics, and under adverse conditions the algae will perish and the pool water will remain clear. Fewer temperature changes occur in large bodies of water, and algal growth is less than in small bodies of water.

For a well-balanced pool, approximately a third of the water surface must be covered with foliage, and the pool must contain a generous number of submerged plants. Using an algicide or a filter will also help produce clear water, but the correct balance of plants is a much more permanent solution to the problem of algae.

Once the pool has its quota of functional plants, others can be selected. Using marginal and bog plants, choose those that are appropriate to the design of the pool. A pool will look more formal if the plants are arranged in some kind of pattern, rather than placed at random. This will be enhanced if specimens of three to five plants are used rather than larger numbers. To enjoy the reflective qualities of the pool to the full, plant low-growing submerged plants which will remain unseen and not obstruct the mirror effect. Informal pools should include a variety of plants that complement the surrounding area to make the feature look as natural as possible. Since the bog area helps merge the pool into the landscape, the bog plants grown should match groups of nearby plants and the pool planting.

Only introduce plants once the pool is full of water; submerged plants will begin to die after an hour or two if deprived of water.

When planting an ornamental pool, one of the most important considerations is the flowering season of the plants. The majority of flowering water plants, including waterlilies, are at their best during the summer months so, for the longest period of seasonal interest, they should be supplemented with spring- and autumn-flowering species and cultivars. Foliage plants have a longer period of interest than flowering plants and add variety to the planting; all should be selected to produce a harmonious effect.

Aspect must also be taken into account. Most flowering plants require sun, so the water surface should not be shaded by any tall-growing, dense marginal aquatics, particularly on the south side of the pool. There are, of course, some plants that will tolerate partial shade, so unavoidable shade is not an insoluble problem.

The majority of water plants, apart from most marginals, will not tolerate moving water. The margins of moving water features can be planted, especially if areas of calm water are provided by carefully placed stones along the edges to direct the flowing water towards the centre of the pool or stream.

Wildlife pools should be planted with native plants. Introduce a selection of food plants to encourage as much wildlife as possible, with one or two areas of tall-growing marginals for shelter and shade.

It is important to grow each plant in the correct depth of water: grow waterlilies, deep-water aquatics and submerged plants in the deeper parts of the pool according to their depth requirements, leaving the shallow areas for marginals and the marshy areas for bog plants. The same principles apply to planting containers; if necessary, place marginals on bricks to lift them to the right level.

Introduce fish several weeks after planting is complete, having top-dressed the soil around the marginal plants with pea gravel. As the pool environment becomes more established, wildlife, such as snails, frogs and toads, will naturally collect by the poolside.

As long as various seasonal tasks are carried out, the pool is properly maintained and the plants looked after, the end result will be an attractive, well-balanced, self-supporting water environment.

A WELL-PLANTED POOL

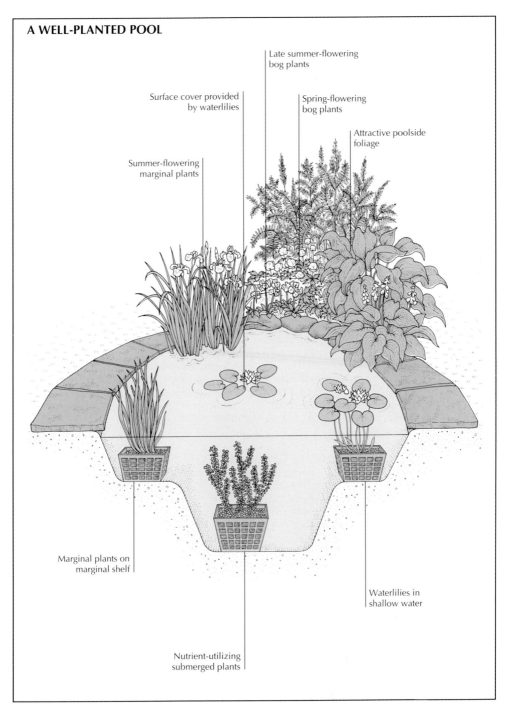

Late summer-flowering
bog plants

Surface cover provided
by waterlilies

Spring-flowering
bog plants

Attractive poolside
foliage

Summer-flowering
marginal plants

Marginal plants on
marginal shelf

Waterlilies in
shallow water

Nutrient-utilizing
submerged plants

Planting mediums/baskets

Aquatic plants do not require a rich growing medium to thrive. They should be grown in a standard aquatic compost or soil rather than a rich medium, as the nutrients will quickly be leached from the medium into the water, encouraging algal growth. Standard aquatic composts are prepared so that the nutrients are released at a rate at which the plants can absorb them. A mixture of rotted cow manure and fresh meadow turf is sometimes recommended, but it is too rich for the water and should not be used.

Making your own planting medium

Garden soil may be used to make compost which is suitable for aquatic plants. A heavy to medium loam with a high clay content is ideal; light, sandy soils are not suitable as the fine particles are soon washed from the baskets into the water.

Make sure the soil is from a border which has produced healthy garden plants. Do not use soil from an area that has recently been dressed with artificial fertilizer, otherwise this may leach into the pool water and encourage algae. Soil from wet or low-lying areas should also be avoided because it is likely to be full of pernicious native weeds which will grow vigorously and jeopardize plant growth.

Run the soil through a coarse sieve to sift out any debris including large stones and sticks. Remove any roots, especially those of couch grass, nettle and ground elder. There is no need to mix the soil with any other material except to introduce additional nutrients once a year in spring, in the form of soil pellets or especially manufactured plant-food sachets pressed into the soil close to the crown of each plant (see page 112).

Commercial planting mediums

Specialist aquatic planting composts are available, but these have been produced with varying degrees of success. A good aquatic compost should consist of heavy soil, some organic matter and slow-release nutrients. Do not use compost that is sold in plain bags which has been mixed on site as it is unlikely to be any more effective than your own mixture and it will be expensive to buy.

If you are purchasing a commercial planting medium, choose a well-known branded product which should have been carefully prepared. Some inconsistency may occur in quality between brands as the major component is soil, itself a variable material. If possible, test the compost before you buy it: it should be free of debris, heavy, smooth and moist, and smear when rubbed between the finger and thumb. When dampened, the compost should mix well with water and bind rather than ooze through the fingers.

SOIL STRUCTURE TEST

Take a small quantity of the proposed soil and dry it out so that it is crumbly and easy to rub through the fingers. Half-fill a large glass jar with water and add the dry soil. Place a lid on the jar and then shake it vigorously to mix the soil and water.

Leave the jar undisturbed for up to five days, and after this time the water should be clear and all the soil particles will have separated into individual layers. After the mixture has settled, there will be a layer of sand, a layer of clay and, floating on the surface, a layer of organic matter.

A suitable soil for aquatic plants will have a clay layer at least twice as deep as the sand layer, with only a light covering of organic debris floating on the surface.

Soil for the bog garden

The soil for the bog garden should be heavy and have about a quarter by volume of well-rotted organic matter added to it.

Planting baskets

Although wildlife and clay-puddled pools are best filled with plants growing in soil on the floor and margin, planting baskets are more appropriate in ornamental pools.

Waterlilies, deep-water aquatics and marginal plants should be planted in planting baskets to stop them spreading too far and invading each other's territory. When growing in a basket, a plant may achieve up to half its maximum spread, depending on the size of the container. Some water plants grow faster than others and will need lifting and dividing at different times; planting baskets provide the facility for dealing with plants separately. They also make it easier to feed individual plants. Furthermore, it is possible to provide special soil conditions if the plants are grown in separate baskets.

There is a wide range of planting baskets from which to choose. Most are square or circular with lattice-work walls which permit water and gas exchange between the soil in the container and the water. They are designed to be as stable as possible with broad bases, so that tall marginal plants will not over-balance. As well as square and round baskets, there are other configurations, the majority of which are manufactured in association with pre-formed pools to provide baskets which will fit any curving edges.

Since submerged plants depend on water rather than soil for their nourishment, they can be grown in ordinary plastic seed trays rather than aquatic planting baskets. Waterlilies, deep-water aquatics and marginal plants may be grown temporarily in large, closed-sided containers, but the plants will die after a relatively short time due to lack of oxygen. Marginal plants will grow in such closed-sided containers for longer periods than waterlilies and other deep-water aquatics because the surface of the soil is occasionally exposed to air and some gaseous exchange occurs.

Lining the baskets

Unless the planting baskets have micro-mesh sides, or very heavy soil is used, baskets need to be lined with hessian or polypropylene mesh. This will stop the soil particles washing through the lattice-work sides and dirtying the water. Cut a square of material approximately twice the size of the basket. Line the basket; if it is to be used for tall marginal plants, place a brick in the bottom before introducing soil and this will anchor the basket so that it is unlikely to tip over.

Lining a basket

1 Place the planting basket on top of the lining material and cut out a square twice the size of the basket.

2 Line the basket; if it is to be used for tall marginal plants, place a brick in the bottom before introducing soil.

Planting 1

April is the best month for planting because the plants will be able to develop to their full potential from the beginning of the growing season. It is acceptable to plant through until late summer, but these plants will have to be cut back prior to planting and will not produce a good display until the following season.

Preparing plants
Waterlilies Purchased from the nursery, the majority of waterlilies are bare-rooted, but container-grown plants are sometimes available. If purchased in containers, the waterlilies will have to be replanted into planting baskets after some preparation. Carefully remove the plant from the container, keeping the soil and roots intact, and plant the waterlily without disturbing the root system. If the roots have not fully spread through the compost, free them of soil and then treat them as bare-rooted plants.

Most of the popular waterlilies have upright, log-like rootstocks with a ruff of smaller roots growing around the top. Strong shoots and leaves are produced from the top of the rootstock. The small group of waterlilies derived from *N. tuberosa* and *N. odorata* have cylindrical-shaped, horizontal, creeping rhizomes, with strong shoots at the end.

Early in the planting season, waterlilies will only have submerged foliage but, as the season progresses, the plants will develop surface foliage and a few flowers. In such cases, both the surface foliage and flowers should be removed before planting; if left, they will die, especially if the plant has been transported in a polythene bag. Without floating leaves, the waterlily is free to adapt to its pool environment and can develop new stems and leaves according to the water depth.

Using a sharp knife, remove the old part of the rootstock below the active roots. Trim off any surface leaves and flowers, but do not remove the submerged foliage. Shorten the ruff of trailing white roots around the neck of the plant to within 1in (2.5cm) of the rootstock, and pare the rootstock back to solid flesh. Dip the rootstock in some powdered charcoal or flowers of sulphur to prevent fungal infection; it is now ready to plant.

Preparing waterlilies

Using a sharp knife, remove the older, inactive portion of the rootstock. Cut off any surface foliage and flowers and trim the ruff around the neck.

Preparing marginals

Trim the roots to within 1in (2.5cm) of the crown. If planting from mid-summer onwards, trim the stems to one third of their optimum height.

Marginal plants These need less preparation. Trim the roots to within 1in (2.5cm) of the crown and, if necessary, trim the stems down to a third of the plant's ultimate height. This will only need to be done if you are planting from mid-summer onwards, when dealing with mature plants. Make sure the cuts are above the water to prevent hollow-stemmed marginals filling with water and rotting.

Deep-water aquatics All deep-water aquatics, apart from *Nuphar*, are treated in the same way as marginals; *Nuphar* are treated in the same way as waterlilies.

Bog plants Little or no preparation is needed for bog plants. If planting takes place from mid-summer onwards, trim the vigorous clump-forming species to a third of their ultimate height and remove any flower heads that are passed their prime.

Submerged plants Neither bunched nor clump-forming submerged plants need any preparation prior to planting.

Floating aquatics Separate any large clumps of floating aquatics into smaller portions if necessary before introducing them.

Preparing the basket

Planting
Waterlilies and deep-water aquatics These are planted in the same way; bare-rooted and container-grown plants are treated differently.
Bare-rooted plants Fill the basket with soil to within 1in (2.5cm) of the rim. Firm the surface and trim off the excess lining material. Water well with a fine-rosed watering can.

PLANTING IN BASKETS

When planting a water feature, grow a single species or cultivar in each basket. Not only does this look better, but it is also more practical, for different plants grow at different rates. Allow room for each plant to spread, to avoid over-crowding. For the most natural effect, the foliage of adjacent plants should mingle: place the baskets slightly closer than the optimum spread of each plant.

Place the planting baskets on the pool floor or marginal shelf, raising them up on a pile of bricks if necessary.

1 Fill the basket with soil to within 1in (2.5cm) of the rim and firm the surface down lightly with your hands; cut off the excess lining material.

2 Using a watering can with a fine rose, thoroughly and evenly soak the medium with water in order to drive out the air trapped in the soil.

Planting 2

With a trowel or your hand, dig a hole large enough to accommodate the roots. Place the plant in the hole and cover the roots with soil. Firm the soil around the roots and water again before covering the surface with a ½in (1.25cm) layer of clean pea gravel.

Container-grown plants Half fill the basket with soil, water well with a fine-rosed watering can and put the plant in without disturbing the compost. Fill the basket to within 1in (2.5cm) of the rim with more soil, firming it down. Water and cover with a ½in (1.25cm) dressing of clean pea gravel.

Marginal plants Follow the instructions for waterlilies and deep-water aquatics.

Bog plants these are normally sold in semi-rigid or flexible black polythene pots, and they should be treated in the same way as ordinary herbaceous plants.

Thoroughly water the plant while it is still in the container. Carefully remove the container without disturbing the compost around the roots of the plant. Using a spade or trowel, dig a planting hole that is slightly wider but the same depth as the pot. Place the plant in the hole; make sure the crown is not buried,

otherwise it will rot in the wet soil of the bog garden. Pack soil around the roots, lightly firm the surface, and water thoroughly with a fine-rosed watering can.

Submerged plants If you have bunches of lead-weighted submerged aquatics, push them into a container of soil or gravel, making sure the lead is completely covered. Exposed lead will rot through and the stems of the submerged plants will free themselves, float to the surface and perish.

Floating plants Float the plants on the surface of the water.

Introducing the planting baskets

Each plant must be placed at the recommended depth, if necessary on a pile of bricks to bring them up to the correct level. Choose the position carefully; once in place the containers should not be moved as this will disturb the growth of the plants.

Gently lower the planting basket into the water. If the water is deep, thread a piece of thick string through each side of the basket and gently release the string until the basket comes to rest on the floor of the pool. Once it

Planting

3 With a trowel or your hand, dig a hole large enough for the roots of the plant, and place the plant in the hole.

4 Cover the roots with the planting medium and firm the surface, especially around the roots of the plants.

is in position, remove the string. If you cannot reach the middle of the pool from the edge, place a broad plank across the pool and carefully crawl along it in order to introduce the basket into the pool.

To place baskets in large pools, you will need the help of a second person. Cut two pieces of string as long as the longest side plus the depth of the pool. Thread these through the sides of the basket near the top, one at either side. Carry the basket to the pool and, with one person on each side, position it over the water. Slowly lower the basket into the pool and when it has come to rest on the bottom, carefully free the string.

Retrieve planting baskets from shallow pools simply by reaching down into the water and lifting them out. If the water is deep, it will be necessary to wade into the pool and take the container out by hand. This should be done as little as possible as it will disturb the pool's environment. If you are wearing waders, make sure they are chest-waders; even in a pool as shallow as 3ft (90cm) thigh-waders may fill with water when you bend down to pick up the basket.

WATERING

Always water the soil in planting baskets thoroughly to remove the air before introducing them to the pool. If this is not done properly, streams of air bubbles will rush up to the surface when the planting basket is introduced to the pool, disturbing the soil and plants.

Use a fine-rosed watering can to ensure an even spray and soak the baskets.

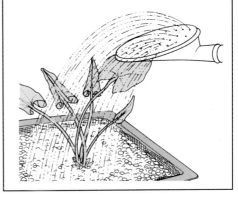

5 After watering the plant in, cover the surface of the planting medium with a ½in (1.25cm) layer of pea gravel.

6 Carefully place the basket in the water; if the water is deep, use lengths of string to lower it in.

Planting 3

Small pools and containers

If the pool or container is too small to accommodate a planting basket, you will have to plant directly into soil on the floor of the pool or container. This should not cause any problems since plants suitable for small water features are fairly restrained in their growing habits so are unlikely to grow into one another. However, should it occur, the plants are easily separated.

Spread a 4-6in (10-15cm) layer of growing medium on the floor and thoroughly soak it to drive out the air, keeping the water level just below the surface of the medium; over-watering at this stage will cause muddy water later on when the pool or container is filled.

Prepare the plants as necessary (see page 100) and push them firmly into the growing medium. Cover with a ½in (1.25cm) dressing of clean pea gravel, and fill the pond or container with water. This must be done very carefully so that the force of the water does not stir up the gravel and soil.

Place a plastic bag on the floor of the pool or container; it must be large enough to cover the area. Put the end of a hosepipe on top of the bag, and slowly turn the tap on with the water at half pressure. The water will gently flow over the bag and down the sides in a fan-like fashion. As the water level rises, the bag and hosepipe will float to the surface; remove the bag as it nears the top and continue filling.

Earth-bottomed pools

While it is perfectly possible to use planting baskets in a wildlife pond or a clay-puddled

Small pools and containers

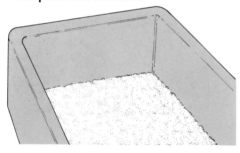

1 Spread a 4-6in (10-15cm) layer of planting medium on the floor and thoroughly soak it with water.

2 Prepare the plants and plant them in the wet soil; cover the surface with a ½in (1.25cm) layer of pea gravel.

3 Place a plastic bag flat over the plants. Take a hosepipe and rest it on top of the plastic bag. Gently turn the tap on.

4 With the tap at half pressure, the bag will gently disperse the water without disturbing the soil and float to the top.

pool, planting directly into soil laid on the floors and marginal shelves will promote a more natural environment.

Waterlilies and deep-water aquatics Mix a generous amount of planting medium with enough water to create a stiff, mud-like consistency. Pack this around the roots of the plant in a 4in (10cm) layer. Next, cut a square of hessian large enough to wrap around the roots, and place the plant in the middle of the square. Using a piece of string, loosely tie the hessian around the neck of the plant to form a sack, and lower the bundle into the water in the desired place. The plant will sink to the pool floor and the roots will push through the hessian and grow into the soil.

Marginal plants These are planted directly into the soil in shallow water. The plants should not become invasive because the steep drop from the marginal shelf to the pool floor will restrict plant growth and the marginals should not spread very far beyond the line of the shelf.

With a trowel or your hand, dig a hole large enough to accommodate the plant. Place the plant in the hole and firm it in, adding more growing medium if necessary. Scatter a ½in (1.25cm) layer of clean pea gravel over the top of the soil.

Submerged bunched aquatics These are easy to plant in earth-bottomed pools. Place them on the surface of the water and the lead weights will pull them down to the pool floor, where they will quickly root.

Floating plants Simply float the plants on the surface of the water.

Making planting sacks

1 Mix some aquatic compost or some heavy garden soil with enough water to make a mud-like consistency.

2 Take a generous handful of the mixture and pack it around the roots of the plant in a 4in (10cm) layer.

3 Place the plant on a square of hessian and, using a piece of string, loosely tie the hessian around the neck of the plant.

4 Carefully lower the sack containing the plant into the pool, making sure it is in the desired place.

Plant propagation 1

Waterlilies

The majority of waterlilies are increased by division of the rootstock or by separating the growth from the eyes. The exception is *Nymphaea tetragona* 'Alba' (syn. *N. pygmaea*), which is raised from seed. Propagation from eyes produces more plants from a rootstock than propagation by division, but this method takes longer to produce flowering plants.

Division

Carefully lift the waterlily out of the basket in late spring or early summer. The crown will have a main fleshy rootstock with smaller side rootstocks branching off it. Remove the outer branches of rootstock with a knife and lightly dust the cut surfaces with flowers of sulphur or powdered charcoal. This will help to prevent fungal infection of the tissue. Discard the old, central part of the rootstock and replant the outer branches of rootstock in planting baskets in fresh soil, and return the baskets to the pool.

Eyes

All mature waterlilies produce eyes along their rootstocks. These eyes are similar to those of a potato, except that in most cases they have tiny shoots on them. If left, the majority of shoots will stay in a semi-dormant state, although a few may develop into branched rootstocks.

Removing eyes Cut the eyes out of the rootstock using the point of a sharp knife. The ones produced by *N. tuberosa* and its cultivars are different; they occur as small protuberances along the rootstock and should be detached by hand or with a knife. Lightly dust the cut surfaces with flowers of sulphur or powdered charcoal.

Potting Pot the adult waterlily in the planting basket and pot the eyes individually, in small pots of heavy garden soil or formulated aquatic planting compost. Stand the pots in a shallow tray of water; the water level should cover the eyes. Place the tray in a greenhouse or in a sheltered part of the garden; as the eyes produce shoots, gradually raise the water level so that it is just above the developing shoots. As they grow, repot the plants into progressively larger pots, immersing each one in a container of water so that the water level is just above the shoots. Once they are a suitable size, introduce them to the pool.

Planting out It can take up to three years to grow a waterlily to a saleable size from eyes,

Division

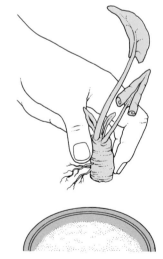

1 Carefully lift the waterlily in late spring or early summer.

2 Remove the outer branches of the rootstock using a sharp knife.

3 Dust the cut tissue to prevent fungal infection and replant the branch.

but if the young plant is being grown for non-commercial reasons, it can be placed in the pool much earlier. Most cultivars can be introduced during the second season; if necessary, stand the pot on some bricks to bring the crown to within 1ft (30cm) of the water surface; this will bring the crown closer to the light and encourage growth.

Seed
Of the hardy waterlilies, only *N. tetragona* 'Alba', which does not produce eyes, can be raised from seed to produce uniform progeny that are true to type. Most other hardy waterlilies do not readily set seed, although mixed seed of larger hybrids are available.

To collect seed, check the large, green, pea-like fruit of the waterlily as it ripens and gather the seed before it is shed. The seed will be embedded in a sticky jelly; do not separate the two.

Preparation Fill small seed trays or pots with a good quality, finely sieved garden soil or aquatic planting compost, and firm the soil.

Planting Using a pair of tweezers, spread the jelly and seed across the planting medium, and cover the surface with a thin layer of the same compost. Place the seed trays or pots in containers of water with the water level just above the soil, and put the containers in a warm room or greenhouse, where there is plenty of light but no direct sunlight.

As the seedlings grow, raise the water level so that they are covered. After three or four weeks the seedlings will appear; raise the water level to cover the seedlings as they grow. At this stage they may be smothered by filamentous algae. To destroy this, spray the seedlings with a proprietary algicide, following the dilution instructions. Remove the dead algae to prevent fermentation of the dying material.

Pricking out Once the first rough leaves appear, the seedlings should be pricked out. Using a small dibber or plant label, lift the clumps of plantlets out of the seed trays or pots. Wash them carefully and tease them apart. Prick out the seedlings so they do not touch in the seed trays which contain good, heavy garden soil or aquatic planting compost. Stand the trays in water with the level above the level of the shoots; as the foliage develops, raise the water level.

Once large enough, repot the plants and grow them in the same way as eyes until they are ready to be introduced to the pool.

Planting eyes

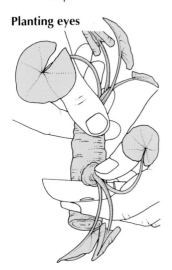  

1 Cut the eyes out of the rootstock with a knife and dust the cut tissue.

2 Pot the eyes individually in small pots of soil or aquatic planting compost.

3 Stand the pots in a tray of water, with the water level just above the eyes.

Plant propagation 2

Other plants

Marginal and bog plants are propagated in one of three ways: by seed, cuttings or division. Most submerged plants are increased from cuttings, and deep-water aquatics are propagated by seed or division. The majority of floating aquatics reproduce freely by division or runners.

For specific requirements, see individual plant entries.

Seed raising

The annual raising of seed is often the most satisfactory and economical form of propagation, especially if certain plants need replacing each year.

Most aquatic seed is sown immediately it ripens in summer and early autumn, or else it can be stored in phials of water until a suitable sowing time.

Very few collected seeds can be kept in seed packets because some are very sensitive to drying out and have a very short life span. These are best sown immediately they ripen. The most notable exceptions to this are *Alisma plantago-aquatica*, *Mentha aquatica*, *Mimulus* and *Myosotis scorpioides*.

Preparation Fill the seed trays or pots to within 1in (2.5cm) of the rims with a soil-based seed compost or aquatic planting compost. Firm down the surface, and water the compost from above using a watering can with a fine rose.

Sowing and germinating Carefully sprinkle the seed thinly over the surface of the growing medium, distributing it as evenly as possible. Large seeds can be sown individually by hand. Lightly cover the surface with sieved sowing medium or silver sand and gently water from above.

The seed of marginals and deep-water aquatics will need wet conditions. Place the trays or pots in a shallow container of water so that the water level is just beneath the surface of the medium. This will allow the moisture to soak through gently, whereas watering from above would disturb the seed; do not raise the water level or the seed will be washed away and will not germinate.

Place the container in a shady part of the greenhouse or in a sheltered place outside. Once the seedlings appear, raise the water level: deep-water aquatics should be completely immersed but marginal plants should only stand in water.

For bog plants, water the freshly-sown seed from above using a can with a fine rose, and place the seed tray in a warm, light corner of the greenhouse or on a window sill. Water regularly until germination occurs.

Pricking out As soon as the cotyledons, or seed leaves, have expanded and the first rough leaf appears, prick out the seedlings. Using a small dibber or plant label, carefully lift out clumps of seedlings and separate each individual to be replanted.

Sowing seed

1 Fill a seed tray with soil-based compost or aquatic planting compost.

2 Firm the compost lightly with your finger tips to 1in (2.5cm) below the rim.

3 Water the compost from above using a watering can with a fine rose.

Fill a seed tray with seed compost and a little coarse bonemeal, about one tablespoon to a bucket of compost. Make small holes 1-2in (2.5-5cm) apart and carefully place one seedling in each hole so that the cotyledons are just above the surface of the compost. Gently water the seedlings from above using a watering can with a fine rose.

If the tray contains deep-water aquatics, place it in a container of water so that the seedlings are covered. Marginal plant seedlings should just stand in water. Raise the level of the water as the plants grow. Bog plants must have plenty of light and they must be watered regularly from above with a fine-rosed watering can.

After approximately six weeks, the seedlings will need lifting and planting in individual pots. The plants will need repotting into progressively larger pots as they grow; each pot must stand in the correct amount of water, according to the type of plant.

When the plants are large enough, they can be planted into baskets and introduced into the pool. Bog plants should be planted directly into the soil of the bog area.

4 Sprinkle the seed thinly and evenly over the surface of the compost.

5 Lightly cover the seed with a layer of sieved compost or silver sand.

6 Place the tray in a container and add the correct amount of water.

7 Lift each seedling free of the compost using a dibber or plant label.

8 Make small holes 1-2 in (2.5-5cm) apart and plant the seedlings.

9 Immerse the tray in the right amount of water for the type of plant.

Plant propagation 3

Hardening off

After the warm, artificial environment of the greenhouse, bog plant seedlings will need to harden off in order to survive outdoor temperatures and conditions. Marginals and deep-water aquatics are unlikely to need hardening off because they are raised in water and are not so sensitive to air temperature changes.

Place the bog plant seedlings in a cold frame, raising the lid gradually over a period of two weeks to allow in cooler air. Alternatively, take the seedlings out of the greenhouse during the day, placing them in a sheltered spot outside, and return them to the greenhouse in the evening. Water regularly; the plants should take on a hardy appearance, with stiff foliage, often a darker colour.

Repot the plants into larger pots as they grow, and introduce them to the bog garden as soon as they are big enough. Once planted, water them in well.

Cuttings

Many aquatic plants are increased from short stem cuttings of non-flowering growths. For some water gardeners, this process of annual renewal is also a good way of keeping plant growth under control.

Taking the cutting

Once growth commences in spring, take short stem cuttings no more than 2in (5cm) in length. Make a straight cut across a leaf joint as it is here that the greatest cellular activity takes place and the cuttings are most likely to root successfully. Trim off any lower leaves.

Planting Aquatic plants will benefit from hormone rooting powders or liquids, although the majority will take root without them. If using a proprietary rooting agent, dip the end of the cutting into the powder or liquid and push it gently into a tray of mud. Place the tray in a container filled with enough water to just cover the surface of the soil; the cuttings will quickly take root. Once well-rooted, the plants can be planted in baskets and introduced to the pool.

Division

Many aquatics can be propagated by division in spring. This involves splitting the root system into smaller clumps, replanting the vigorous outer portions and discarding the exhausted central woody portion. Division is also a way of controlling aquatics (see page 116), in such cases only after selected outer portions are retained and replanted.

Cuttings

1 Take a short stem cutting 2in (5cm) long by cutting straight across the stem at a leaf joint.

2 Dip the base of the stem into the hormone rooting powder or liquid; knock off any excess powder.

3 Insert the cutting up to its leaves in a tray of mud. Place the tray in a container of water.

Dividing into clumps Gently pull the roots apart, using a sharp knife if necessary. If division takes place in summer, the leaves or stems of each plant should be trimmed to a height of 2in (5cm) above the water level. Repot the clumps in planting baskets using soil or aquatic planting compost, and introduce them into the pool.

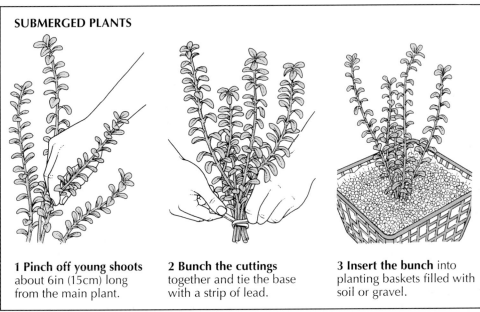

SUBMERGED PLANTS

1 Pinch off young shoots about 6in (15cm) long from the main plant.

2 Bunch the cuttings together and tie the base with a strip of lead.

3 Insert the bunch into planting baskets filled with soil or gravel.

Division

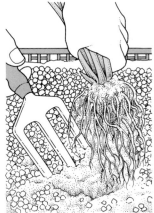

1 Gently lift the plant with a hand fork, taking care not to damage the roots. Knock off the excess soil.

2 Divide the plant by carefully cutting through the roots with a sharp knife to form small portions.

3 Retain the vigorous outer portions for replanting and discard the old, woody central pieces.

111

Feeding plants

Water plants absorb nourishment through their leaves as well as their roots and, to a certain extent, the condition of the pool water will determine the health of the plants.

Waterlilies, deep-water aquatics, bog plants and marginals will all benefit from plant fertilizers, although some marginal plants rapidly exhaust their growing medium and are better divided and replanted rather than fed, as the resulting plants will be healthier. Waterlilies in particular need large amounts of nutrients in order to thrive. Most pools are able to sustain their floating and submerged aquatic population with regular additions of nutrient-rich fresh water in summer. If the pool water is lacking in nutrients, these plants will go into decline; floating aquatics will deteriorate and submerged plants will turn yellow. In such cases, feed the submerged plants in their baskets and sufficient nutrients will leach into the water to satisfy the floating plants.

Feed plants once a year in spring, as soon as they show signs of active growth; slow-release fertilizers will last throughout the summer and into autumn. Do not overfeed as excess fertilizer will leach into the water and encourage algal growth.

Aquatic fertilizers

Most aquatic fertilizers are sold in perforated plastic packets: peel the tape off the perforations and push the sachet down into the container next to the plant's crown. This ensures that the slow-release fertilizer will be used by the plant before it is able to escape into the water and encourage algae.

Home-made bonemeal balls provide an economical method of feeding plants. Mix a handful of moist clay or heavy soil with a teaspoon of coarse bonemeal and roll the mixture into balls the size of golf balls. Push one ball into the growing medium, next to the crown of the plant.

ACIDIC AND ALKALINE WATER

Very acid or alkaline water will affect plant health (see pages 8 and 184). Iron is an essential trace element plant food and, in alkaline conditions, it becomes unavailable. This deficiency can be corrected by spraying affected foliage with a properly formulated iron supplement. Plants in very acid conditions cannot be fed in a similar manner; fertilizers do not help and in some cases turn the leaves of waterlilies brown. The only remedy is to clean the pool, refill it and repot the plants.

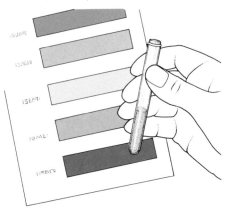

1 Take a beaker of pool water and pour this into a test tube; mix in some of the solution included in the kit.

2 Check the colour of the liquid against the range of colours on the chart in the kit; this will indicate the pH value.

Aquatic fertilizers

1 If using a proprietary aquatic fertilizer, peel the tape off and insert the sachet in the soil, next to the crown of the plant.

2 Once the sachet is in place, cover it with soil and pea gravel; this will prevent the fertilizer leaching into the water.

Home-made fertilizers

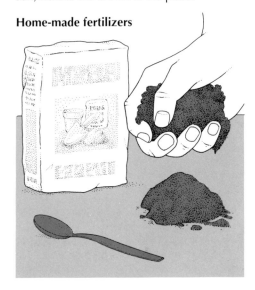

1 Take a handful of moist clay or heavy soil and add approximately 1 teaspoon of coarse bonemeal; thoroughly mix the soil or clay and bonemeal.

2 Roll a small portion of the mixture between the palms of your hands to form a ball the size of a golf ball, and insert the pellet next to the crown of the plant.

Plant pests and diseases

Aquatic plants are subject to a number of pests and diseases. Although these are relatively few in number, their control can be difficult, for the smallest trace of insecticide or fungicide in the pool can lead to the total loss of fish and snail life. Recognizing the symptoms at an early stage is necessary if an effective cure is to be administered.

Brown China mark moth
Pest: a common pest, the moth lays its eggs on floating foliage in late summer, and these hatch into leaf-eating caterpillars.
Effect: the caterpillars burrow into the plant stems and eat the foliage. They also cut and shred the leaves and use the material for building shelters. Feeding off the foliage continues after winter hibernation.
Treatment: hand pick affected leaves or defoliate; plants will regenerate healthy growth.

Great pond snail (see page 174)
Pest: this common and destructive pest has a voracious appetite for aquatic plants as well as algae. It is also the intermediary host for some fish parasites.
Effect: the snails eat waterlily pads and other foliage, reducing them to shreds and leaving a mess of floating debris behind.

Treatment: remove the eggs as soon as they are seen and pick the snails off by hand.

Caddis flies
Pest: there are many species of caddis fly. During summer evenings, the female adult deposits eggs wrapped in protective jelly on and around submerged foliage. The resulting larvae live in protective shelters.
Effect: the larvae feed voraciously, devouring leaves, stems, flowers and roots.
Treatment: chemical control is not very effective as the larvae are protected by their shelters. Fish act as an adequate control, feeding off the larvae.

Waterlily aphid
Pest: a troublesome pest that attacks all types of waterlilies with emergent foliage. The eggs laid in early autumn on plum and cherry trees hatch in spring into winged females. These fly to pond plants and reproduce asexually on aquatics, producing large numbers of wingless females which, in turn, produce a generation of winged males and females in late summer. These return to plum or cherry trees in autumn and lay eggs that overwinter.
Effect: the aphids suck the sap of leaves and flowers, damaging and killing them.
Treatment: forcibly spray the affected plants

Pests and diseases

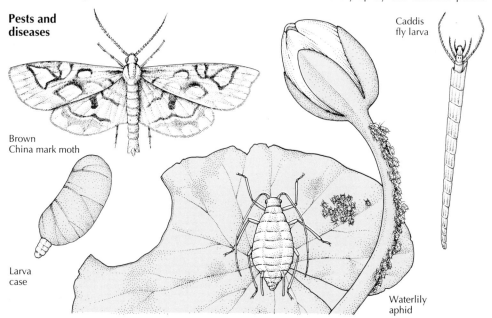

Caddis fly larva

Brown China mark moth

Larva case

Waterlily aphid

with a jet of water in summer to dislodge the aphids for fish to eat. In winter, spray all plum and cherry trees with tar oil wash.

Waterlily beetle

Pest: very difficult to deal with, this pest is fortunately only of local occurrence. After winter hibernation in poolside vegetation, the tiny, grey-brown beetles migrate to waterlily pads and lay their eggs. The resulting yellow-bellied larvae feed on the foliage until pupation occurs. There can be as many as four broods per season.

Effect: the larvae strip waterlilies of their leaves, causing them to decompose.

Treatment: spray the affected plants forcibly with a jet of clear water to dislodge the pests for fish to eat. Hand pick damaged leaves; remove the fading foliage of marginal plants during early autumn to reduce overwintering sites for the adult beetles.

Waterlily leaf spot

Disease: a fairly common disfiguring disease which is an irritation rather than a threat.

Effect: dark patches appear on the foliage of some plants; the leaves rot and disintegrate or develop brown, dry, crumbling edges.

Treatment: remove any affected leaves as soon as possible and burn them.

Waterlily crown rot (see page 124)

Disease: this troublesome disease is believed to be a relative of potato blight.

Effects: yellow cultivars are most susceptible but all types are vulnerable. The leaves and flower stems turn black and begin to rot; the rotting rootstock becomes foul-smelling and gelatinous.

Treatment: remove affected plants and the soil in their container and destroy them to stop the disease spreading.

WARNING

An extremely virulent form of waterlily crown rot, which may not even be related to the original disease, has become established among commercial waterlilies. It affects all waterlilies, irrespective of colour, causing the crown to decompose into an unpleasant brown mass, quickly killing the plant. To date there is no known cure, so infected plants should be destroyed and the pool sterilized with a solution of sodium hypochlorite. Once clean, the pool can be re-filled with water and new plants introduced.

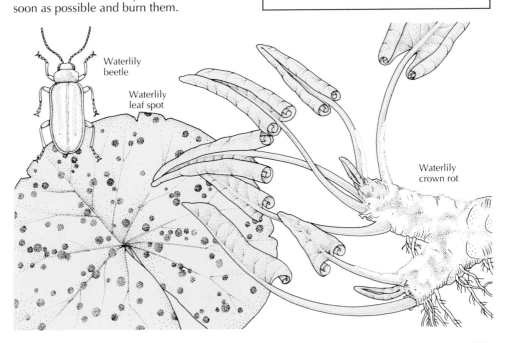

Waterlily beetle

Waterlily leaf spot

Waterlily crown rot

The plant year

SPRING
Plant care
For the best results, propagate and introduce plants in spring (see pages 100 and 106).

Take planting baskets out of the water and examine the plants. Replace weak plants, remove vigorous or tall specimens that have outgrown their space and either divide them or replace them with smaller plants, using fresh soil or compost. Once replanted, feed the plants (see page 112) and return the baskets to the water.

Division
Thin overcrowded and congested plants in spring by dividing them: gently split the root system into smaller clumps by hand or with a sharp knife, and select several choice outer portions for replanting. Do not divide all the plants at once because the pool will look very sparse when the newly divided plants are replanted; choose different groups every year.

Waterlilies The majority of waterlilies need dividing every three or four years. This will become apparent the preceding summer, when the leaves will become congested and there will be far fewer flowers than normal. As soon as the danger of severe frost has passed and the pool is unlikely to freeze over completely, the plant can be lifted and divided.

Deep-water aquatics Deep-water aquatics are treated in the same way as waterlilies: the thick tuberous rootstocks of plants which have outgrown their positions are divided in spring, normally every three or four years.

Marginal plants These require more regular division, every two or three years, or when they begin to escape from their containers and invade other areas of the pool.

Bog plants Divide bog plants every couple of years when they become invasive; when needing attention, they will start to die from the middle outwards. Divide the plants once they have started to grow and when the danger of frost has passed.

Floating aquatics Floating aquatics will reappear in spring, having overwintered on the bottom of the pool as submerged dormant or resting buds. They do not need dividing in spring; later on in the season, if they outgrow their space in the pool, they can be divided into smaller clumps.

Submerged aquatics Only clump-forming submerged plants need dividing, although some may have to be replaced. Do not be too hasty when assessing submerged plants: many die back completely for the winter and look inactive in the early part of the year. If grown in containers, they can be lifted out and replaced if the warm water does not stimulate them into growth.

SUMMER
Dead-heading
Dead-head all flowering plants if possible, to prevent them setting seed. Water plantain and musk can be particularly troublesome: their light seed is carried on the surface of the water to other containers, where it will germinate freely. Dead-heading is, however, often impractical on a regular basis in very large, well-planted pools.

Remove dying foliage and keep the pool tidy by tying up sprawling plants. Remove clumps of unwanted floating and submerged plants by hand.

Weeding
Keep the bog garden and the containers of marginal plants free of weeds.

AUTUMN
Plant care
Remove all waterside foliage as soon as it starts to fade and turn brown, otherwise it will decompose and pollute the water. This also helps control the waterlily beetle (see page 114) which, if allowed to, will hibernate among dead foliage.

Cutting back
When cutting the foliage back, make sure the cut is just above the maximum expected winter water level; hollow-stemmed marginal plants cut beneath the water may rot.

Waterlilies and deep-water aquatics Allow these to die back naturally; the foliage decomposes leaving only a short-term oily scum on the surface of the water. Only if the leaves are showing signs of leaf spot is it necessary to remove them in autumn to prevent further spread of this disease.

Marginal and bog plants Leave these to die back naturally.

Floating plants Mature specimens produce winter buds which fall to the bottom of the pool. The foliage becomes brittle, gradually breaks up and sinks to the floor, where it decomposes without causing problems.

Submerged aquatics These behave in a similar way to floating aquatics; one or two produce winter buds, but the majority remain as dormant root systems.

Bog plants Bog plants will die back naturally; cover any tender ones with a layer of straw at the first sign of frost.

WINTER
Tender plants
The majority of aquatics listed in the plant directories are hardy enough to withstand most winters, but any tender plants should be removed to a frost-free place indoors for the winter months.

Plants grown in sinks, tubs and other containers are more vulnerable in winter than those grown in pools because the water in relatively shallow containers is more likely to freeze. To avoid frost damage, the containers should be drained of water so the plants remain in mud; they can be protected with an appropriate material. Alternatively, place the containers in a frost-free place. Plants can then be left until spring. Immediately new growth appears, the plants should be lifted, divided and planted in fresh planting medium, and the container refilled with water and placed outside.

If you want to remove the containers from their sites during the winter, waterlily and lotus rootstocks can be lifted in late autumn once the foliage has faded and stored in airtight tins of damp sand in a frost-free place. Any marginals can be repotted and kept in frost-free conditions.

Tropical waterlilies and lotus grown in frost-free containers or indoors will continue to grow if the environment is kept warm and the water temperature is well above freezing. If the temperature drops, however, they will die back naturally. If you wish, lift and store them in airtight tins full of damp sand and replant them in the pool in spring as soon as growth starts again.

OVERWINTERING
Most floating and some submerged aquatics produce turions and bulbils. These can be collected from the plants in late autumn and overwintered indoors. Place them in a container of water with a 1in (2.5cm) layer of soil on the bottom. Put the container in a frost-free place for the winter and the turions and bulbils will develop into vigorous young plants the following spring. They will be encouraged into early growth by the warm indoor environment and can be introduced into the pool before other plants have started to grow to minimize the problem of algae.

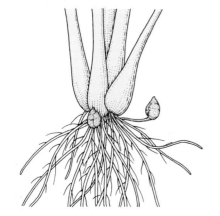

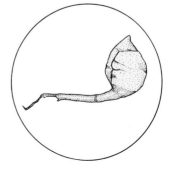

Turion

Hardy waterlilies 1

Plants for mid-depth water

Waterlilies, with their floating foliage and blossoms of great beauty, are a familiar sight in most garden pools. They are available in a wide array of colours, shapes and fragrances, in a range of sizes suitable for any pool. They provide a good splash of colour and flower more or less continuously from early summer until the first autumn frosts.

All these waterlilies are hardy in zones 5-9. They require full sun and still water; in the garden pool they are best grown in planting baskets (see page 100). Those listed below are ideal for the average sized pool with a surface area of 6 x 8ft (1.8 x 2.4m) and a depth of 1½-2½ft (45-75cm). The figures at the end of each entry indicate the depth (d) at which that cultivar grows. For the most part, the surface spread of the plant is between one and one-and-a-half times the depth at which it grows, depending on the size of the planting basket. See page 106 for propagation details.

N. 'Albatros' This white-flowered cultivar has star-shaped blossoms up to 6in (15cm) across. The juvenile purple foliage changes to deep green as the plant matures. d 1-2ft (30-60cm)

N. 'Amabilis' This is one of the finest of the salmon pink cultivars, with blossoms up to 6in (15cm) across. As the star-shaped flowers start to fade to soft rose pink, the bright yellow stamens turn fiery orange. The leaves are large and spreading. d 1½-2½ft (45-75cm)

N. 'American Star' This is similar in character to a tropical waterlily but is hardy in a cold climate. The star-like pink flowers, up to 6in (15cm) across, are held above the water among the leaves. The young purplish-bronze foliage matures to bright green. d 1½-2½ft (45-75cm)

N. 'Andreana' The brick red, cup-shaped blossoms of this cultivar are streaked and shaded with cream and yellow. They grow up to 8in (20cm) across and are held above the

NYMPHAEA AND NUPHAR

It is important to differentiate between waterlilies (**Nymphaea**) and pondlilies (**Nuphar**). Although they are related and look superficially alike, their behaviour is very different. Pondlilies are vigorous plants, ill-suited to small or shallow pools, much preferring large expanses of water. Waterlilies are happy in small pools as long as they are not overcrowded and the water is deep enough for the variety.

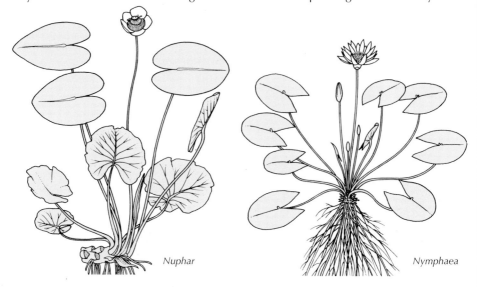

Nuphar

Nymphaea

foliage. The small glossy green leaves are sparingly blotched with maroon and have very distinctive overlapping lobes. d 2-2½ft (60-75cm)

N. **'Arc-en-ciel'** The only waterlily that is grown primarily for its foliage, although it does have pleasing, blush pink, papery blossoms which complement the leaves. The colourful leaves are dark olive green and boldly splashed with purple, rose, white and bronze. d 1½-2½ft (45-75cm)

N. **'Atropurpurea'** A real delight with soft, satiny, deep crimson blossoms of incurved petals and contrasting pale yellow stamens. The foliage is infused with red when young, but changes to green as it matures. d 1-1½ft (30-45cm)

N. **'Comanche'** This popular waterlily has deep orange, rounded blossoms which change to bronze with age. The leaves are purplish-green when young but mature to plain green. d 1½-2ft (45-60cm)

N. **'Conqueror'** The cup-shaped blossoms, up to 6in (15cm) across, are crimson with white flecks and have central clusters of bright yellow stamens. The young purple foliage turns green as it matures. d 2-2½ft (60-75cm)

N. **'Firecrest'** A colourful waterlily with deep reddish-pink, starry flowers which have distinctive red-tipped stamens. The dark green leaves have a strong purple cast. d 1½-2½ft (45-75cm)

N. **'Froebelii'** This is a popular red cultivar for the small pool. The handsome, open-tulip-shaped, deep blood red blossoms have bright orange stamens and are produced among purplish-green leaves. d 1½-2½ft (45-75cm)

N. **'Gloire de Temple-sur-Lot'** This exquisite waterlily has a fully-double array of delicately incurved petals and bright yellow stamens. The rosy pink blossoms fade to pale pink; the leaves are large and plain green. Although one of the finest waterlilies in cultivation, it is

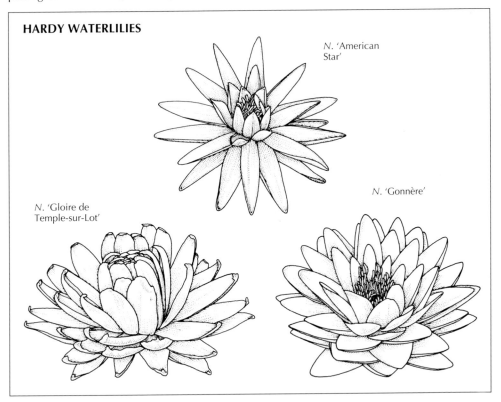

HARDY WATERLILIES

N. 'American Star'

N. 'Gonnère'

N. 'Gloire de Temple-sur-Lot'

Hardy waterlilies 2

slow to settle and rarely flowers well until its second season. d 2-2½ft (60-75cm)

N. 'Gonnère' Also known as 'Crystal White', this is one of the finest hardy waterlilies. The fully-double, pure white blossoms, with bright green sepals, sit among round, pea-green leaves. d 2-2½ft (60-75cm)

N. 'Hermine' This lovely white-flowered *Nymphaea* has tulip-shaped blossoms which are often held just above the surface of the water. This tough cultivar has dark green, medium-sized leaves that are more oval than round. d 1½-2½ft (45-75cm)

N. 'Indiana' The small, orange-red, cup-shaped flowers gradually change colour to deep red as they fade. The green foliage is heavily blotched and stained with purple. d 1½-2½ft (45-75cm)

N. 'James Brydon' Large, crimson, peony-shaped flowers sit among dark purplish-green leaves which are sparingly flecked with maroon. d 1½-2½ft (45-75cm)

N. 'Louise' The double, deep red, cup-shaped blossoms, up to 6in (15cm) across, have yellow stamens and brownish-green sepals. The leaves are plain. d 2-2½ft (60-75cm)

HARDY WATERLILIES

N. 'Hermine'

N. 'James Brydon'

N. 'Marliacea Albida'

N. 'Masaniello'

N. **'Marliacea Albida'** The best known and most widely cultivated white waterlily, this has scented, cup-shaped blossoms, some 6in (15cm) across, held just above the water. The reverse of the petals is sometimes flushed pink; the deep green leaves have purplish undersides. d 1½-2½ft (45-75cm)

N. **'Marliacea Chromatella'** The canary yellow, cup-shaped flowers, up to 6in (15cm) across, often have pink-flushed sepals and outer petals. The large, olive green leaves are splashed with maroon and bronze. d 1½-2½ft (45-75cm)

N. **'Marliacea Flammea'** A colourful cultivar with bright red, cup-shaped flowers flecked with white; the outer petals are deep pink and the stamens are rich orange. The large, olive green leaves are heavily mottled with brown and maroon. d 1½-2½ft (45-75cm)

N. **'Masaniello'** The fragrant, rounded blossoms are rose pink flecked with crimson and fade to deep carmine red. The stamens are deep orange; the leaves are plain green. d 1½-2½ft (45-75cm)

N. **'Moorei'** The soft yellow flowers are similar to those of *N.* 'Marliacea Chromatella'. The leaves are spotted with purple. d 1½-2½ft (45-75cm)

N. **'Odorata Sulphurea Grandiflora'** Fragrant, star-shaped, yellow blossoms are held above heavily mottled, dark green foliage. d 1½-2ft (45-60cm)

N. **'Pink Sensation'** This colourful and prolific pink cultivar has attractive, fragrant, star-shaped blossoms and deep green, rounded leaves which have reddish undersides. d 1½-2½ft (45-75cm)

N. **'Rose Arey'** A popular scented waterlily which smells strongly of aniseed. The large, star-shaped flowers have rose pink petals and bright yellow stamens; the young foliage is crimson and matures to a greenish-red. d 1½-2½ft (45-75cm)

N. **'Sultan'** This attractive waterlily has iridescent, star-shaped, cherry red flowers which are irregularly streaked with white. The leaves are dark green and rounded. d 1½-2½ft (45-75cm)

N. **'Sunrise'** Probably the largest-flowering yellow waterlily, with individual papery blossoms that reach 8in (20cm) across. The dull green leaves are sparingly blotched with brown and they have red undersides. d 2-2½ft (60-75cm)

N. **'Virginalis'** This pure white waterlily has broad, semi-double blossoms with yellow stamens and pink-flushed sepals. These sit among attractive purple-tinged green leaves. d 1½-2½ft (45-75cm)

N. **'William Falconer'** This striking waterlily has medium-sized, rounded, blood red flowers with yellow stamens. The juvenile purple leaves change to olive green as they mature. d 1½-2½ft (45-75cm)

HARDY WATERLILIES

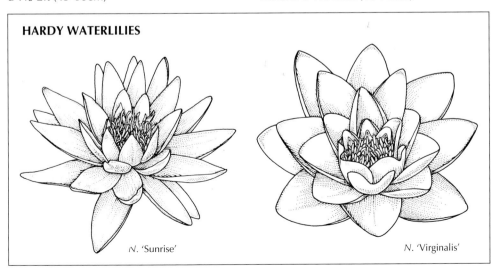

N. 'Sunrise'

N. 'Virginalis'

Hardy waterlilies 3

Plants for shallow water

Due to their diminutive size, dwarf and pygmy waterlilies are ideal plants for shallow water 6in-1½ft (15-45cm) deep, as well as for containers (see page 144). Some of them are genuine pygmy forms while others are more modest versions of our traditional kinds.

Dwarf and pygmy waterlilies should be grown in planting baskets (see page 100) or planted straight into the soil of very small ponds or containers (see page 104) and placed in still water and full sun. They are hardy in zones 5-9. The figures at the end of each entry indicate the depth (d) at which that plant grows. For the most part, the surface spread of the plant is between one and one-and-a-half times the depth at which it grows, although this will depend on the size of the basket. See page 106 for propagation.

N. 'Aurora' This chameleon waterlily is one of the finest waterlilies for tub culture. The creamy-coloured buds open out into cup-shaped, yellow flowers which pass through orange to blood red as they age. Each colour phase lasts one day. The olive green foliage is mottled with purple. d 1-1½ (30-45cm)

N. candida This charming and very hardy species produces an abundance of pure white, small, cup-shaped blossoms. These have bright golden stamens which are tipped with crimson stigmas. The leaves are plain green. d 1-1½ft (30-45cm)

N. 'Caroliniana' This delightful waterlily has fragrant, blush pink, papery blossoms made up of slender petals and bright yellow stamens. It is not a true dwarf or pygmy but grows well in shallow water and does not spread too far. Its various selections 'Caroliniana Nivea' (pure white), 'Caroliniana Perfecta' (salmon pink) and 'Caroliniana Rosea' (rose pink) are also popular. They all have plain green foliage. d 1-1½ft (30-45cm)

N. 'Ellisiana' This cultivar will flourish in shallow water although it is not a true dwarf. Of modest spread, it is prolific and free-flowering, and produces startling open-tulip-shaped, wine red flowers with bright orange stamens. The leaves are small and plain green. d 1-1½ft (30-45cm)

N. 'Graziella' Not a true dwarf, this cultivar will grow in up to 2ft (60cm) of water, although it is happiest in half that depth. The orange, cup-shaped flowers have deep orange stamens and sit among heavily mottled purple and olive green foliage. d 1-1½ft (30-45cm)

N. Laydekeri hybrids This race of small, tulip-shaped hybrids is excellent for tub culture and small pools. They all prosper in as little as 1ft (30cm) of water, although they will tolerate twice that depth.

N. 'Laydekeri Alba' The pure white blossoms with yellow stamens sit among plain green leaves. The flowers have an unusual fragrance of tea.

N. 'Laydekeri Fulgens' This fragrant cultivar has bright crimson flowers with reddish stamens. The foliage is dark green on top and purple underneath.

N. 'Laydekeri Lilacea' The scented, soft pink flowers with bright yellow stamens age to a deep rosy crimson. The green leaves are occasionally blotched with brown.

N. 'Laydekeri Purpurata' Rich vinous-red blossoms with bright orange stamens sit among small green leaves. These have purple undersides and are occasionally splashed with black or maroon.

N. 'Laydakeri Rosea' The small, deep rose-coloured flowers have bright orangey-red stamens and turn crimson with age. The green leaves have reddish undersides.

N. odorata var. minor Often known as the millpond waterlily, this is a dwarf version of the vigorous and sweetly scented North American *N. odorata*. Rarely spreading more than 1½ft (45cm) across the surface of the water, this waterlily has fragrant, white, star-like blossoms and rounded, plain green leaves which have dark red undersides. d 1-1½ft (30-45cm)

N. tetragona (syn. *N. pygmaea*) These true pygmy waterlilies are miniature replicas of the popular waterlilies rather than merely dwarf forms, and all are good for tub culture. They are capable of growing in as little as 6in (15cm) of water, tolerating up to 1ft (30cm).

N. t. 'Alba' The smallest waterlily: each white, star-shaped blossom is no more than 1in (2.5cm) across. The leaves are tiny, oval and dark green with purple undersides.

N. t. 'Helvola' This free-flowering cultivar has star-shaped, canary yellow flowers and

HARDY DWARF AND PYGMY WATERLILIES

N. 'Aurora'

N. 'Caroliniana'

N. 'Laydekeri Fulgens'

N. tetragona 'Helvola'

orange stamens. The olive green leaves are heavily mottled with purple and brown.

N. t. 'Johann Pring' A true pink pygmy with elegant, satiny, starry blossoms and plain green leaves.

N. t. 'Rubra' This beautiful, shy-flowering cultivar has startling blood red, star-like blossoms and bright orange stamens; the tiny purplish-green leaves have reddish undersides.

123

Hardy waterlilies 4

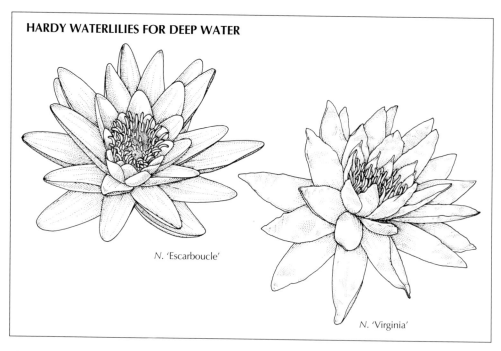

HARDY WATERLILIES FOR DEEP WATER

N. 'Escarboucle'

N. 'Virginia'

Plants for deep water

There are many waterlilies that prosper in water up to 10ft (3m) deep. Most benefit from a larger pool with a minimum surface area of 10ft (3m) sq, although they will tolerate a smaller pool.

These waterlilies require full sun and still water, and they are hardy in zones 5-9. Grow them in planting baskets or plant them in the earth floor of natural pools (see pages 100 and 104). The figures at the end of each entry indicate the depth (d) at which that species or cultivar grows. For the most part, the surface spread of the plant is between one and one-and-a-half times the depth at which it grows, although this will depend on the size of the basket. See page 106 for propagation details.

N. alba (common white waterlily) A good choice for large expanses of water and for wildlife pools (see page 140). The attractive, cup-shaped, pure white blossoms have bright yellow stamens, and the foliage is fresh green. d 10ft (3m)

N. **'Charles de Meurville'** A very vigorous cultivar with large, star-shaped blossoms made up of plum-coloured petals that are tipped and streaked with white. These darken to a very attractive deep port-wine colour with age. The leaves are large and deep olive green. d 3-4ft (90cm-1.2m)

N. **'Colonel A. J. Welch'** A tough, vigorous cultivar, it produces numerous cup-shaped, soft yellow blossoms which peep from the foliage rather than standing well clear of it. This is the only hardy waterlily that reproduces viviparously, with the flower stems carrying young plants. d 2½-4ft (75cm-1.2m)

N. **'Colossea'** Fragrant, flesh pink blossoms, up to 9in (23cm) across, sit among dark olive green leaves. d 3-6ft (90cm-1.8m)

N. **'Escarboucle'** One of the best known and most frequently encountered red cultivars with large, fragrant blossoms up to 1ft (30cm) across. These crimson, cup-shaped flowers have bright yellow stamens. The deep green leaves grow up to 1ft (30cm) in diameter. d 3-6ft (90cm-1.8m)

N. **'Gladstoneana'** A real giant with cup-shaped flowers which reach more than 1ft (30cm) across in deep water. The waxy white petals surround dense clusters of bright

PLANTING DEPTHS

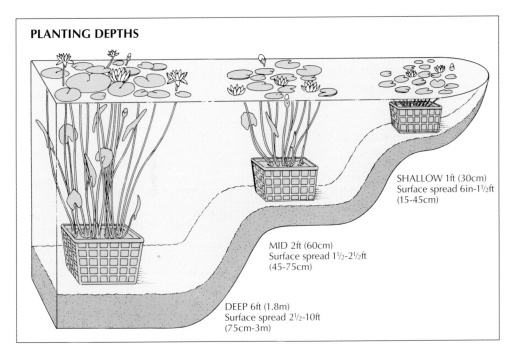

SHALLOW 1ft (30cm)
Surface spread 6in-1½ft
(15-45cm)

MID 2ft (60cm)
Surface spread 1½-2½ft
(45-75cm)

DEEP 6ft (1.8m)
Surface spread 2½-10ft
(75cm-3m)

yellow stamens, and the large, circular, dark green leaves have leaf stalks that have characteristic brown markings. d 3-8ft (90cm-2.4m)

N. 'Marliacea Carnea' This popular pink-flowered waterlily is too large for the majority of garden pools. The pretty, vanilla-scented blossoms, up to 8in (20cm) across, are cup-shaped and have conspicuous central clusters of bright golden stamens. The juvenile foliage is purplish in colour but turns dark green with age. White flowers are often produced the first year after planting. d 2½-5ft (75cm-1.5m)

N. 'Picciola' This lovely waterlily has large, star-shaped, deep crimson flowers, up to 8in (20cm) in diameter, which sit just above the surface of the water. The green leaves have a reddish cast and are spotted and splashed with maroon. d 2½-3½ft (75cm-1.05m)

N. tuberosa 'Rosea' The pink, cup-shaped blossoms have bright red stamens; the leaves are pale green. d 2½-4ft (75cm-1.2m)

N. tuberosa 'Richardsonii' The enormous, magnolia-like white blossoms have yellow stamens and conspicuous green sepals. It will tolerate fairly shallow water but requires a considerable surface area to develop to its full potential. d 2½-4ft (75cm-1.2m)

N. 'Virginia' The star-like, papery, white flowers have broad petals. The green sepals are flushed with brown and the rounded green leaves have reddish undersides. d 2½-4ft (75cm-1.2m)

CROWN ROT DISEASE

It is believed that the devastating crown rot disease (see page 114) originated on imported Japanese N. 'Attraction'. Unless you are certain that a specimen of this plant has not been imported from Japan you should not buy it. This is a pity because it is a lovely waterlily with immense, cup-shaped flowers, up to 9in (23cm) across. The garnet red blooms are flecked with white and the rich mahogany stamens have conspicuous yellow tips; off-white sepals have a rosy flush. It has large plain green leaves and should be planted at a depth of 3-4ft (90cm-1.2m).

Deep-water aquatics

If a plant has its roots at the bottom of a pool and its leaves floating on the surface of the water it is known as a deep-water aquatic.

Deep-water aquatics make an attractive display in the garden pool and, unlike water-lilies, are tolerant of some adverse conditions, such as moving water. This group of plants is grown in planting baskets (see page 100) or straight into the soil of earth-bottomed pools (see page 104). They need a minimum of 1ft (30cm) of water and require the same cultural treatment as waterlilies.

All the following require sun apart from the pondlily, which tolerates partial shade. The figures at the end of each entry indicate: the zones of hardiness (z) and the depth (d) at which that plant grows. For the most part, the surface spread of the plant is between one and one-and-a-half times the depth at which it grows, although this will depend on the size of the planting basket. See page 106 for propagation details.

Aponogeton distachyos (water hawthorn) This reliable plant is capable of providing a continuous display of blossoms from early spring until autumn. The white flowers are forked and bear a double row of bract-like organs, at the base of which are clusters of jet black stamens. A sweetly scented plant, it carries its floating blossoms among dull green, oblong-shaped leaves, which are often heavily splashed and spotted with purple. Increase by division in spring although it will often seed itself. z 7-9; d 1-3ft (30-90cm)

Hottonia palustris (water violet) A beautiful plant with large whorls of bright green foliage and spikes of whitish or lilac-tinted blossoms in summer. It is not easy to grow and rarely succeeds when introduced to a newly estab-lished pool; a thriving plant indicates near perfect water conditions. It grows turions which produce plants the following season. Increase from summer stem cuttings. z 6-9; d 1-1½ft (30-45cm)

Nuphar hybrids (pondlilies) The pondlily is related to the waterlily, but it is less dec-orative, with small, bottle-shaped, button-like flowers and large, leathery, floating foliage. It is better suited to informal or wild-life ponds (see page 140), and is ideal for shade and gently moving water.

N. advenum (American spatterdock) This species produces globular flowers, up to 3in (8cm) across, during summer. These are yellow tinged with purple or green, and have bright coppery-red stamens. The large, thick, fresh green leaves are broadly oval, and float on the surface of the water; clusters of upright leaves stand erect from the vigorous crown. Increase by division in spring. z 4-9; d 1½-5ft (45cm-1.5m)

N. japonicum (Japanese pondlily) Small yellow flowers, up to 3in (8cm) across, are produced throughout the summer. They sit among large but slender arrow-shaped, float-ing leaves and curled, translucent underwater foliage. Increase by division during the spring. z 5-9; d 1½-2ft (45-60cm)

N. lutea (yellow pondlily) This large, coarse plant requires a lot of room and is particularly well-suited to wildlife pools (see page 140). Small, bottle-shaped, yellow flowers are pro-duced for much of the summer among masses of leathery, green leaves. Easy to propagate by division in early spring. z 5-9; d 1-8ft (30cm-2.4m)

N. polysepala (Indian pondlily) This pondlily has golden flowers, occasionally tinged with red. They are up to 6in (15cm) across and are produced during summer. The large, dark green leaves are broad and lance-shaped, growing as much as 1ft (30cm) in length. z 5-9; d 1-5ft (30cm-1.5m)

Nymphoides peltata (water fringe) Often re-ferred to as 'the poor man's waterlily', this cultivar provides a wonderful display of deli-cately fringed, buttercup-like flowers during late summer. The handsome foliage is mottled green and brown. Raise from seed or increase from spring and summer division of the scrambling rootstock. z 5-9; d 1-2½ft (30-75cm)

Orontium aquaticum (golden club) A useful plant for moving water, this relative of the arum will also grow in the muddy shallows, although it is happier in deeper water. This popular plant produces a striking display of very fine yellow and white, pencil-like flowers during late spring, which stand clear of the water among the handsome, narrow, waxy, glaucous leaves. Easy to increase from seed provided it is sown while it is still green. z 4-9; d 1½ft (45cm)

Polygonum amphibium (amphibious bistort)
In mid- and late summer, this creeping plant
has short, dense spikes of reddish flowers
which rise out of the attractive lance-like
floating foliage. This is green with a red flush.
Amphibious bistort is a popular plant for
wildlife pools (see page 140); it will also grow
successfully in slow-moving water. Increase
by division in early spring, although it will
often seed itself quite freely. z 5-9; d 1-4ft
(30cm-1.2m)

Ranunculus aquatilis (water crowfoot)
During early summer, this fine aquatic produces clover-like, toothed, floating leaves
and a profusion of delicate, white, chalice-
like flowers with yellowish-gold centres. The
fine, grass-like submerged foliage is bright
green and much divided. This lovely aquatic
will tolerate moving water and is useful for
streamside planting. Increase from stem cuttings before any floating leaves appear. z 6-9;
d 1-1½ft (30-45cm)

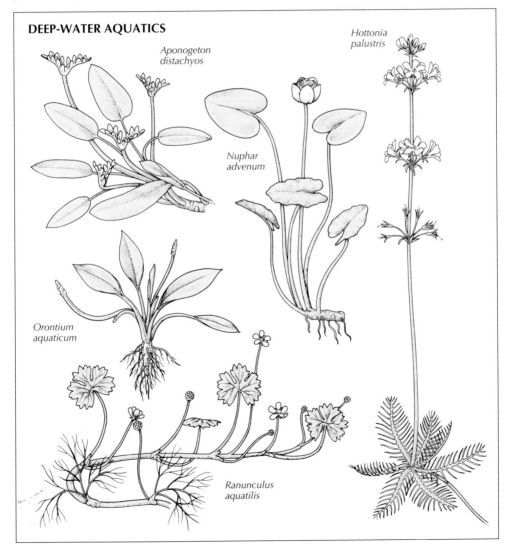

DEEP-WATER AQUATICS

Aponogeton distachyos

Hottonia palustris

Nuphar advenum

Orontium aquaticum

Ranunculus aquatilis

Submerged plants

For the most part, submerged plants have totally submerged foliage and emergent flowers. Although not the most attractive of plants, they play a vital role in maintaining water clarity by starving algae and slimes of their life-giving mineral salts. Their foliage provides excellent cover for fish spawn, making these plants popular with fish and wildlife enthusiasts. They can be overwintered indoors for early spring growth to help combat algae (see page 182).

Very few submerged plants are sold as growing plants; the majority are purchased as lead-weighted bunches of cuttings; the lead is not harmful. Insert these cuttings, still held together with the strips of lead, in planting baskets and totally submerge them in a maximum of 3ft (90cm) of water (see page 102). In natural pools they can be inserted directly into the soil on the pool floor or just placed in the water, in which case they will sink to the floor and take root.

The spread of these plants is indefinite, they will grow until checked: remove unwanted growth by hand or with a net. They will grow in partial shade but they prefer sun; all will tolerate a degree of moving water. They are hardy in zones 6-9. See page 106 for propagation details.

Callitriche hermaphroditica (autumnal starwort) Also known as *C. autumnalis*, this totally submerged, cress-like aquatic only prospers in well-established pools. Fish love to feed on the foliage, which also provides a haven for insect life. A good plant for the wildlife pool (see page 140). Increase by spring and summer stem cuttings.

C. platycarpa More popularly known as *C. verna*, this starwort produces floating leaves in shallow water; the bright green, cress-like foliage disappears completely in winter. Increase by summer stem cuttings.

C. stagnalis This is the least popular of the starworts with gardeners, but it is widely grown by fish fanciers. It has bright green foliage, fruits freely, and loses its leaves in late summer.

Ceratophyllum demersum (hornwort) This and the very similar *C. submersum* are sold under the generic name *Ceratophyllum*. Both are very useful plants for deep and partially shaded ponds. They have dark green, bristly leaves arranged in dense whorls around brittle, wiry stems. In early spring the plants root on the pool floor or in containers, but as summer progresses they detach themselves from their rootstock and float just beneath the surface of the water. They remain free-floating

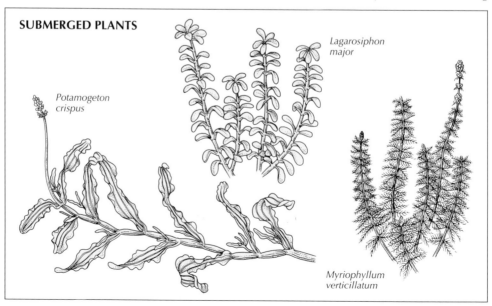

SUBMERGED PLANTS

Lagarosiphon major

Potamogeton crispus

Myriophyllum verticillatum

until the approach of autumn, when they form winter buds which break away and fall to the pool floor. Increase by spring and early summer stem cuttings.

Eleocharis acicularis (hair grass) A plant with fine grass-like leaves that rapidly forms creeping underwater colonies, especially when established in containers of good soil or aquatic planting compost. It is excellent for formal pools as it cannot be seen from above. Sold as plants rather than lead-weighted bunches, it does not root from cuttings; propagate by division any time during the growing season. A good container plant (see page 144).

Elodea canadensis (Canadian pondweed) One of the most versatile and successful of submerged plants. Small, dark green, lance-like leaves are carried in dense whorls along extensive branching stems. Easy to increase by bunched cuttings.

Fontinalis antipyretica (willow moss) A reliable evergreen plant with dark olive green mossy foliage. It prospers under most conditions, but looks best in moving water. It is often grown by fish fanciers as it is an excellent plant for spawning purposes. Increase by bunched cuttings. A good container plant (see page 144).

Lagarosiphon major Also known as *Elodea crispa*, this submerged aquatic has long, trailing, dark green stems clothed in dense whorls of dark green, crispy foliage. It tends to become a little straggly after winter and should be cut back to encourage more compact growth. Easy to increase from cuttings that are taken any time during the active growing season.

Lobelia dortmanna An interesting rather than inspiring plant for shallow water which forms dense carpets of narrow, dark green foliage. In mid- to late summer it produces clusters of delicate lavender-coloured blossoms on wiry stems just above the surface of the water. Increase by division. A good plant for containers (see page 144).

Myriophyllum aquaticum (syn. *M. proserpinacoides*) (parrot's feather) This aquatic has feathery blue-green foliage which often turns red or copper-coloured. The long, scrambling stems are not always submerged and sometimes float on the surface of the water. It is

---

PLANTING DENSITY

To ensure reasonable clarity, submerged aquatics should be placed at an average density of one bunch to every 1 sq ft (0.093 sq m) of surface area (the total pool area excluding marginal shelves). They do not have to be distributed chequerboard style across the floor of the pool, as the important factor is the total volume of plant material. Bunches planted in two or three strategically placed containers are equally effective and much easier to manage.

---

generally a frost tolerant plant but it will not survive very severe winters; overwinter late summer cuttings in a tray of mud in a frost-free place. Increase from spring or summer cuttings.

M. spicatum (spiked milfoil) The handsome, much-divided foliage on long, slender stems provides an excellent spawning ground for goldfish. The whorls of tiny leaflets are coppery green in spring but turn bronze as summer progresses. In mid- to late summer the stems push up tiny crimson and yellow flower spikes. Increase by stem cuttings at any time in the growing season before flower buds appear. A good wildlife plant (see page 140).

M. verticillatum (whorled milfoil) Fine, bright green, needle-like foliage is borne in whorls on slender, trailing stems; small yellowish-green flowers are produced above the water during mid- to late summer. A good aquatic for fish spawning and wildlife pools. Increase any time before flowering.

Potamogeton crispus (curled pondweed) This very fine plant looks rather like crinkly, bronze-green seaweed. Beautiful translucent foliage supports small spikes of striking crimson and cream flowers in mid- to late summer. These peep just above the surface of the water. Increase from spring and early summer stem cuttings.

P. pectinatus (fennel-leafed pondweed) A lovely but delicate-looking submerged plant with very slender, bronze-green foliage. A good choice for still or moving deep water. Easy to increase from spring and early summer stem cuttings.

Floating aquatics

Floating aquatics play a major role in maintaining a well-balanced pool. Along with the floating foliage of waterlilies and deep water aquatics, they reduce the amount of sunlight that falls into the water and absorb mineral salts, making it difficult for algae to survive.

Floating aquatics do not need planting, just placing on the surface of the water. As the majority reproduce freely by division or runners, they grow rapidly and should be controlled by removing unwanted clumps by hand or with a net. The figures at the end of each entry indicate the zones of hardiness (z) for that plant. All the following require sun. See pages 116 and 106 for overwintering and propagation details.

Azolla caroliniana (fairy moss) A small floating fern which congregates in dense but controllable masses. The individual plantlets are a bluish-green colour and lacy in appearance; they turn purplish-red in autumn and in strong sunlight. It will not survive severe weather: overwinter indoors. Increase by redistributing the plantlets. z 7-9

Hydrocharis morsus-ranae (frogbit) In mid- to late summer simple three-petalled white flowers with bright yellow centres rise out of neat rosettes of small, dull green, kidney-shaped leaves. The frogbit forms turions which can be overwintered indoors or left in the pool, in which case they will sink to the bottom during early autumn and reappear on the surface in late spring when the water temperature starts to rise. z 5-9

Stratiotes aloides (water soldier) An unusual, semi-evergreen plant that resembles a pineapple top. The leaves are dark olive green, spiny and carried in neat rosettes which float on, or just above, the surface of the water. Creamy-white, papery flowers are produced in the axils of the leaves during mid- to late summer. It is a persistent plant that reproduces freely from runners; the young plants can be overwintered indoors or left in the pool where they will start to grow in spring. A good plant for the wildlife pool (see page 140). z 4-9

Trapa natans (water chestnut) Each plant consists of a neat rosette of dark green, floating, rhomboidal leaves out of which emerge delicate white blossoms during mid- to late summer. It is an annual that persists by means of spiny, hard, black, nut-like fruits. These fall to the bottom of the pool in autumn and release seed that germinates the following spring. The fruits may be overwintered indoors in a jar if they are kept damp. z 6-9

Utricularia minor (lesser bladderwort) A small carnivorous plant with soft, delicate, finely divided olive green leaves that floats just beneath the surface of the water. The lacy foliage bears many tiny translucent bladders which capture and ingest minute aquatic insects. The flowers are carried on delicate spikes above the surface of the water during summer. They are pale primrose-coloured, rounded and pouched, similar to antirrhinums. Increase by redistributing the tangled foliage. z 5-9

U. vulgaris (greater bladderwort) This larger version of *U. minor* produces a tangled mass of bright green filigree foliage with insect-trapping bladders, and spikes of bright yellow summer blossoms. Increase by redistributing the foliage. z 5-9

Wolffia arrhiza Many gardeners find *Wolffia* appealing because it is believed to be the smallest-flowering plant in the world. It is minute, with tiny greenish flowers and bright green leaves; best in small pools or containers (see page 144). z 6-9

DUCKWEED

The genus **Lemna** are known as duckweeds. They are tiny floating plants which are disliked by pool owners as they rapidly cover the water surface and are difficult to control and remove. A single plantlet caught up in a marginal plant can trigger or restart an invasion. Although duckweed provides useful spawning ground for fish in wildlife pools (see page 140), **Lemna trisulca** (ivy-leafed duckweed) is the only one that can be recommended for a garden pool as it will not invade the entire water surface. It is a lovely little plant with dark green, crispy, translucent foliage which floats in congested masses just beneath the surface of the water. Increase by redistributing the plantlets; it is hardy in zones 5-9.

FLOATING AQUATICS

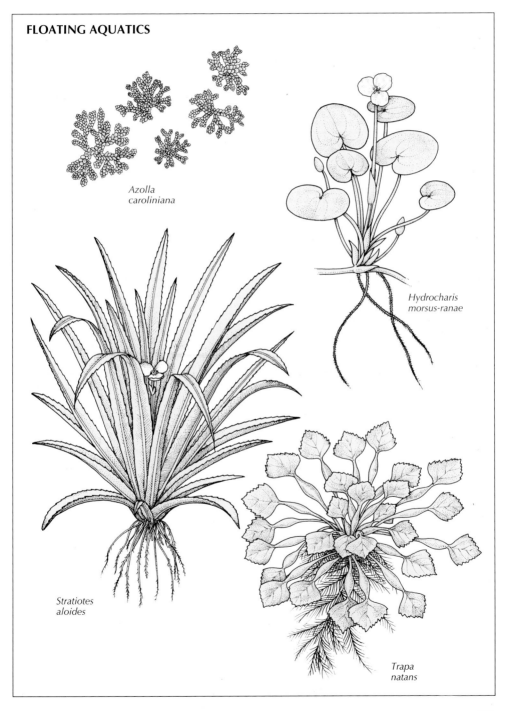

Azolla
caroliniana

Hydrocharis
morsus-ranae

Stratiotes
aloides

Trapa
natans

Marginal aquatics 1

As well as being decorative and adaptable, marginal aquatics are useful for masking and softening the area where land and water meet. They contribute little to the balance of the watery environment but provide an ideal refuge for all manner of aquatic insect life.

Marginal plants grow around the edge of the pool, preferring mud or a few inches of water, although most will tolerate a depth of up to 6in (15cm). All the following marginal plants will tolerate periodic inundation and moving water; grow them in planting baskets or plant them in the soil of earth-bottomed pools (see pages 100 and 104).

The figures at the end of each entry indicate: zones of hardiness (z) for that plant and height (h) and spread (s)* achieved by that plant at maturity under optimum conditions. Suitable light intensity is also given for each plant. See page 106 for propagation details for marginal aquatics.

*If grown in a planting basket, the plant will achieve as little as half the given spread, depending on the size on the container.

Acorus calamus (sweet flag) The shiny, fresh green, iris-like foliage has a strong tangerine fragrance and complements the curious greenish-yellow, horn-like flower spikes produced in summer. The cultivar 'Variegatus' has handsome cream, green and rose striped foliage and is of more modest habit. Increase by division in spring. z 4-9; h 4ft (1.2m); s 2ft (60cm); sun/partial shade

Alisma plantago-aquatica var. parviflorum A very hardy species with distinctive rounded leaves and short pyramids of pink and white flowers during mid-summer. Increase by seed sown as soon as it ripens, or by division during spring. z 4-9; h 2½ft (75cm); s 1½ft (45cm); sun

Calla palustris (bog arum) This is a useful plant for disguising the edge of the pool; it also tolerates shallow water. It spreads by means of stout, creeping rhizomes which are clothed in handsome, glossy, heart-shaped foliage. The small white flowers appear in late spring and are followed in summer by spikes of bright red berries. These contain seed that germinates freely if sown immediately. Winter buds form along the trailing rhizomes and may be used for propagation in spring

before they start to grow. If placed in trays of mud, they will quickly form young plants. z 5-9; h 1ft (30cm); s 1ft (30cm); sun

Caltha palustris var. palustris (syn. *C. polypetala*) (Himalayan marsh marigold) A giant of a plant with dark green leaves up to 10in (25cm) across. It produces large trusses of golden flowers in late spring. Increase by seed or division in spring. z 5-9; h 3½ft (1.05m); s 1½ft (45cm); sun/partial shade

Cotula coronopifolia (brass buttons) A lovely little plant which produces bright golden blossoms in profusion all summer long above strongly scented, light green foliage. It is a short-lived perennial, dying as soon as flowering is over. However, if left undisturbed, it usually seeds freely. z 6-9; h 6in (15cm); s 1ft (30cm); sun

Glyceria maxima 'Variegata' (syn. *G. aquatica* 'Variegata') (variegated water grass) A perennial grass with cream and green striped foliage which, on emerging in early spring, is infused with deep rose pink. Increase by division in early spring. z 4-9; h 4ft (1.2m); s 1½ft (45cm); sun

Houttuynia cordata This plant has bluish-green, heart-shaped leaves and produces four-petalled white flowers with hard central cones in summer. In the beautiful double form 'Flore Pleno', these cones are lost in a dense central ruff of petals. There is also a cultivar called 'Chameleon' which has pink, yellow and green variegated foliage. Excellent plants for carpeting the ground between taller marginal aquatics. Increase by division during spring. z 6-9; h 1ft (30cm); s 1ft (30cm); sun/partial shade

Hypericum elodes (marsh hypericum) An extremely useful plant for shallow water or muddy soil, where it forms a dense carpet of foliage and hides the point where pool meets land. During late summer it produces showy yellow flowers. Propagate by spring division or summer cuttings rooted in mud. z 5-9; h 9in (23cm); s 1ft (30cm); sun

Iris laevigata A lovely blue iris which has given rise to innumerable attractive hybrids. Among the best are 'Alba' (white), 'Colcherensis' (violet and white) and 'Rose Queen' (soft pink). There is also the fine 'Variegata', or 'Elegantissima', which has variegated leaves. All flower during summer and are best

MARGINAL AQUATICS

Calla
palustris

Acorus
calamus

Juncus
effusus
'Spiralis'

Iris
versicolor

Marginal aquatics 2

MARGINAL AQUATICS

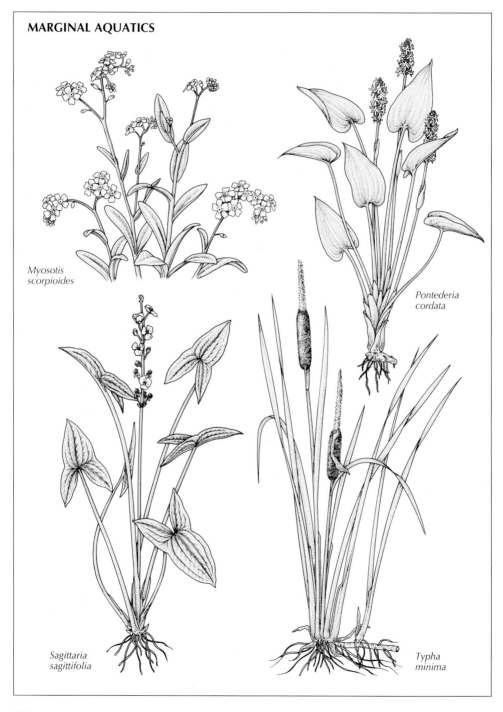

Myosotis
scorpioides

Pontederia
cordata

Sagittaria
sagittifolia

Typha
minima

divided immediately flowering is over. z 4-9; h 3ft (90cm); s 1ft (30cm); sun

I. versicolor Strong violet-blue flowers veined with purple and splashed with gold are produced during summer and make this a popular plant. The cultivar 'Kermesina' is even more lovely, with blooms of deep velvety-plum and similar distinctive markings. Plain green, sword-like leaves complement the flowers. Increase by division during summer directly after flowering. z 4-9; h 3ft (90cm); s 1ft (30cm); sun

Juncus effusus (soft rush) There are only two forms of this plant freely available and of any merit for the small water garden. These are: 'Spiralis' (corkscrew rush) with curiously malformed stems that grow in a spiralling corkscrew (a good container plant, see page 144); and 'Vittatus', a golden variegated cultivar with foliage that has alternate longitudinal stripes of green and yellow. As with many variegated plants, remove any vigorous plain green foliage as it emerges. Propagate both forms by division in spring. z 5-9; h 2ft (60cm); s 1ft (30cm); sun/partial shade

Myosotis scorpioides (water forget-me-not) During early summer, this charming little plant, tolerant of shallow water, is smothered in sky blue flowers that are almost identical to those of the familiar bedding plant forget-me-not. An improved form called 'Semperflorens' is even more lovely, being more compact and producing fewer leaves. Best increased by seed, although division in early spring is generally successful. Occasionally seed-raised plants have attractive white flowers. A good plant for containers (see page 144). z 5-9; h 9in (23cm); s 1ft (30cm); sun

Peltandra virginica (arrow arum) This handsome member of the arum family has bright green, narrow spathes during summer. These rise out of dark green, glossy, arrow-shaped foliage which grows from a short, fleshy rootstock. Readily increased by division in early spring. z 5-9; h 2½ft (75cm); s 1½ft (45cm); sun/partial shade

Pontederia cordata (pickerel) A plant of noble proportions that produces numerous stems, each consisting of an oval or lance-like shiny green leaf and a leafy bract. Spikes of soft blue flowers emerge from among these during late summer. Propagate by division of the rootstocks in early spring or germinate seed when they are still green. z 6-9; h 3ft (90cm); s 1½ft (45cm); sun

Ranunculus lingua (greater spearwort) A tall-growing decorative buttercup with erect, hollow stems which are well-clothed with narrow, dark green leaves and large, golden blossoms. The most popular form is 'Grandiflora', which flowers for much of the summer. Increase by division in the spring. z 5-9; h 3ft (90cm); s 1½ft (45cm); sun

Sagittaria sagittifolia (arrowhead) A popular, handsome native plant with arrow-shaped foliage, good for wildlife pools (see page 140). Tiered spikes of white-petalled flowers with dark centres emerge during summer. It grows from large winter buds which look like bulbs; these can be lifted and redistributed in the spring. Alternatively, increase by division. z 5-9; h 2ft (60cm); s 2ft (60cm); sun

Schoenoplectus lacustris subsp. *tabernaemontani* 'Zebrinus' (syn. *Scirpus tabernaemontani* 'Zebrinus') (zebra rush) A popular mutant which grows best in very shallow water. Its stems are alternately barred with green and white; any plain green stems should be removed as soon as they emerge. Propagate by late spring division. z 7-9; h 3ft (90cm); s 1½ft (45cm); sun

Typha minima This splendid little plant produces masses of spikes of short, fat, brown flowers in late summer among dark green, grassy foliage. It can be successfully accommodated in the tiniest pool. The dried heads are excellent for flower arrangements. A good container plant (see page 144). Increase by division during early spring. z 6-9; h 1½ft (45cm); s 1ft (30cm); sun

Veronica beccabunga (brooklime) Although not a spectacular plant, brooklime is useful as it climbs out of the water and masks the area where pool meets land. It will also spread across the surface of the water, providing shade for fish, and its hanging roots are a suitable repository for spawn. During summer its dark green, glossy foliage is sprinkled with tiny blue and white flowers. Propagate annually in spring by pushing short stem cuttings into the mud in the pool or into trays of wet soil. z 5-9; h 9in (23cm); s 1½ft (45cm); sun/partial shade

Bog plants 1

The bog is the very wet peripheral area of the water garden, as compared to the margins which refer to the shallows of the pool. It is difficult to distinguish between bog and marginal plants, but most gardeners agree that those plants which prosper in standing water are marginal plants, while the ones which require very wet conditions, but will not tolerate long periods of inundation, are bog plants. Unlike marginal plants, bog plants are planted directly into the soil of the bog garden. All the following can be recommended for the garden pool with a bog area, and some are also suitable for the wildlife bog garden (see page 140).

The figures at the end of each entry indicate: zones of hardiness (z) and height (h) and spread (s) achieved by that plant at maturity under optimum conditions. Suitable light intensity is also given for each plant entry. See pages 102 and 106 for planting and propagation details.

Ajuga reptans (bugle) Dense, creeping, herbaceous plants that are invaluable for disguising the harshness of the pool edge. The common bugle is not particularly attractive but its cultivars are most handsome. 'Atropurpurea' has purplish-bronze leaves, while 'Multicolor' has cream variegations on a green background, with a pinkish-buff cast. Both have spikes of dark blue flowers during summer. Increase by division of the creeping stems or plantlets any time between early autumn and early spring. z 4-9; h 6in (15cm); s 1ft (30cm); sun/partial shade

Aruncus dioicus (syn. *A. sylvester*) (goat's beard) A tall plant with frothy plumes of creamy-white summer flowers. It has pale green, deeply cut and lobed leaves, and stems that are hard and green, rather like bamboo. The dwarf form 'Kneiffii' is similar, but has much more finely divided foliage and attains no more than 3ft (90cm) in height. Both are easy to increase by division during winter. z 4-9; h 5ft (1.5m); s 2ft (60cm); sun/shade

Astilbe hybrids (false goat's beard) A wideranging group of perennials with handsome feathery plumes of flowers which are produced above bold clumps of attractive divided foliage. All flower from mid- to late summer. Among the more popular hybrids are 'Fanal' (bright crimson), 'Peach Blossom' (salmon pink), 'Venus' (pale pink) and 'White Gloria'. All are easy to increase by division of the coarse woody rootstock during winter or early spring. z 4-9; h up to 4ft (1.2m); s 2ft (60cm); sun/partial shade

Cardamine pratensis (cuckoo flower) A pretty spring-flowering plant with single rosy-lilac flowers produced above tufts of pale green, ferny foliage. There is a double form called 'Flore Pleno' which is even more lovely. Both are easily raised from seed or increased by division during winter. A good plant for the wildlife pool. z 4-9; h 1½ft (45cm); s 1ft (30cm); sun/partial shade

Eupatorium purpureum (Joe Pye weed) an attractive perennial with crowded, terminal heads of small, tubular, pinkish-purple flowers in late summer and early autumn. The leaves are oval in shape and coarse, and are arranged in whorls along purplish stems. Increase by division in winter or seed sown in early spring. z 4-9; h 4ft (1.2m); s 2ft (60cm) sun/partial shade

Filipendula ulmaria (meadowsweet) Frothy spires of creamy-white blossoms are produced during summer above handsome, deeply-cut, dark green foliage. The double form has the most attractive flowers, while the golden-leafed 'Aurea' has the most striking foliage. A good plant for the wildlife pool. Increase by division during winter or early spring. z 4-9; h 5ft (1.5m); s 2ft (60cm); sun/partial shade

F. vulgaris (syn. *F. hexapetala*) (dropwort) An attractive fern-leafed plant related to common meadowsweet with similar creamy-white flowers produced in summer. There is also a fully-double form called 'Flore Pleno'. Increase by division during winter or early spring. z 4-9; h 2ft (60cm); s 1ft (30cm); sun/partial shade

Gunnera manicata One of the largest and most remarkable herbaceous plants that can be grown outside in this country. Rather like a giant rhubarb, it has large kidney-shaped leaves, up to 6ft (I.8m) across, with deeply indented margins. The undersides and stalks of the leaves are liberally sprinkled with unpleasant bristly hairs. The reddish, branching flower spike, produced in mid-summer, resembles a huge bottlebrush, growing up to 3ft (90cm) high. This rises from a thick, creeping

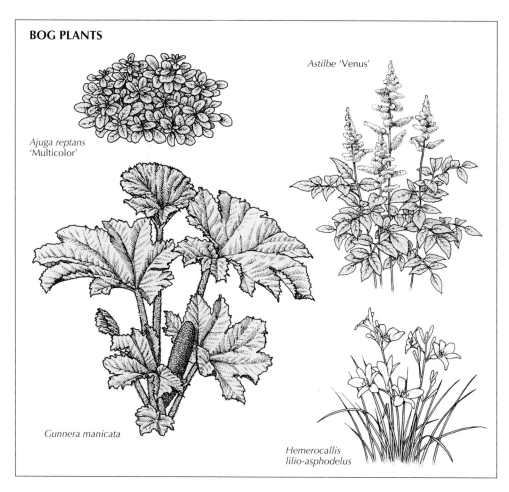

BOG PLANTS

Ajuga reptans
'Multicolor'

Astilbe 'Venus'

Gunnera manicata

Hemerocallis
lilio-asphodelus

rhizome that is densely clothed in brown, papery scales. Gunneras like a moist, cool position: alongside a stream or pool, where their huge spreading leaves can be mirrored in the water, is aesthetically and culturally ideal; they are also welcome additions to the wildlife pool. The plant is susceptible to frost and will need winter protection in frosty areas; a covering of straw, bracken or, with established plants, their own frost-blackened leaves, is usually sufficient. Increase by division in spring or sow fresh seed; the former is more reliable. z 7-9; h 8ft (2.4m); s 8ft (2.4m); sun/partial shade

Hemerocallis (daylily) While many daylilies are grown successfully in the herbaceous border, they enjoy life to the full in the bog garden. All form large clumps of narrow, arching, strap-like leaves which produce wiry stems with a succession of large, brightly-coloured, trumpet-like flowers. Each blossom lasts a single day, but so many buds are produced that the display continues for much of the summer. There are innumerable cultivars including 'Pink Damask', the bright orange 'Mikado' and the tall-growing lemon yellow 'Hyperion', and several species like *H. lilio-asphodelus*, which has fragrant, yellow-chrome flowers, are also suitable for bog gardens. All daylilies are easily propagated by division during winter. z 4-9; h 4ft (1.2m); s 2ft (60cm); sun

Bog plants 2

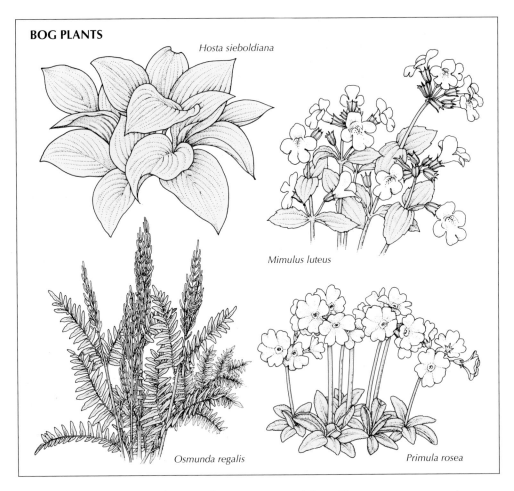

BOG PLANTS

Hosta sieboldiana

Mimulus luteus

Osmunda regalis

Primula rosea

Hosta sieboldiana (syn. *H. glauca*) (plantain lily) One of the largest of the plantain lilies. Big, bold, glaucous, heart-shaped leaves, up to 6in (15cm) across and often twice as long, make an attractive summer feature. Slender flower spikes support pendent, dull white, bell-like blossoms in summer. Easily increased by division in spring just as the shoots are emerging. z 4-9; h 2ft (60cm); s 2ft (60cm); sun/shade

H. lancifolia A green foliage species with long, lance-shaped leaves which complement the erect sprays of lilac blossoms that appear in mid-summer. Propagate by spring division. z 4-9; h 2ft (60cm); s 1½ft (45cm); sun/shade

H. undulata The two most commonly grown variegated forms both have brightly-coloured cream, green and white leaves which are somewhat twisted and undulating. Remove any flower buds as these tend to detract from the beauty of the foliage. Increase by spring division. z 4-9; h 1ft (30cm); s 1½ft (45cm); sun/shade

Iris ensata (syn. *I. kaempferi*) (Japanese clematis-flowered iris) This beautiful mid-summer-flowering swamp iris has tufts of broad grassy foliage crowned with exotic clematis-like flowers. Among the best cultivars are 'Blue Heaven' (rich purple-blue velvety petals marked with yellow), 'Landscape at Dawn' (fully-double, pale rosy lavender blooms) and 'Mandarin' (deep violet flowers). 'Variegata' is also very attractive, with cream and green variegated foliage and small, deep violet-blue flowers. Increase named cultivars by division immediately after flowering; good mixed colours can be raised from seed which should be sown during early spring. Unlike the majority of other irises, *I. ensata* must be grown in acid soil. z 5-9; h 2½ft (75cm); s 1ft (30cm); sun

I. sibirica (Siberian iris) An easy-to-grow summer-flowering iris, tolerant of almost any moist soil conditions. It has smaller blossoms and narrower, more grassy leaves than *I. ensata*. *I. sibirica* is fairly subdued, with pale blue flowers, but its selected cultivars and hybrids are striking and colourful. Among the most popular are 'Ottawa' (deep violet), 'Perry's Blue', 'Perry's Pygmy' (a blue-flowered dwarf form) and 'Snow Queen' (white). Increase by division after flowering. z 4-9; h 2½ft (75cm); s 1ft (30cm); sun

Lysimachia nummularia (creeping Jenny) This evergreen carpeting plant is ideal for masking the edge of a pool and provides attractive ground cover between tall marsh plants in boggy areas. It is studded with starry, buttercup-like flowers during mid-summer; the cultivar 'Aurea' has bright yellow foliage. Increase by spring division, or short cuttings in summer. z 5-9; h 2in (5cm); s 1½ft (45cm); sun/shade

Lythrum salicaria (purple loosestrife) Bushy stems carry slender spikes of deep rosy purple blooms in late summer. Named cultivars include 'The Beacon', 'Lady Sackville' and 'Robert', which range in colour from purple, through rose-pink, to pink. A good plant for wildlife pools. Common purple loosestrife is increased from seed, cultivars may be divided in early spring. z 4-9; h 4ft (1.2m); s 2ft (60cm); sun/partial shade

Mimulus species and hybrids (musk) The majority of *Mimulus* prefer boggy conditions; those best suited to the bog garden are *M. luteus* and *M. guttatus*. Among the finest are the pastel-coloured 'Monarch', the mixed 'Queen's Prize' and the bright red 'Bonfire'. All the popular cultivars flower from mid-summer until autumn. Easy to raise from seed sown in spring. z 6-9; h 1ft (30cm); s 1ft (30cm); sun

Osmunda regalis (royal fern) A tall handsome fern with bright green, large, leathery fronds throughout the summer, which turn bronze in autumn. There are a number of crested and tasselled forms. Increase by division of the crowns in spring. z 5-9; h 6ft (1.8m); s 2½-3ft (75-90cm); sun/shade

Primula A large number of species and hybrids flourish in the damp of the bog garden. The following provide a continuity of colour. All can be raised successfully from seed sown either immediately after it ripens or during early spring.

P. aurantiaca An early-flowering candelabra primula with tiers of bright orange blossoms in late spring. z 5-9; h 2½ft (75cm); s 1ft (30cm); sun/partial shade

P. beesiana A mid-summer-flowering candelabra species with attractive rich rosy purple flowers. z 5-9; h 2ft (60cm); s 1ft (30cm); sun/partial shade

P. bulleyana A candelabra species of primula with orange-yellow flowers during mid-summer. z 5-9; h 2½ft (75cm); s 1ft (30cm); sun/partial shade

P. denticulata (drumstick primula) Rounded heads of blue or lilac flowers are produced on short, stout stems in spring. z 5-9; h 1ft (30cm); s 1ft (30cm); sun/partial shade

P. florindae (Himalayan cowslip) This primula produces flowers in mid- to late summer which resemble large cowslips. z 5-9; h 3ft (90cm); s 1½ft (45cm); sun/partial shade

P. japonica Crimson blossoms in dense, tiered whorls are held above bright green, cabbage-like leaves during mid-summer. 'Miller's Crimson' and 'Postford White' are excellent cultivars. z 5-9; h 2ft (60cm); s 1ft (30cm); sun/partial shade

P. rosea One of the earliest and tiniest primulas for the bog garden. Brilliant rosy pink blossoms smother the ground-hugging foliage during early spring. z 5-9; h 6in (15cm); s 6in (15cm); sun/partial shade

Trollius europaeus (globe flower) A bold, buttercup-like plant which produces yellow flowers during spring. There are some excellent cultivars available, including 'Canary Bird' (soft yellow), 'Fire Globe' (intense orange) and 'Orange Princess'. Increase by division during the dormant period. z 4-9; h 3ft (90cm); s 1ft (30cm); sun

Wildlife plants 1

All wildlife plants are chosen for their ability to attract wildlife, rather than for their decorative appeal. Native plants provide the best resources as they are part of our natural ecosystem. Insects, mammals and birds all benefit from these, be it for food or nesting. Cover is also an important feature of the wildlife pool: there must be enough foliage to protect and encourage the native fauna.

The following marginal plants can be planted in planting baskets or straight into the earth of natural-bottomed pools (see pages 100 and 104); plant the bog plants directly into the soil (see page 102). The figures at the end of each entry indicate: zones of hardiness (z) for that plant and height (h) and spread (s)* achieved by that plant at maturity under optimum conditions. The suitable light intensity for each plant is also given. See page 106 for propagation details for wildlife plants.
* If grown in planting baskets, the plant will achieve as little as half the given spread, depending on the size of the container.

Alisma plantago-aquatica (water plantain) An easy-going marginal with attractive oval foliage and, in summer, loose pyramidal panicles of pink and white flowers. The seeds are a source of food for various fauna. Increase by seed sown as soon as it ripens or divide during spring. z 4-9; h 2½ft (75cm); s 1½ft (45cm); sun

Butomus umbellatus (flowering rush) Throughout late summer, this handsome native marginal aquatic produces spreading umbels of dainty rose pink flowers on stout, erect stems which grow through masses of narrow, twisted foliage. It attracts pollinating insects and the rootstock is a source of food for small mammals. Increase by pushing the bulbils from the basal axils of the leaves into mud just beneath the water. z 4-9; h 3ft (90cm); s 1½ft (45cm); sun

Caltha palustris (marsh marigold) A familiar marginal plant, useful for shallow water, which attracts insect life early in the year. During spring, it is garlanded with waxy blossoms of intense golden yellow. It is a compact plant with glossy, dark green foliage. Increase by seed sown immediately it ripens or divide the crowns in spring. z 4-9; h 2ft (60cm); s 1ft (30cm); sun/partial shade

Carex pendula (pendulous sedge) This semi-evergreen marginal provides winter cover. It has attractive, broad, green leaves and, in spring, long, drooping, khaki, catkin-like flowers that look particularly good reflected in water. It prefers wet soil rather than standing water. Easy to increase from seed sown during spring. z 5-9; h 4ft (1.2m); s 1½ft (45cm); sun/partial shade

Cyperus longus (sweet galingale) This is a striking native marginal with fresh green, grassy foliage and terminal umbels of stiff, spiky leaves which radiate from the stem like the ribs of an umbrella. It has insignificant flowers which are small and brownish in colour. A useful plant, it adapts to most pool conditions, but is happiest when growing beside water and creeping down to colonize the mud at the water's edge. Its roots create a carpet which help prevent the erosion of steep banks. Increase by spring division or seed sown immediately it ripens in late summer. z 5-9; h 3½ft (1.05m); s 1½ft (45cm); sun

Damasonium alisma (starfruit) A small marginal plant similar to the water plantain with whorls of white blossoms during summer, followed by curious star-shaped fruits in autumn which provide food for small animals and birds. The leaves are strap-like and grow from a stout rootstock. Easily increased from seed sown as soon as it ripens. z 5-9; h 7½in (19cm); s 6in (15cm); sun

Iris pseudacorus (yellow flag) A large, mid-summer-flowering, vigorous marginal with flowers that attract insects and seeds that are eaten by small animals. The soft primrose var. *bastardii* is particularly attractive, as is the bright golden yellow 'Golden Queen'. The most spectacular is 'Variegata', with its variegated foliage, although this rarely attains the height of the other kinds. Increase by division in summer immediately after flowering. z 4-9; h 4½ft (1.35m); s 2ft (60cm); sun

Ludwigia palustris (false loosestrife) Grown for its foliage rather than its strange, tiny, petalless flowers, this native marginal plant has long, smooth, mid-green leaves. Its stems spread across the surface of the water and produce small hanging roots; these harbour aquatic insects and provide spawning ground for fish. Easily increased by summer stem cuttings. z 6-9; h 9in (23cm); s 1ft (30cm); sun

WILDLIFE PLANTS

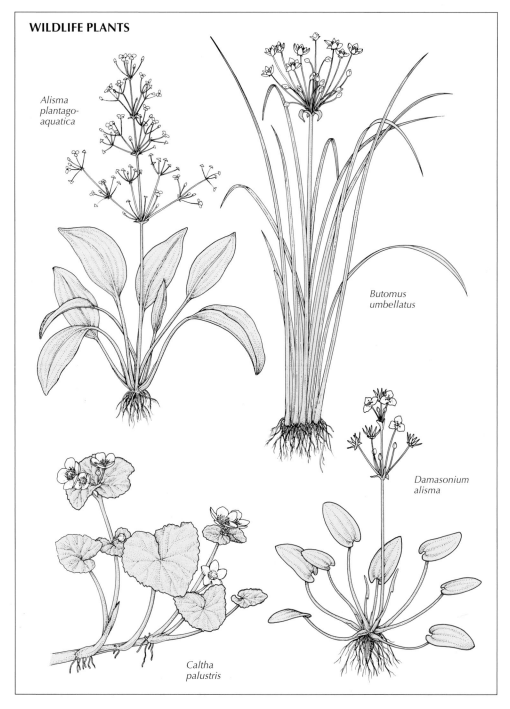

*Alisma
plantago-
aquatica*

*Butomus
umbellatus*

*Damasonium
alisma*

*Caltha
palustris*

Wildlife plants 2

WILDLIFE PLANTS

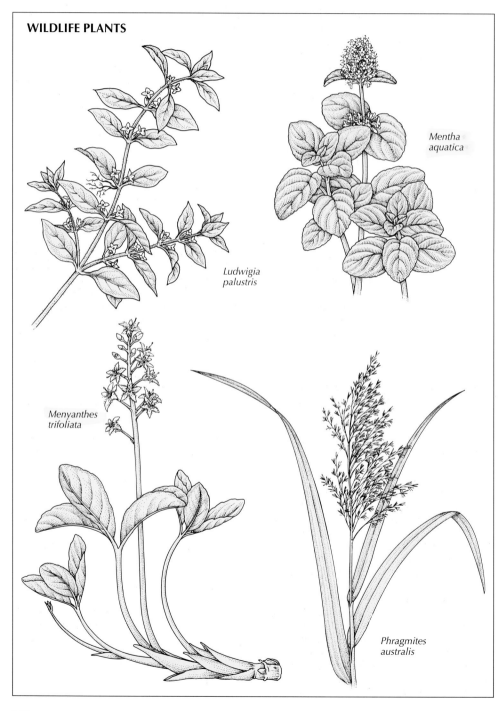

Mentha
aquatica

Ludwigia
palustris

Menyanthes
trifoliata

Phragmites
australis

Mentha aquatica (water mint) This strongly scented marginal plant attracts pollinating insects. It enjoys shallow water or mud, and when growing happily it produces dense, terminal whorls of lilac pink flowers during late summer, amidst an abundance of hairy, greyish-green foliage. Unfortunately, it is inclined to spread rather rapidly by means of its slender, white rhizomes and therefore cannot be recommended for the small pool. Easily increased by summer cuttings, division during early spring or by seed. z 5-9; h 1½ft (45cm); s 1½ft (45cm); sun

Menyanthes trifoliata (bog bean) A very distinctive bog plant for shallow water which attracts a variety of pollinating insects. It bears decorative, white, fringed flowers during late spring above dark green, trifoliate leaves, much like those of the broad bean. Both the leaves and flowers are protected by a short, scaly sheath situated towards the end of each sprawling, olive green stem. If the creeping stem is chopped into sections, each with a root attached, these will rapidly start to develop into small plants. z 5-9; h 1ft (30cm); s 1ft (30cm); sun

Narthecium ossifragum (bog asphodel) A small native bog plant with narrow, almost iris-like leaves from which slender heads of yellow flowers appear in summer. Although this plant enjoys marginal conditions during the summer, it is much happier in boggy soil near the edge of the water. Increase from seed during the spring or summer or by division during summer. z 5-9; h 6in (15cm); s 6in (15cm); sun

Phragmites australis (reed) A well-known, strong-growing bog plant with stems like thin bamboo, handsome grassy foliage with purplish-silver plumes and silky flower heads. This plant is a favourite with birds and small mammals for nesting material. Increase by division in spring. z 3-9; h 5½ft (1.65m); s 3ft (90cm); sun

Rumex hydrolapathum (water dock) This marginal plant, which is an enlarged version of the common garden dock, has bold, dark green foliage that turns bronze in summer and crimson in autumn. It provides good cover for fauna. Readily increased from seed or by division of the long, woody roots. z 5-9; h 6ft (1.8m); s 2ft (60cm); sun

Schoenoplectus lacustris (syn. *Scirpus lacustris*) (bulrush) This marginal is the true bulrush. It has stiff, dark green, needle-like leaves growing from short, hardy, creeping rhizomes, and it produces pendent tassels of crowded, reddish-brown flowers in summer. It produces almost evergreen cover, and the dying stems make excellent nesting material. It is an extremely useful plant for shallow water. Increase by spring division. z 5-9; h 4ft (1.2m); s 1½ft (45cm); sun

Sparganium erectum (syn. *S. ramosum)* (bur reed) A coarse, rush-like marginal which has bright green foliage and, in late summer, clustered heads of brownish-green flowers. The flowers give rise to spiky seed heads rather like small teasels. Being semi-evergreen, this plant provides winter cover for fauna. Propagate by division of the rootstocks during spring or by seed sown as soon as it ripens. z 5-7; h 3ft (90cm); s 2ft (60cm); sun/partial shade

Typha angustifolia (narrow-leafed reedmace) A very impressive marginal aquatic with bold, poker-like seed heads, used by birds for nesting material. This narrow-leafed cousin of the common reedmace, *T. latifolia*, should only be grown in large expanses of water. Increase by early spring division. z 5-9; h 8ft (2.4m); s 2ft (60cm); sun

---

OTHER PLANTS

There are a number of other aquatics suitable for wildlife pools. See individual plant directories for details. The floating aquatic *Stratiotes aloides* is a sanctuary for insect life and the *Lemna* species are an excellent source of green food for fish. The submerged *Callitriche hermaphroditica* also provides fish food, and *Myriophyllum spicatum* and *M. verticillatum* are good spawning plants for fish. The genus *Nuphar (N. luteum* in particular) and *Polygonum amphibium* are deep-water aquatics which provide good surface cover, as does *Nymphaea 'Alba'*. *Cardamine pratensis, Filipendula ulmaria, Gunnera manicata* and *Lythrum salicaria* are all bog plants that attract insect life, and the marginal *Sagittaria sagittifolia* is a source of food.

Container plants

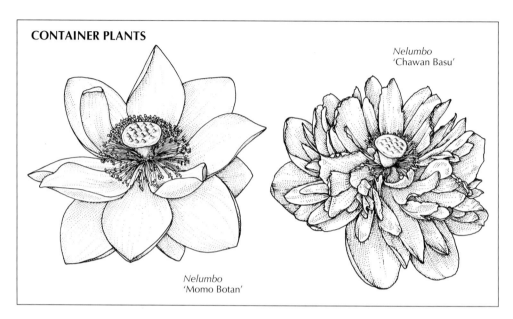

CONTAINER PLANTS

Nelumbo
'Chawan Basu'

Nelumbo
'Momo Botan'

Containers, such as sinks, tubs and urns, provide a good opportunity for growing an interesting and unusual range of aquatic plants. The body of water warms up more rapidly than in conventional pools, and it is likely to remain much warmer throughout the summer. Under these circumstances, both hardy and half-hardy aquatics co-exist happily.

Container plants should be grown in planting baskets or planted into the soil in the bottom of the containers (see pages 100 and 104), and overwintered in a warm place (see page 116). Where applicable, the figures at the end of the entries indicate the depth (d) at which that plant grows. The surface spreads of waterlilies and pondlilies are between one and one-and-a-half times the depth at which they grow. See page 106 for propagation details.

Nelumbo (lotus) The following cultivars of dwarf lotus, along with N. 'Pygmaea Alba' (see page 146), can be grown outdoors in containers during the summer months. Their ability to flower is largely dictated by the intensity of light, but even without flowers their foliage is a delight, providing a tropical touch. Propagate by dividing the banana-like rootstock bearing terminal shoots. They are hardy in zone 10 and require sun.

N. 'Chawan Basu' This semi-dwarf, free-flowering lotus has beautiful white blossoms edged with pink, up to 6in (15cm) across, and plain green foliage. d 1ft (30cm)

N. 'Momo Botan' This largest-flowering of the dwarf varieties has striking fully-double, carmine-coloured blossom and rounded green leaves which have a bluish-green cast to them. A good indoor plant (see page 146). d 1½ft (45cm)

N. 'Pygmaea Rosea' Tiny flowers of intense rose pink rise above rounded green leaves which have stout stalks. d 1ft (30cm)

Nuphar (pondlily) While not generally recommended for small areas owing to their rather aggressive growing habits, there are two species of pondlilies that are well adapted to tub culture. Although not perhaps comparable to waterlilies in terms of quantity of blossoms, they do have a simple charm of their own. Pondlilies are hardy in zones 5-9 and are happy growing in both sun and partial shade.

N. pumila (dwarf pondlily) A small pondlily with pleasant, bright green, almost heart-shaped leaves and tiny, rounded, yellow blossoms which are produced for much of the summer. Increase by division during early spring. d 1-1½ft (30-45cm)

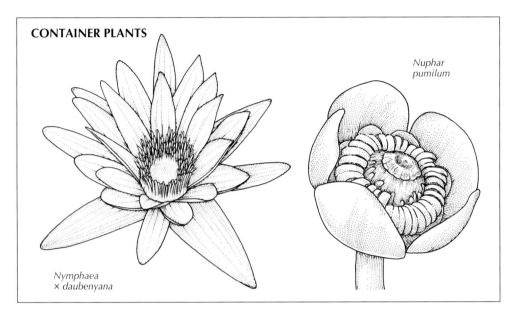

CONTAINER PLANTS

Nuphar
pumilum

Nymphaea
× daubenyana

N. sagittifolium (Cape Fear spatterdock) This fascinating plant remains almost totally submerged and has striking bright green, translucent leaves. It occasionally produces groups of floating foliage in which attractive soft yellow blossoms nestle. d 1ft (30cm)

Nymphaea (waterlily) All those hardy waterlilies described as dwarf or pygmy cultivars (see page 122) can be cultivated in containers provided that the water is deep enough for the chosen cultivar. It is also important to ensure that the container can accommodate the spread of each plant. In addition to these, the following sub-tropical waterlilies can be grown in tubs for the summer months. They are all hardy in zone 10 and require sun.

N. × daubenyana (Daubeny's waterlily) This is the hardiest of the tropical blue-flowered waterlilies. It has small, star-shaped, fragrant blossoms which have a greenish cast. The leaves are almost arrow-shaped and are brownish-green, splashed with brown. d 6-12in (15-30cm)

N. 'Margaret Mary' The small, star-like, soft blue blossoms of this attractive waterlily have prominent yellow stamens. The rounded leaves are dark green on top and light brown beneath. Reproduces viviparously. d 6-12in (15-30cm)

N. 'Patricia' This startling waterlily has bright crimson blossoms which sit among rounded, pale green leaves. Reproduces viviparously. d 1-1½ft (30-45cm)

OTHER PLANTS

Many marginal plants are well suited to tub culture. These include **Juncus effusus 'Spiralis'**, **Myosotis scorpioides** and **Typha minima** (see page 132). The plants will sometimes grow together but should be controlled by annual lifting and dividing. Many submerged aquatics are too invasive for growing in containers, but the clump-forming hair grass **Eleocharis acicularis** is excellent, creeping along the floor of the container. The willow moss **Fontinalis antipyretica** is another good choice, although this does not enjoy very warm conditions. **Lobelia dortmanna** will produce carpets of erect, blunt underwater foliage, and clusters of lavender-coloured blossoms (see page 128). The tiny floating aquatic **Wolffia arrhiza** (see page 130) is an excellent plant for tubs and other containers as it is so small.

Indoor plants

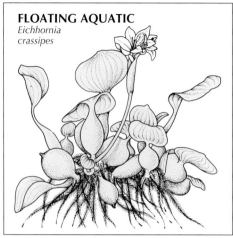

FLOATING AQUATIC
Eichhornia crassipes

MARGINAL AQUATIC
Cyperus haspan

There are many opportunities for growing aquatics indoors, and the choice of plants for this warm, sheltered, frost-free environment is rich and varied.

Most indoor plants prosper in temperatures around 13°C (55°F) but will tolerate up to 32°C (90°F). They must have plenty of light; the following selection will all succeed in the natural light of a greenhouse or sun room, although extra artificial light may prolong the flowering season of some plants. As the flowering season is determined by light rather than temperature in the indoor environment, plant growth slows down in winter when the light level drops. For this reason, it is easier to allow the plants to die back and store them during the winter rather than struggle to keep them growing (see page 116).

Where applicable, the figures at the end of the entries indicate: zones of hardiness (z) for that plant; depth (d) at which that plant grows and spread (s)* and height (h) achieved by that plant at maturity under optimum conditions. The required light intensity is also given for each plant. Where relevant, grow in planting baskets (see page 100); see page 106 for propagation details.

* If grown in planting baskets, the plant will achieve as little as half the given spread, depending on the size of the container. The surface spreads of waterlilies are between one and one-and-a half times the depth at which they grow.

Colocasia esculenta (taro) This handsome marginal plant is a member of the arum family. It has large, green, heart-shaped leaves; the cultivars 'Fontanesii' and 'Illustris' have darker veins or leaf stalks. Grow from tubers which can be lifted and divided during the dormant season. z 10; h 3½ft (1.05m); s 3ft (90cm); sun/shade

Cyperus haspan A manageable and compact version of the papyrus, *Cyperus papyrus*, this delicate-looking marginal has finely-divided, umbrella-like heads of foliage on strong green stems. Easily increased by division. z 10; h 3ft (90cm); s 1ft (30cm); sun

Eichhornia crassipes (water hyacinth) A very handsome, tender floating aquatic with dark glossy green and rather flattened leaves, which have inflated bases that are honey-combed inside to give the plant buoyancy. From the strange cluster of balloon-like foliage emerge strong spikes of delicate-coloured blue and lilac orchid-like blossoms, each with a bright peacock eye. A first-class aquatic which reproduces freely from runners during the summer months. z 10; h 7½in (19cm); s indefinite; sun

Nelumbo (lotus) The lotus family comprises wonderful plants with large, waxy, plate-like leaves held well above the water on stout stems. The flowers are like large satiny water-lily blossoms, but with a pepperpot-like ovary in the centre. They are very adaptable plants and tolerate shallower water than waterlilies.

LOTUS
Nelumbo nucifera

OTHER PLANTS

The following submerged aquatics grow best in water in excess of 16°C (60°F), and when submerged in a minimum of 15in (38cm) of water. Plant at an average density of one bunch per 1 sq ft (0.093 sq m) in containers (see page 144).

Egeria densa Dark green, crispy leaflets are borne in dense whorls. Increase by cuttings during the active growing season. z 10; s indefinite; sun

Vallisneria spiralis (tape grass) Broad, tape-like foliage, which is bright green and almost translucent, grows in dense masses. Increase by division of the plantlets. z 10; s indefinite; sun/shade

The following, along with *N.* **'Momo Botan'** (see page 144), are all suitable for indoor culture. They must have full sun and they only grow and flower well when subjected to consistently warm temperatures of 16-27°C (60-80°F). All are hardy in zone 10. Propagate in spring by division of fleshy rootstock which have terminal shoots (see page 106).

N. **'Kermesina'** A Japanese cultivar with fully-double, bright red blooms and bluish-green foliage. d 1-2ft (30-60cm)

N. lutea (American lotus) The hardiest lotus, with pale yellow blossoms up to 8in (20cm) across and leathery, rounded green leaves. d 1-2ft (30-60cm)

N. nucifera (East Indian lotus) Very large pink blossoms reach 1ft (30cm) across; the large, blue-green leaves are plate-like and grow on strong stems. d 1-2ft (30-60cm)

N. **'Pygmaea Alba'** A true dwarf lotus with small, white, tulip-like blossoms, no more than 4in (10cm) across, and plain green foliage. A good container plant (see page 144). d 6in (15cm)

Nymphaea (waterlily) Unlike their hardy counterparts, tropical waterlilies are available in both day and night blooming varieties and in a wide range of colours, including blue. Many are also deliciously fragrant. Avoid vigorous cultivars; the following will all adapt to the space limitations of an average pool. They are hardy in zone 10 and require sun.

N. **'Aviator Pring'** Star-like yellow blossoms are held above bold green leaves which have toothed and waved margins. d 1½-2½ft (45-75cm)

N. **'Blue Beauty'** The most frequently grown blue waterlily, this is a lovely plant with star-shaped blossoms, bright yellow stamens and sepals that are distinctively marked with black. The dark green leaves are speckled with brown. d 1½-3ft (45-90cm)

N. **'Independence'** A colourful waterlily with rich rose-coloured, star-shaped flowers. The rounded leaves are green, tinged with red. d 1½-2½ft (45-75cm).

N. **'Red Flare'** Brilliant red, fragrant, star-like blossoms are held above dark brownish-green foliage. Night blooming. d 1½-2½ft (45-75cm)

Pistia stratiotes (water lettuce) This floating aquatic is a relative of the arum lily and resembles a soft, green, downy lettuce. The small, green, arum-like flowers are of little significance. Easy to increase by separating out the clusters of young plants that appear around the parent. z 10; h 5in (13cm); s indefinite; sun/partial shade

Thalia dealbata An almost-hardy plant with foliage similar to the bedding canna, but with a white, mealy coating. Long wands of violet blossoms are produced during summer. Increase by division although seed, if available, germinates readily. z 10; h 5ft (1.5m); s 3½ft (1.05m); sun

147

Planting plans 1

FORMAL POOL 1

Dimensions: 6 x 10ft (1.8 x 3m)
Depth: 2½ft (75cm); margin 9in (23cm)
These two planting schemes are based on formal arrangements and colours. The first is made up of predominantly bright-coloured crimson and deep blue plants while the second consists of softer, paler tones of white and pink. The pool has a marginal shelf with extended corners.

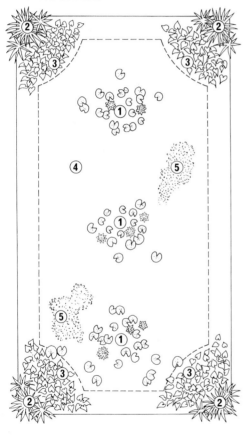

1 *Nymphaea* 'Hermine' (waterlily) 1 basket: 1 plant
2 *Peltandra virginica* (marginal) 3 baskets: 3 plants each
3 *Alisma plantago-aquatica* (marginal) 1 basket: 3 plants each
4 *Eleocharis acicularis* (submerged) 4 baskets: 8 bunches each
5 *Trapa natans* (floating) 2 portions

Alternative planting

1 *Nymphaea* 'Froebelii' (waterlily) 1 basket: 1 plant
2 *Iris laevigata* 'Variegata' (marginal) 1 basket: 3 plants
3 *Houttuynia cordata* 'Flore-Pleno' (marginal) 3 baskets: 3 plants each
4 *Potamogeton crispus* (submerged) 4 baskets: 8 plants each
5 *Azolla caroliniana* (floating) 2 portions

FORMAL POOL 2

Dimension: 6ft (1.8m) in diameter
Depth: 2½ft (75cm); margin 9in (23cm)
These schemes could also be used in an oval or square pool. Symmetrical plantings emphasize the formality of the feature.

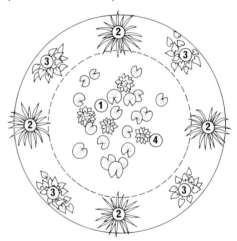

1 *Nymphaea* 'Rose Arey' (waterlily) 1 basket: 1 plant
2 *Iris laevigata* 'Colcherensis' (marginal) 1 basket: 3 plants
3 *Calla palustris* (marginal) 1 basket: 1 plant
4 *Lobelia dortmanna* (submerged) 2 baskets: 8 plants each

Alternative planting

1 *Nymphaea* 'Gonnère' (waterlily) 1 basket: 1 plant
2 *Juncus effusus* 'Vittatus' (marginal) 3 baskets: 3 plants each
3 *Cotula coronopifolia* (marginal) 1 basket: 1 plant
4 *Myriophyllum verticillatum* (submerged) 2 baskets: 8 bunches each

FORMAL ORIENTAL-STYLE POOL
Dimensions: 5 x 8ft (1.5 x 2.4m)
Depth: 2ft (60cm); margin 9in (23cm)
Note the architectural-looking line of rocks
and the small, protruding shelf.

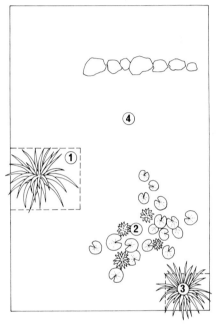

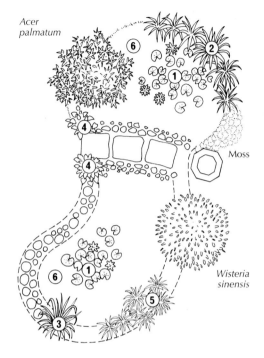

1 *Schoenoplectus lacustris* subsp. *tabernae-montani* 'Zebrinus' (marginal) 1 basket: 1
plant
2 *Nuphar polysepala* (deep water) 1 basket: 1
plant
3 *Typha minima* (marginal) 1 basket: 3 plants
4 *Eleocharis acicularis* (submerged) 4 bas-kets: 8 plants each
Alternative planting
1 *Acorus calamus* (marginal) 1 basket: 3 plants
2 *Nymphaea* 'James Brydon' (waterlily) 1 bas-ket: 1 plant
3 *Juncus effusus* 'Spiralis'(marginal) 1 basket:
3 plants
4 *Eleocharis acicularis* (submerged) 4 bas-kets: 8 plants each

INFORMAL ORIENTAL-STYLE POOL
Dimensions: 5 x 8ft (1.5 x 2.4m)
Depth: ½-2ft (15-60cm)
Beach and stepping stones are important
features of an Oriental-style pool.

1 *Nymphaea candida* (waterlily) 1 basket: 1
plant
2 *Iris versicolor* (marginal) 3 baskets: 3 plants
each
3 *Juncus effusus* 'Vittatus' (marginal) 1 basket:
3 plants
4 *Schoenoplectus lacustris* subsp. *tabernae-montani* 'Zebrinus' (marginal) 3 baskets: 1
plant each
5 *Iris laevigata* 'Rose Queen' (marginal) 3 bas-kets: 3 plants each
6 *Callitriche hermaphroditia* (submerged) 2
baskets: 4 bunches each
Alternative planting
1 *Nymphaea* 'Caroliniana Nivea' (waterlily) 1
basket: 1 plant
2 *Iris laevigata* 'Alba' (marginal) 3 baskets: 3
plants each
3 *Acorus calamus* 'Variegatus' (marginal) 1
basket: 3 plants
4 *Acorus calamus* (marginal) 2 baskets: 3
plants each
5 *Iris laevigata* 'Dorothy' (marginal) 3 bas-kets: 3 plants each
6 *Lobelia dortmanna* (submerged) 2 baskets:
4 plants each

Planting plans 2

INFORMAL POOL 1
Dimensions: 4 x 9ft (1.2 x 2.7m)
Depth: 1½ft (45cm); margin 9in (23cm)
The first scheme comprises yellow, white and blue plants, the second mainly foliage plants.

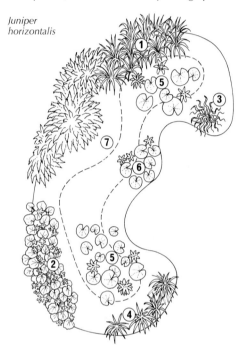

Juniper
horizontalis

3 *Juncus effusus* 'Spiralis' (marginal) 1 basket: 3 plants
4 *Iris versicolor* 'Kermesina' (marginal) 3 baskets: 3 plants each
5 *Nymphaea tetragona* 'Alba' (waterlily) 1 basket: 1 plant
6 *Nymphoides peltata* (deep water) 1 basket: 1 plant
7 *Fontinalis antipyretica* (submerged) 4 baskets: 8 bunches each

INFORMAL POOL 2
Dimensions: 4 x 6ft (1.2 x 1.8m)
Depth: 2ft (60cm); margin 9in (23cm)
The first scheme of this kidney-shaped pool is based on pink and white, while the alternative planting plan is a mixture of different colours, for more of an informal, cottage garden look. Both pools contain striking, colourful waterlilies.

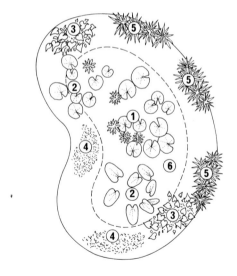

1 *Acorus calamus* (marginal) 2 baskets: 3 plants each
2 *Caltha palustris* (marginal) 2 baskets: 3 plants each
3 *Juncus effusus* 'Vittatus' (marginal) 1 basket: 3 plants
4 *Iris laevigata* (marginal) 3 baskets: 3 plants each
5 *Nymphaea* 'Odorata Sulphurea Grandiflora' (waterlily) 1 basket: 1 plant
6 *Nymphaea tetragona* 'Helvola' (waterlily) 1 basket: 1 plant
7 *Myriophyllum spicatum* (submerged) 4 baskets: 8 bunches each
Alternative planting
1 *Schoenoplectus lacustris* subsp. *tabernaemontani* 'Zebrinus' (marginal) 2 baskets: 1 plant each
2 *Glyceria maxima* 'Variegata' (marginal) 2 baskets: 1 plant each

1 *Nymphaea* 'Firecrest' (waterlily) 1 basket: 1 plant
2 *Aponogeton distachyos* (deep water) 1 basket: 3 plants
3 *Houttuynia cordata* (marginal) 1 basket: 3 plants
4 *Azolla caroliniana* (floating) 1 portion
5 *Iris versicolor* 'Kermesina' (marginal) 1 basket: 3 plants
6 *Myriophyllum verticillatum* (submerged) 4 baskets: 8 bunches each

Alternative planting

1 *Nymphaea* 'Amabilis' (waterlily) 1 basket: 1 plant
2 *Orontium aquaticum* (deep water) 1 basket: 1 plant
3 *Veronica beccabunga* (marginal) 1 basket: 1 plant
4 *Trapa natans* (floating) 1 portion
5 *Glyceria maxima* 'Variegata' (marginal) 1 basket: 1 plant
6 *Potamogeton crispus* (submerged) 4 baskets: 8 bunches each

BOG GARDEN 1

Dimensions: 4 x 6ft (1.2 x 1.8m)
A bog garden helps integrate a pool into the surrounding landscape. Choose plants that complement the planting of the pool and any nearby borders; the following designs are colourful, suitable beside any informal pool.

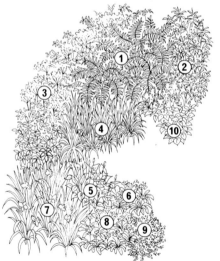

1 *Osmunda regalis* (bog) 1 plant
2 *Aruncus dioicus* 'Kneiffii' (bog) 1 plant
3 *Filipendula vulgaris* (bog) 3 plants
4 *Iris sibirica* 'Ottawa' (marginal) 3 plants
5 *Pontederia cordata* (marginal) 1 plant
6 *Primula japonica* 'Miller's Crimson' (bog) 3 plants
7 *Hemerocallis* 'Hyperion' (bog) 1 plant
8 *Primula bulleyana* (bog) 3 plants
9 *Lysimachia nummularia* (bog) 1 plant
10 *Hosta lancifolia* (bog) 1 plant

Alternative planting

1 *Lythrum salicaria* (bog) 1 plant
2 *Astilbe* 'Fanal' (bog) 2 plants
3 *Eupatorium purpureum* (bog) 2 plants
4 *Iris ensata* 'Landscape at Dawn' (marginal) 3 plants
5 *Peltandra virginica* (marginal) 1 plant
6 *Ajuga reptans* (bog) 1 plant
7 *Aruncus dioicus* (bog) 1 plant
8 *Hosta sieboldiana* (bog) 1 plant
9 *Primula rosea* (bog) 3 plants
10 *Trollius europaeus* (bog) 1 plant

BOG GARDEN 2

Dimensions: 3½ x 7ft (1 x 2.1m)
Both schemes consist of planting in drifts using contrasting colours and foliage.

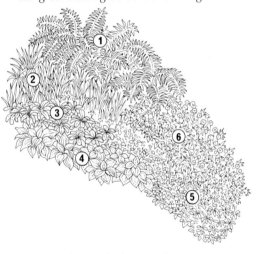

1 *Osmunda regalis* (bog) 2 plants
2 *Iris ensata* 'Blue Heaven'(bog) 3 plants
3 *Primula japonica* 'Postford White' (bog) 5 plants
4 *Hosta sieboldiana* (bog) 3 plants
5 *Mimulus luteus* (bog) 3 plants
6 *Trollius europaeus* 'Canary Bird' (bog) 3 plants

Alternative planting

1 *Gunnera manicata* (bog) 1 plant
2 *Filipendula vulgaris* (bog) 3 plants
3 *Primula florindae* (bog) 5 plants
4 *Hosta undulata* (bog) 3 plants
5 *Cardamine pratensis* (bog) 5 plants
6 *Lythrum salicaria* 'The Beacon' (bog) 3 plants

Planting plans 3

WILDLIFE POOL 1
Dimensions: 5 x 8ft (1.5 x 2.4m)
Depth: ½-2ft (15-60cm); margin 9in (23cm)
This plan consists of plants that will attract a variety of insects, such as gnats, water boatmen and dragonflies. These will help provide a balanced ecosystem.

WILDLIFE POOL 2
Dimensions: 6 x 8ft (1.8 x 2.4m)
Depth: ½-2ft (15-60cm); margin 9in (23cm)
This pool with boggy margins has good surface cover and some winter marginal cover for fauna. The submerged plants are a source of green food for fish, and there are food plants which produce seeds for wildlife. There is also spawning ground for fish.

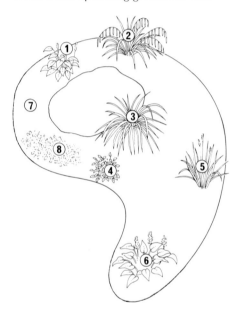

1 *Gunnera manicata* (bog) 1 plant
2 *Caltha palustris* (wildlife) 1 plant
3 *Iris pseudacorus* (wildlife) 3 plants
4 *Nymphaea alba* (waterlily) 1 plant
5 *Menyanthes trifoliata* (wildlife) 1 plant
6 *Cardamine pratensis* (bog) 1 plant
7 *Carex pendula* (wildlife) 1 plant
8 *Myriophyllum spicatum* (submerged) 24 bunches
Alternative planting
1 *Phragmites australis* (wildlife) 1 plant
2 *Mentha aquatica* (wildlife) 1 plant
3 *Cyperus longus* (wildlife) 1 plant
4 *Stratiotes aloides* (floating) 1 plant
5 *Sagittaria sagittifolia* (marginal) 1 plant
6 *Filipendula ulmaria* (bog) 1 plant
7 *Sparganium erectum* (wildlife) 1 plant
8 *Callitriche hermaphroditica* (submerged) 24 bunches

1 *Rumex hydrolapathum* (wildlife) 1 plant
2 *Carex pendula* (wildlife) 1 plant
3 *Phragmites australis* (wildlife) 1 plant
4 *Ludwigia palustris* (wildlife) 1 plant
5 *Schoenoplectus lacustris* (wildlife) 1 plant
6 *Alisma plantago-aquatica* (wildlife) 1 plant
7 *Myriophyllum spicatum* (submerged) 24 bunches
8 *Lemna trisulca* (floating) 1 portion
Alternative planting
1 *Butomus umbellatus* (wildlife) 3 plants
2 *Cyperus longus* (wildlife) 1 plant
3 *Sparganium erectum* (wildlife) 1 plant
4 *Caltha palustris* (wildlife) 1 plant
5 *Narthecium ossifragum* (wildlife) 7 plants
6 *Damasonium alisma* (wildlife) 3 plants
7 *Callitriche hermaphroditica* (submerged) 24 bunches
8 *Stratiotes aloides* (floating) 3 plants

SUNKEN INDOOR POOL

Dimensions: 4 x 8ft (1.2 x 2.4m)
Depth: 1½ft (45cm); margin 6in (15cm)
This sunken indoor pool could be constructed from a liner or a pre-formed unit. It is a large feature, needing a light, sunny conservatory or sun room with a lot of space. The lotus and indoor waterlily add an exotic, tropical touch.

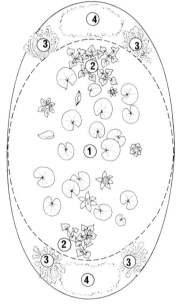

1 *Nelumbo nucifera* (indoor) 1 basket: 1 plant
2 *Eichhornia crassipes* (indoor) 1 plant
3 *Colocasia esculenta* (indoor) 1 basket: 1 plant
4 *Egeria densa* (indoor) 1 basket: 10 bunches
Alternative planting
1 *Nymphaea* 'Blue Beauty' (indoor) 1 basket: 1 plant
2 *Pistia stratiotes* (indoor) 3 plants
3 *Nelumbo* 'Pygmaea Alba' (indoor) 1 basket: 1 plant
4 *Vallisneria spiralis* (indoor) 1 basket: 10 plants

INDOOR CONCAVE CORNER POOL

Dimensions: 5ft (1.5m) sides
Depth: 1ft (30cm); margin 9in (23cm)
This pool and the one below provide alternative designs for corner sites.

1 *Nelumbo nucifera* (indoor) 1 basket: 1 plant
2 *Pistia stratiotes* (indoor) 3 plants
3 *Colocasia esculenta* (indoor) 1 basket: 1 plant
Alternative planting
1 *Nelumbo lutea* (indoor) 1 basket: 1 plant
2 *Nelumbo* 'Pygmaea Alba' (indoor) 1 basket: 1 plant
3 *Cyperus haspan* (indoor) 1 basket: 1 plant

INDOOR CONVEX CORNER POOL

Dimensions: 5ft (1.5m) sides
Depth: 1ft (30cm); margin 9in (23cm)
Both pools could be raised or sunken.

1 *Nymphaea* 'Margaret Mary' (container) 1 basket: 1 plant
2 *Eichhornia crassipes* (indoor) 3 plants
3 *Thalia dealbata* (indoor) 1 basket: 1 plant
Alternative planting
1 *Nelumbo* 'Kermesina' (indoor) 1 basket: 1 plant
2 *Pistia stratiotes* (indoor) 3 plants
3 Leave unplanted

Planting plans 4

HALF-BARREL CONTAINER
Dimensions: 2½ft (75cm) in diameter
Depth: 2ft (60cm)
A variety of indoor plants as well as container plants can be grown in barrels outside. If necessary, place marginal plants on piles of bricks in order to bring them up to the required height.

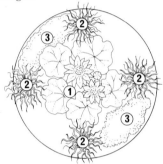

1 *Nelumbo* 'Chawan Basu'(container) 1 plant
2 *Typha minima* (marginal) 1 plant
3 *Wolffia arrhiza* (floating) 2 portions
Alternative planting
1 *Nelumbo* 'Momo Botan' (container) 1 plant
2 *Juncus effusus* 'Spiralis' (marginal) 1 plant
3 Leave unplanted
Alternative planting
1 *Nelumbo* 'Pygmaea Rosea' (container) 1 plant
2 *Myosotis scorpioides* (marginal) 1 plant
3 *Fontinalis antipyretica* (submerged) 3 bunches

Alternative planting
1 *Nymphaea* 'Margaret Mary' (container) 1 plant
2 *Typha minima* (marginal) 1 plant
3 *Wolffia arrhiza* (floating) 2 portions

Alternative planting
1 *Nymphaea* x *daubenyana* (container) 1 plant
2 *Juncus effusus* 'Spiralis' (marginal) 1 plant
3 *Lobelia dortmanna* (submerged) 3 plants
Alternative planting
1 *Nymphaea* 'Patricia' (container) 1 plant
2 *Myosotis scorpioides* (marginal) 1 plant
3 *Eleocharis acicularis* (submerged) 3 plants

SINK
Dimensions: 1½ x 2ft (45 x 60cm)
Depth: 1ft (30cm)
Sinks can be planted with a mixture of container and indoor plants. The positioning of the plants as well as the types will determine the overall effect; a symmetrical arrangement will look more formal than an asymmetrical one. Sinks make good indoor and outdoor features.

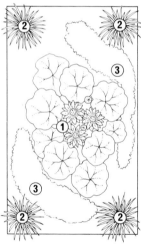

1 *Nelumbo* 'Chawan Basu' (container) 1 plant
2 *Juncus effusus* 'Spiralis' (marginal) 1 plant
3 *Wolffia arrhiza* (floating) 2 portions
Alternative planting
1 *Nelumbo* 'Momo Botan' (container) 1 plant
2 *Typha minima* (marginal) 1 plant
3 *Eleocharis acicularis* (submerged) 3 plants
Alternative planting
1 *Nelumbo* 'Pygmaea Alba' (indoor) 1 plant
2 *Myosotis scorpioides* (marginal) 1 plant
3 *Lobelia dortmanna* (submerged) 3 plants

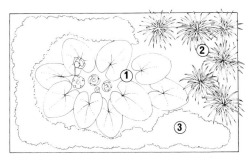

1 *Nuphar pumila* (container) 1 plant
2 *Typha minima* (marginal) 1 plant
3 *Fontinalis antipyretica* (submerged) 3 bunches
Alternative planting
1 *Nuphar sagittifolium* (container) 1 plant
2 *Myosotis scorpioides* (marginal) 1 plant
3 *Lobelia dortmanna* (submerged) 3 plants
Alternative planting
1 *Nelumbo* 'Pygmaea Alba' (indoor) 1 plant
2 *Typha minima* (marginal) 1 plant
3 *Wolffia arrhiza* (floating) 2 portions

INDOOR SINK WATERSCAPE
Dimensions: 1½ x 2ft (45 x 60cm)
Depth: ½-1ft (15-30cm)
A sink provides the ideal opportunity for a miniature indoor waterscape. Using small rocks, pebbles and stones, recreate a natural-looking landscape.

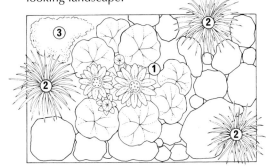

1 *Nelumbo* 'Pygmaea Alba' (indoor) 1 plant
2 *Cyperus haspan* (indoor) 1 plant
3 *Egeria densa* (indoor) 1 plant
Alternative planting
1 *Nelumbo* 'Pygmaea Alba' (indoor) 1 plant
2 *Juncus effusus* 'Spiralis' (indoor) 1 plant
3 *Pistia stratiotes* (indoor) 1 plant

OUTDOOR GROUP OF CONTAINERS
Dimensions: 1½ x ¾ft (45 x 23cm); ½ x ½ft (15 x 15cm); ½ x 2ft (15 x 60cm)
Depths: 1½ft (45cm); 1½ft (45cm); 1ft (30cm)
Containers can be arranged in groups to create more of a feature. Both indoor and container plants can be grown as both types enjoy the warm conditions provided by containers. If necessary, place marginal plants on a pile of bricks to bring them up to the required height.

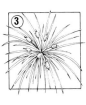
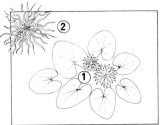

1 *Nymphaea* x *daubenyana* (container) 1 plant
2 *Cyperus haspan* (marginal) 1 plant
3 *Iris laevigata* 'Variegata' (marginal) 1 plant
4 *Myosotis scorpioides* (marginal) 1 plant
5 *Wolffia arrhiza* (floating) 2 portions
Alternative planting
1 *Nymphaea* 'Margaret Mary' (container) 1 plant
2 *Typha minima* (marginal) 1 plant
3 *Acorus calamus* 'Variegatus' (marginal) 1 plant
4 *Typha minima* (marginal) 1 plant
5 *Wolffia arrhiza* (floating) 2 portions
Alternative planting
1 *Nymphaea* 'Patricia'(container) 1 plant
2 *Typha minima* (marginal) 1 plant
3 *Acorus calamus* (marginal) 1 plant
4 *Cyperus haspan* (marginal) 1 plant
5 *Eichhornia crassipes* (indoor) 2 plants

Introduction

No pool is really complete without a good mixture of fish; they add life and colour to the water and help control insects and pests. The ideal colour, shape and conformity of the fish are a matter of personal taste, but most fish species have now been so interbred that it is possible to find almost any colour or shape of fish you want.

Take care to choose fish suited to the pond in question. Native fish such as dace, roach and rudd are not ornamental fish and their dull colours rarely show up in the water. These are fish for the wildlife pool (see page 140). On the other hand, the bright colours and often metallic scales of Koi carp are well-suited to formal pools. Some fish, like orfe, prefer moving water where a fountain is playing. An indoor pool gives the opportunity to show off decorative goldfish and shubunkins; veiltails, fantails, lionheads and orandas can all be recommended. For the majority of pool owners, goldfish are the most reliable and colourful standby. They can be mixed quite happily in all sizes and varieties, they usually blend with most water features and they are both placid and tame.

Any pool that is well planted is ideal for fish. Submerged plants provide a fine spawning ground, protective cover and green food. Deep water aquatics and floating plants create shade which is invaluable during the heat of summer. Popular pond fish do not have any special requirements; provided that the recommended stocking rate is not exceeded, they will live happily under the most modest conditions.

STOCKING RATE

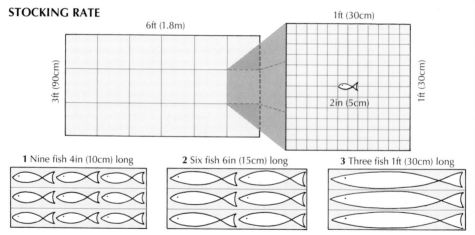

1 Nine fish 4in (10cm) long   **2** Six fish 6in (15cm) long   **3** Three fish 1ft (30cm) long

Before making a selection, it is vital to know how many fish your pool will accommodate by allowing a certain number of fish per unit of surface area. This takes into account the oxygen intake of the pond; depth is not a consideration as it does not affect this rate.

The stocking rate for decorative fish is 2in (5cm) of fish to every 1 sq ft (0.093 sq m) of surface area, excluding that occupied by the marginal plants. The length of fish includes the tail. For example, an 18 sq ft (1.67 sq m) pool measuring 3 x 6ft (90cm x 1.8m) can have a fish population which consists of: nine fish 4in (10cm) long (1); six fish 6in (15cm) long (2); three fish 1ft (30cm) long (3); or any combination that results in a total of 36in (90cm). This allows for growth and development as well as encouraging natural breeding.

A number of fish fanciers stock more heavily than this, but the absolute maximum is 6in (15cm) of fish for every 1 sq ft (0.093 sq m) of surface area, unless a filtration system is used (see page 14). The minimum rate can be as little as just three or four fish, enough to keep mosquito larvae and other pests at bay.

It is best to introduce fish in late spring or early summer when, because the water is warm, they are least likely to suffer from any temperature-related disorders. Do not introduce fish until planting is complete as newly planted aquatics are extremely vulnerable to disturbance and take time to settle down and root sufficiently to withstand fish activity. Even quite small fish will poke around among the plants and retard their growth. A generous layer (about 1/2in/1.25cm) of pea gravel covering the compost in planting baskets will help reduce the problem.

The fish year

For the most part, fish take care of themselves. Having been dormant for the winter months, they begin to stir in early spring when the water gets warmer, looking around for food. They will need to be fed only a little at first (see page 160), the amount being increased when protein-rich food is required in early summer. In summer, the mature fish spawn and young fry will need protecting (see page 162); during autumn the fish will once again need feeding with high-protein foods in preparation for winter.

Fish will grow more torpid as the weather gets colder and may need protection against predators: a section of drainpipe on the pool floor is ideal. Apart from moving any tender fish to a frost-free aquarium, winter poses no problems unless the pool freezes over for more than a couple of days, in which case the fish will need a ventilation hole to breathe through (see page 176).

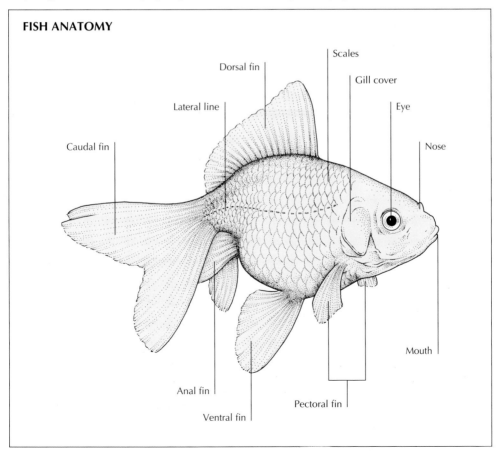

FISH ANATOMY

Scales

Dorsal fin

Gill cover

Lateral line

Eye

Caudal fin

Nose

Mouth

Anal fin

Pectoral fin

Ventral fin

Selecting fish

The retailer

It is important to purchase your fish from a good dealer whose tanks are not over-crowded, and it is worth visiting a few specialist retailers or water garden nurseries first to find the best stock.

Most suppliers sell their fish in tanks which do not have plant life in them but which are supplied with oxygen from an airline instead. This allows uninterrupted views of the fish on display. Although this looks very clinical, these conditions are perfectly acceptable.

Do not buy fish from interconnected tanks as these accelerate the spread of water-borne diseases. Also avoid buying from tanks which have a constant through-flow of fresh tap water, a system used to wash away the free-swimming stage of white spot disease. Fish can only tolerate a certain amount of tap water before the chlorine begins to affect their protective body slime and gills.

When purchasing fish, take into account the colour of the water in the tank: it should be a warm amber hue.

Observing quarantine

Fish are often still under stress when displayed for sale. They have been rushed from the breeder to the wholesaler and on to the garden centre in a matter of a few days, so it is useful to have some idea of how long they have been in the country. The colour intensity of the fish will give some indication of this: the brighter the fish, the more recent the import. Only buy fish that have been in quarantine for a period of three weeks or more and carefully check them for signs of disease.

Healthy fish: what to look for

Colour intensity: once removed from the muddy waters of a breeding pond to the clear environment of the selling tank, fish will start to lose their brightness after a month or so; bright red fish fade to salmon pink and bright yellow fish soften to ochre. This dullness is a good indication that they have had a suffi-cient period of quarantine. Once faded fish are re-introduced to a pool, they quickly re-gain their vivid hues.

Upright fins: one of the best indications that a fish is in good health is the condition and stance of its fins. A stout, upright dorsal fin and well-expanded ventral fins are both indica-tions of a healthy fish.

Bright eyes: clear and bright eyes are a sign of good health and fish with eyes that are cloudy should not be purchased.

Liveliness: an obvious consideration when choosing fish is their liveliness. However, while a lively fish is likely to be a healthy fish, it could just as easily be a hungry one. It is not uncommon for fish in display tanks to be kept a little hungry so that they swim and dart about, searching for food in a lively, excited manner which makes them more appealing to the purchaser.

Unhealthy fish: what to avoid

Damage: it is vital that small fish do not have any damaged or missing scales; exposed tis-sue is very susceptible to secondary fungal infection. The same applies to larger speci-mens, although the likelihood of finding a large fish that has no scales missing is fairly re-mote. If an otherwise healthy fish has a few scales missing, dip the fish in a proprietary fungus cure based on either methylene blue or malachite green prior to introducing it to the pool.

White spot: (see page 164). Sometimes white spots, rather like tiny raised pin-heads, may be seen distributed in an irregular fashion along the bodies and tails of the fish. These are almost certainly symptoms of white spot disease which, although curable, takes a lot of time and effort to defeat. Never purchase any fish from a garden centre where there are fish with this disease as it is easily transferable from one tank to another on a net, and it is almost inevitable that all the fish on the pre-mises will have some degree of infection. Take care not to confuse white spot disease with the nuptial tubercles that appear in pro-fusion on the gill plates, head and sometimes front or pectoral fins of normal healthy male fish during the breeding season. While look-ing very much like white spot disease, the tubercles will be mostly concentrated around the head area. Normal healthy fish in breed-ing condition will have upright fins and bright eyes rather than folded-down dorsal fins and clouded, milky eyes.

'Big-head': some species of fish are afflicted by disorders that are specific to them. These should not be confused with natural variations when you are making a selection. One of the most serious problems is the condition in carp known as 'big head'. It is thought by many to be some kind of tubercular infection. A carp with this disorder will have an enlarged and distorted head and often a pinched body as well. When selecting carp it is essential to avoid any that appear to have larger heads than normal, even if they seem to be otherwise healthy. If you are not sure what normal carp should look like, visit several retailers to get an overview before making any final decision.

Crooked spine: when selecting green tench watch out for individuals with a crooked backbone, which is often accompanied by a very dark coloration. The cause of this disorder is not known but it almost invariably results in death.

Transporting the fish

Once the fish have been selected they must be carefully packaged for the journey home. The best way of transporting live fish is in a large, heavy gauge polythene bag filled with a small amount of water (sufficient to ensure that they can swim, but no more) and blown up with oxygen. On hot, sultry days when the oxygen level is low, species like orfe should not be moved at all. These fish have a high oxygen requirement and are best transported during cool weather.

Introducing the fish

As a precaution against disease, it is wise to disinfect all newly purchased fish with a fungus cure based on malachite green or methylene blue (see page 164) before introducing them to the pond. Quickly dip the fish into the solution and return it to the bag.

Once this has been done, float the bag on the surface of the water until the temperature of the water inside and outside the bag is equal before releasing the fish. If this is not done the fish may suffer from swim bladder disorder, causing it to move around in an unstable fashion until it becomes accustomed to the new water temperature. When the weather is very hot, however, it is better to tip the fish into the pool immediately. The risk of temporarily upsetting the swim bladder is less than that of the fish expiring in a hot, floating polythene bag.

Feeding the fish

Once the fish are swimming around happily they can be fed a pinch of food per fish on alternate days (see page 160). To begin with, the new fish will be rather shy, but persistent feeding in the same place regularly will soon pay off. In the early stages of feeding not all the food will be cleared up owing to the diffident nature of the fish. After twenty minutes, remove any uneaten fish food otherwise it will decompose on the floor of the pool and encourage fungal infections.

Transporting the fish

Fill the bag with a little water, enough to ensure that the fish can swim around quite happily. Add some oxygen from a cylinder.

Introducing the fish

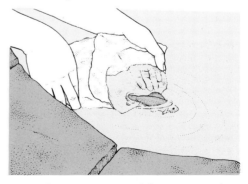

Once the temperature of the water inside and outside the bag is equal, release the fish into the pool.

Feeding fish

Feeding fish is an enjoyable rather than essential practice. In any well-established pool there will be enough insects around to satisfy their needs, but most pool owners derive enormous pleasure from feeding fish, especially when they swim to the surface in response to a shadow or the sound of footsteps. Regular feeding sessions from the same spot each time will result in the almost magical appearance of the fish population at the surface of the water.

Manufactured food

There are three main types of fish food:

Crumb food is mostly a by-product of biscuit manufacturing and is very variable in quality. Its nutritional value is questionable, although it does provide roughage and minimal nourishment.

Flaked food consists of very thin, papery, multi-coloured slivers. In most cases, these foods have been scientifically prepared to provide all the nutrients necessary to maintain healthy fish.

Floating pellets are another scientifically produced fish food. These are usually brownish in colour and are both carefully balanced and highly nutritious.

Like flaked foods, pellets have the advantage of floating on the surface of the water for a considerable length of time and so uneaten food is easily removed with a net. On windy days, however, flaked fish food may be blown from the pool altogether.

Specialist foods

Fish will appreciate some variety in their diet. This can be provided by specialist foods such as dried flies, shredded shrimps and ants' eggs (really pupal cocoons), all rich in protein. While these are generally very nutritious, packaged ants' eggs can sometimes lose their nutritional value. Fish much prefer the real thing; while not suggesting an expedition to seek out fresh ants' eggs, when a nest is located it is worth setting up a trap in which to gather the eggs (see below).

Live food

All fish like high-protein live foods like gnat and mosquito larvae and *Daphnia* (water fleas). These are occasionally found in water butts and can be removed with a fine mesh net. It is quite practical to culture *Daphnia* to provide a constant food supply for the fish throughout the summer.

Culturing *Daphnia*: add 1in (2.5cm) of soil to a container of rain water and allow it to settle on the bottom. Next, introduce a small quantity of live *Daphnia*. These will reproduce rapidly and produce a succulent harvest of tiny creatures each week.

Which food

It does not really matter which food you choose since this will automatically be supplemented by the live foods which live in the pool. Fish are not fussy and adapt readily to a

Manufactured foods

Flakes

Pellets

Crumbs

Ants' eggs trap

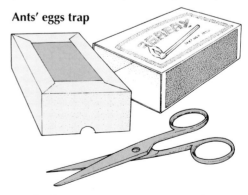

1 Take the tray out of a large matchbox and make a ½in (1.25cm) hole at the top of it at one end.

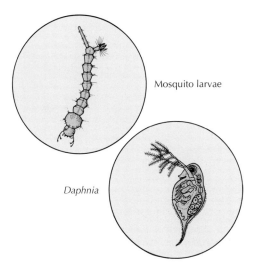

Mosquito larvae

Daphnia

natural food they will be forced to swim to the surface in search of food.

How much and when to feed your fish

During winter fish are dormant and live off their fat reserves and so do not need feeding. As spring approaches and the water warms up, they will need feeding a little at a time, enough for them to eat in a couple of minutes. As the fish become more active they will need an increased diet, including protein-rich foods. This will build up their energy levels and their resistance to disease, so they will be less likely to develop any fungal infections or diseases.

During summer the fish should be fed one pinch per fish of normal fish food on alternate days. To check the quantity, observe the pool for twenty minutes: if the food is eaten rapidly then give the fish a little more, but if there is still food floating on the surface then they have been given too much and the surplus food should be removed with a net. Over-feeding can be dangerous, not because the fish will overeat, but because any excess will fall to the floor, decompose and pollute the water, encouraging fungus which may spread to the fish as a secondary infection.

As the days shorten in autumn, the water temperature drops and the fish will grow sluggish. To help them to prepare for winter, their diet should once again be supplemented with high-protein foods provided about once a week.

change of diet. In some cases, it is preferable to feed certain fish with a particular type of food. Carp, for example, should be fed floating pellets as this will ensure that they come right to the surface where their colours can be enjoyed. Otherwise, they will lurk in the middle regions of the pool, catching the fish food as it sinks. Goldfish enjoy any food, but golden orfe seem to prefer leaping for flies and other insects, although they will eat any available floating pellet and flaked fish food. Scavenging fish tend to mop up the food that falls to the pool floor and eat frogs, snails and small fry, but in a crowded pool with little

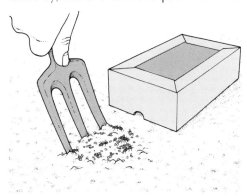

2 Invert the tray and place it close to the ants' nest. Disturb the nest to make the ants active.

3 The ants will transport their eggs from the nursery to the safety of the tray. Gather up the eggs and feed them to the fish.

Breeding fish

The breeding season for ornamental cold water fish lasts from late spring to late summer and is believed to be activated by the intensity of light and the temperature of the water. Bright summer sunshine for two or three days usually stirs healthy, sexually mature fish into fervent activity. Fish will only breed when they have reached a certain length: goldfish, shubunkin and carp must be over 3in (8cm) long; orfe, rudd, roach, dace, tench and catfish over 4in (10cm) long; minnows over 1in (2.5cm) long and bitterling over 1½in (3.75cm) long.

Natural breeding

Fish will naturally breed to make up any deficiencies in number. If the fish population is at its maximum, the female will re-absorb her spawn and existing fry are unlikely to survive. In most well-kept, balanced pools there will almost certainly be at least one male capable of servicing a dozen or more females. They will breed quite happily left to their own devices, providing there is adequate plant cover for the deposition of spawn and that the water is warm enough.

Spawning

Spawning is the mating of fish in the water. In most cases, the female is chased around the pool by the male, who knocks and brushes against her in an effort to get her to release her spawn onto the plants. When this has been done, the male deposits his milt over the eggs and fertilization takes place.

After three or four days, the fry begin to develop. At first the tiny, transparent pin-like fry are difficult to see but, after two or three weeks, they become recognizable as transparent or bronze fish. With goldfish and shubunkin, the lower the water temperature at spawning, the longer it takes for full adult colours to develop, although they will all eventually attain their bright adult colour.

The instinct to save every fry is strong but should be resisted, as it is natural for the smaller and weaker individuals to perish and provide nourishment for the other inhabitants of the pool. You can, if you wish, move the fry to a separate pond empty of fish, until they grow larger.

Alternatively, you can transfer the spawn-covered foliage to a bucket of water or an

---

GENDER

During the breeding season, all male fish develop white, pimple-like nuptial tubercles on their gills and heads. In some cases it is also possible to identify the fish by its shape: male goldfish, shubunkin and carp are more slender than the females, and from above the male is slim in outline while the female is more pear-shaped.

Female

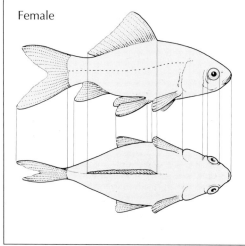

Male

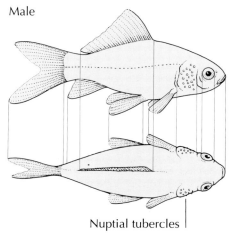

Nuptial tubercles

CONTROLLED BREEDING

To prevent indiscriminate spawning, select your own breeding stock and place them in an aquarium when they are on the point of spawning (1). The water must be the same temperature and chemical composition as the pool water, and the aquarium must contain submerged plants.

The male will chase the female into the foliage where she will deposit her eggs (2). Once spawning has taken place, the fish must be removed in case they eat the spawn. The eggs will hatch into fry after about four days (3) and will need feeding as soon as they become free-swimming.

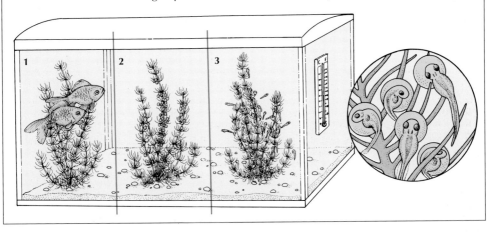

aquarium. It is important that the water is taken from the pool so it is the same temperature and chemical composition as the pool water. Place the bucket or aquarium in a cool place where the temperature will remain at a steady 7-16°C (45-60°F).

The fry will gradually develop and in the Spartan conditions of the bucket or aquarium they will need feeding. Special baby fish foods are available, but scrambled eggs are just as good. Move the fish into the pool when they are about 1in (2.5cm) long. As with freshly purchased fish, slowly introduce them and do not subject them to any violent changes in water temperature.

Stripping

There is no guarantee that selected breeding stock will breed with each other in the pool. Controlled fertilization by stripping is the only way of ensuring a desired cross. This is best done in mid-summer and is only recommended for the experienced fish breeder as it is easy to harm the fish.

Carefully net and examine a chubby female which has the preferred characteristics. If the vent is slightly reddened and distended, the fish is in a suitable condition for stripping. Hold it in wet hands over a flat-bottomed dish containing a little water. Apply gentle pressure to the sides of the body, slowly progressing towards the vent. When stroked rhythmically like this, the eggs tumble into the dish.

Net the chosen male carefully: a sudden jolt could result in the premature emission of milt. Hold it over the spawn and gently stroke the flanks so that the milt is distributed as evenly as possible over it. After fertilization, which takes about twenty minutes, gently rinse the spawn in luke-warm water to reduce the incidence of fungal attacks. It is possible to hatch the eggs in the dish, but it is better to transfer them to an aquarium, if you have one, where there is much more room and it is easier to maintain clinical conditions. Feed the fry when they develop with special baby fish food or scrambled eggs, and introduce them to the pool once they are approximately 1in (2.5cm) long.

Fish pests and diseases

There are many pests and diseases which can affect ornamental coldwater fish although, generally speaking, the better maintained the pool, the fewer the ailments. The majority of pests and diseases are incubated in over-crowded dealers' tanks (see page 158) and are introduced to the pool on new stock.

Most pests and diseases can be treated with manufactured cures based on certain chemicals, available from pet shops and garden centres. IT IS IMPORTANT TO DILUTE ALL CURES ACCORDING TO THE INSTRUCTIONS, USING CLEAN TAP WATER. Catch the affected fish in a net and lower it in the net into the solution for the recommended time.

Unfortunately, in some cases it is more humane to destroy the suffering fish. This is best done by smartly dashing the creature against a concrete floor or path and carefully disposing of it.

Anchor worm: a fairly common pest with a slender, tube-like body about ¼in (0.5cm) long and a barbed head; not technically a worm but a tiny crustacean. It spreads rapidly in crowded, commercial tanks.
Effect: the barbed head embedded in the flesh of the fish causes lesions and tumour-like growths to develop.
Treatment: proprietary parasite cures based on dimethyltrichlorohydroxyethylphosphonate are quick and effective.

Fish leech: this flat, greyish-brown, worm-like creature which crawls and swims in looping motions seldom causes serious problems.
Effect: it clings to the body of the fish, which rubs against the bottom and sides of the pool to relieve the irritation.
Treatment: dip the fish in a three percent salt solution and the leeches will drop off.

Fish lice: a fairly common affliction. Each group of fish is attacked by a specific louse; all look superficially alike with flattened ends, shell-like bodies, small projecting abdomens and feeler-like appendages.
Effect: it clings to the body and gill plates of the fish causing severe damage to its tissues; a bad infestation causes death.
Treatment: hold the fish in a wet net and dab a drop of paraffin onto the lice using a small paint brush. Dip the fish in a solution of malachite green to reduce the risk of a secondary infection before re-introducing it to pool. Alternatively, use a proprietary parasite cure based on dimethyltrichlorohydroxyethylphosphonate.

Fin and tail rot: this is a fairly common disease. A whitish line develops along the outer fin and tail, advancing down as the disease progresses.
Effect: it first attacks the dorsal fin, fraying the outer margin, and quickly spreads to other fins and the tail; the fish will die if the infection reaches its flesh.
Treatment: only effective when administered in early stages. Hold the fish in a wet net. Remove the frayed tissue with sharp scissors and dip the fish in a fungus cure based on malachite green or methylene blue to arrest the infection. Lost tissue will regenerate.

Fungus: a common disease, also known as cotton wool disease, it affects damaged fish and fish spawn, and is encouraged by bad pool hygiene.
Effect: patches of fungal, cotton wool-like growth develops on the damaged area. Untreated secondary infection leads to death.
Treatment: only effective for large fish; destroy fry and small fish. Use a fungal cure based on malachite green or methylene blue. Good pool hygiene helps prevent fungus developing in the first place.

Gill flukes: this minute worm invisible to the naked eye affects the gills.
Effect: the fish swims in a violent and irrational manner, bangs against the sides of the pool and rushes to the surface as if gasping for air. There is a sharp increase in rate of breathing and the fish develops constant fin twitch.
Treatment: use a proprietary parasite cure based on dimethyltrichlorohydroxyethylphosphonate; if the treatment is ineffective, destroy the fish.

Slime and skin diseases: a number of single-celled organisms cause various disorders.
Effect: the fish moves restlessly, brushing against the bottom and sides of the pool to relieve the irritation. Its fins start to fold and the fish develops bluish-white slimy deposits.
Treatment: use a proprietary parasite cure based on chloramine T or malachite green; treatment is only effective if administered in the early stages of the disease. Destroy badly diseased fish.

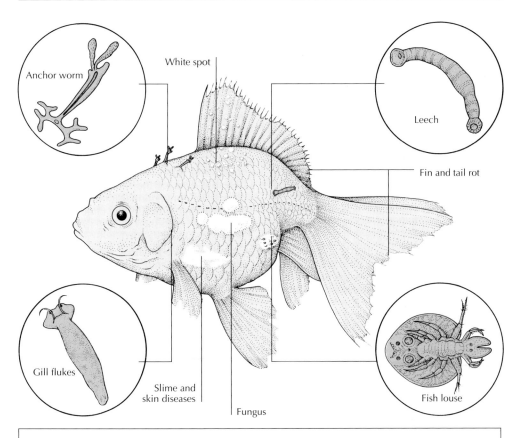

Anchor worm

White spot

Leech

Fin and tail rot

Gill flukes

Slime and skin diseases

Fungus

Fish louse

WHITE SPOT (ICH) DISEASE

Disease: a very common, widespread and destructive disease, particularly in warm aquariums, usually introduced on newly purchased fish. Tiny parasites, less than 0.04in (1mm) long, burrow into skin.

Effect: white spots grow on body, fins and tail, the fish develops a pinched appearance and swims in a drunken fashion.

Treatment: only effective in early stages when the disease appears as a light sprinkling of spots on the tail or fins. Cure depends on breaking the life-cycle: place the fish in water and raise the temperature to 16-18°C (60-65°F) in order to encourage the swarming stage in the parasite. Add a cure based on acriflavine or quinine salts, often mixed with methylene blue, chloramine T or malachite green. Untreated fish die.

SUMMARY OF CHEMICALS

When choosing a manufactured cure, make sure it has the right active chemical ingredient in it. The following chemical bases can be recommended:

Chloramine T

Effective against slime and skin diseases, white spot disease and skin flukes.

Dimethyltrichlorohydroxyethylphosphonate

Effective against fish lice, anchor worm, gill flukes and other parasites.

Malachite green

Effective against fungus, slime and skin diseases, white spot, skin flukes and other parasites

Methylene blue

Effective against fungus and also white spot disease.

Shubunkins

While many people believe shubunkins are completely distinct from goldfish, technically they belong to the same genus.

Like other goldfish, they all grow to a size of 2-15in (5-38cm), except the calico fantail and telescope fantail, which grow to a size of 2-8in (5-20cm). The ultimate size of the fish depends on the size of the pool and the extent of the fish population in it.

Unlike the true goldfish, the shubunkin has nacreous (pearly) scales and is available in a much greater range of colours including blue, violet and grey. While single and bi-coloured specimens are sometimes seen, the majority of shubunkins are a mixture of many different colours.

Despite their somewhat tropical appearance, most shubunkins are hardy, although the more exotic types are not as resilient. The figures at the end of each entry indicate the zones of hardiness (z) for that fish.

Bristol This is a slim and elegant fish with long fins; the tail fins are clearly forked and have rounded lobes. A typical fish is bright blue with black speckles and generous splashes of red, yellow and black. z 7-10

Calico Comet This comet-tailed version of the common shubunkin has a bluish or grey ground colour splashed with red, orange, yellow and peppered with black spots. The tail is flowing and almost as long as the body.

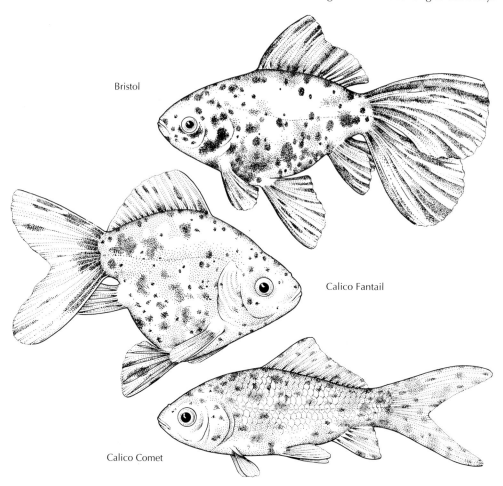

Bristol

Calico Fantail

Calico Comet

This graceful fish is a fast swimmer, and the combination of its brilliant colour and agile movements makes it a very popular choice for the garden pool. z 9-10

Calico Fantail This fantail version of the shubunkin comes in similar colour combinations to the calico comet. Its body is round and dumpy, and it has a spreading tail. Like its goldfish counterpart, it is less hardy than other types of shubunkin and its shape and ungainly swimming technique make it vulnerable to environmental extremes and predators. z 9-10

Calico Telescope Exactly the same in every respect as the calico fantail, but with bulbous, telescopic eyes. z 9-10

Cambridge Blue This is the same shape as the common shubunkin. It has a powder blue base colour and is overlaid with violet and occasionally splashed with ochre. The enthusiast will seek fish without the ochre. z 7-10

Common A smaller version of the common goldfish, the common shubunkin is available in a wide range of colours and colour combinations. The majority are red, white and yellow, often on a blue or grey ground, with a sprinkling of black spots or patches. z 7-10

London The London shubunkin is exactly the same shape as the typical common goldfish but rarely grows as large. It is bright blue with a stippling of black, and also has patches of red, yellow and black. z 7-10

Calico Telescope

Common

London

Carp

With the advent of the Japanese Koi, or Nishi-kigoi, there is now a much greater range of carp from which to choose. The choice of size, shape and colour has increased to such an extent that a whole new hobby has developed devoted to these fish.

In an average garden pool of around 10 x 8 ft (3 x 2.4m) it is unwise to have more than two or three carp. They are boisterous fish and can cause all kinds of problems when present in great numbers, uprooting the plants and disturbing the soil in the baskets. They also produce a considerable amount of detritus which, in turn, provides nutrients for water-discolouring algae. Some are better suited to the wildlife pool (see page 140). Apart from their slightly unruly antics, they are in every other way like goldfish and should be treated as such.

Carp inhabit the middle depth of the pool. They can grow 3-24in (8-60cm) in length, their ultimate size depending on the size of the pool and the extent of the fish population in it. They are all hardy in zones 6-10, apart from the bronze carp, which is only hardy in zones 7-10.

Bronze Carp and goldfish are members of the same family. Bronze carp are really nothing more than uncoloured goldfish conceived at a low water temperature and graded out of coloured goldfish stocks; they often develop into red goldfish. In some cases, the bronze colour is caused by a dominant gene, and if

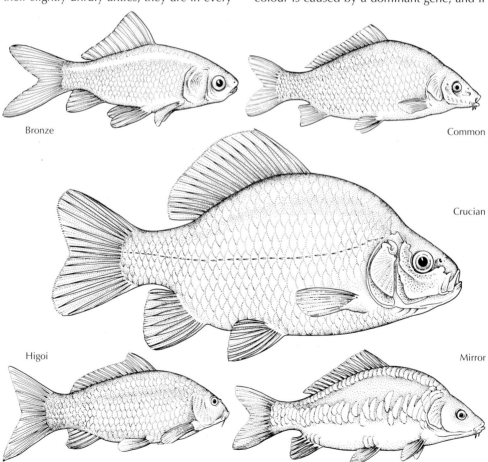

Bronze

Common

Crucian

Higoi

Mirror

interbreeding with common goldfish occurs, this gene is often passed on.

Common This chubby, bronze-copper-coloured fish has a wide body, narrow head and four pendent barbels. This is not a fish for the small, ornamental pool as it tends to be rather boisterous and it is difficult to see. It is much better suited to the larger informal or wildlife pool.

Crucian Very similar to the common carp, but without the barbels, this fish is a chocolate bronze colour which lightens to gold or greenish-yellow on the belly. It does not have a high level of visibility compared with other brightly coloured fish and it is also very boisterous; not a fish for the small, ornamental garden pond.

Gibel Also known as the Prussian carp, this is a variation on the crucian carp, of similar colour and hardiness, but with a slimmer body and a more forked caudal fin. Again, not a fish for the small pool.

Higoi This Chinese Red carp is believed to be a variation of the common carp. A most attractive salmon or orange-pink fish, it has a depressed head and pendent barbels. Like the Koi carp, it grows rapidly and it is unwise to introduce more than two or three to a well-planted garden pool.

Mirror A grey fish with a smooth body that has shiny scales around the head and sometimes on the tail or back as well. It lives in the garden pool but is not as visible as Higoi or Koi carp.

KOI CARP

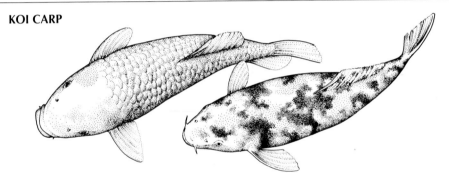

Unquestionably the most striking of the carp family, Koi carp, also known as Nishi-kigoi carp, are available in many colours, ranging from yellow to pink, from grey to violet, and also in many colour combinations. For the most part, their body shape is like that of the Higoi, but sometimes the barbels are much reduced or absent. Some varieties have a metallic look, while others have scales with a conventional flat matt finish.

Breeding a consistent colour line is particularly difficult: very few fry come true to type. Koi are classified into recognized scale types, colours (single, two-colour, three-colour) and patterns, and often the fish are named after their description in Japanese: a fish with the name of Hi Matsuba, for example, is plain red with the Matsuba pine cone pattern.

The major scale types are:

Scaled	The usual fully-scaled carp type
Doitsu	A fish which only has scales along the central lateral line and in the area of the dorsal fin
Leather	A glossy-looking fish with no visible scales except a few small ones near the dorsal fin
Gin Rin	A fish with scales of a glossy, mirror-like appearance

The major colours and patterns are:

Gin	Silver metallic
Hi	Red
Ki	Yellow
Kib	Gold metallic
Kohaku	Red-and-white pattern
Matsuba	Pine cone pattern
Sanke	Three-coloured pattern
Shiro	White
Sumi	Black

Other fish

There are a number of other fish suitable for both garden and wildlife ponds (see page 140). Take care, however, to buy farmed native breeds rather than captured wild stock as some imported fish may be protected species. Wild fish may also harbour diseases injurious to pool fish. The figures at the end of each entry indicate the zones of hardiness (z) for that fish.

Golden and Silver orfe The sleek and elegant orfe are a popular choice. They are surface fish, rarely venturing below the top 6in (15cm) of the water, and they enjoy the spray of a fountain or waterfall and will leap into the air for gnats.

Orfe are hardy fish, long and slender with small, blunt heads. The popular golden orfe is orange-pink, often with dark-coloured or black blotches on and around the head. The silver orfe is long and slender like its golden cousin, but plain silver with no dark markings. The golden orfe is one of the fastest growing fish; both variants grow 3-18in (8-45cm) long. Neither type breeds readily in small pools.

Orfe have a high oxygen requirement and should never be purchased on hot days when the oxygen level is low. Only purchase small fish as large specimens do not travel well; introduce a shoal for the best effect. z 7-10

Golden and Silver rudd These native fish are not as slender as the orfe and are like goldfish in shape, but with more subdued coloration. The silver rudd has an almost metallic appearance and conspicuous red fins, while its golden counterpart is burnished copper rather than true gold or yellow. They grow 3-10in (8-25cm) long.

Both types breed freely where there is an abundance of underwater foliage and enough space. Only purchase small fish; large specimens do not travel well. z 6-10

Roach and dace These native species are not fish for the very small pool, but are excellent additions to the larger wildlife pond. They demand well-oxygenated water, and enjoy the spray of a waterfall or fountain. The dace glides through the water just beneath the surface, leaping at passing flies, while the roach is a more solitary fish, preferring the middle depth of the pool. The dace is a handsome steely-grey fish with a bold, strong head and a long, almost cylindrical body; the roach is similar but with a silvery body and very distinctive eyes with red irises. Both grow 3-10in (8-25cm) long. z 6-10

Minnows Native minnows are a delight in shallow moving water and are best suited to wildlife ponds. They are gregarious small fish up to 3in (8cm) long and should be introduced in groups of eight or ten. For much of the year they are steely-grey, but during the summer breeding season the males turn almost black and sport red bellies and crimson marks at the corners of their mouths. z 7-10

Scavenging fish These fish are carnivorous and invaluable for keeping the pool free from uneaten goldfish food, as well as clearing up mosquito larvae and troublesome aquatic insects such as caddis fly. The broad, greyish-olive-coloured green tench is the most common scavenging fish and will grow up to 12in (30cm) under favourable conditions. It has an elegant body and narrow tapering head but, like all scavengers, is rarely seen as it lurks on the bottom of the pool among the submerged plants. The catfish can be introduced with caution: its scavenging often includes snails, small fry and fancy fish. It is an aggressive fish with long barbels or whiskers and, under favourable conditions, will grow up to 12in (30cm) in length. z 6-10

FISH FOR CONTAINERS

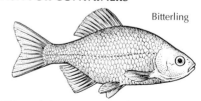

Bitterling

Although happy in a small pool, the tiny bitterling is seen at its best in a container where its delightful antics can be closely observed. It is similar to the common carp in shape, but it has a lustrous metallic sheen which glints in the light as it darts about. z 8-10

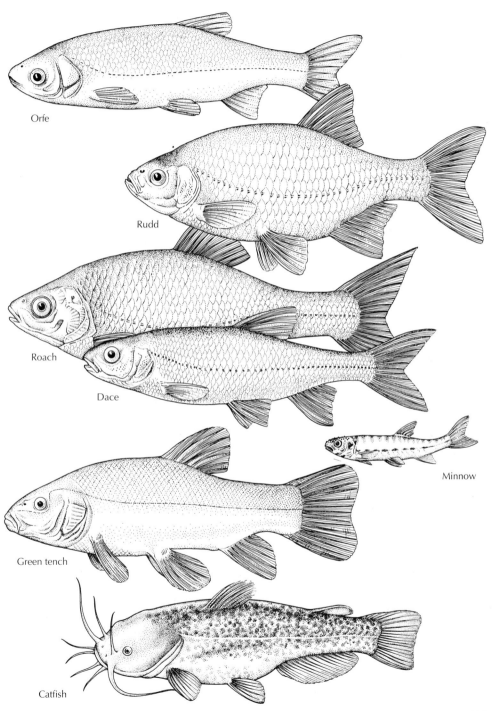

Orfe

Rudd

Roach

Dace

Minnow

Green tench

Catfish

Crustaceans/other livestock

Many crustaceans and amphibians are welcome additions to the pool, and are particularly encouraged by wildlife enthusiasts (see page 140). A number of snails clean and scavenge, grazing upon and slowly removing algae and rotting vegetation, and fresh water mussels help keep the pool free of algae by sucking in the green water and retaining the suspended algae. Frogs, toads and newts are useful as they eat many garden pests. Snails also give some indication of the water conditions: thin and pitted shells are a sign of acid water, while smooth and lustrous shells show the water is alkaline (see page 184).

Snails There are several dozen different species of snail that may appear in a garden pool. Many of them will arrive unannounced, either as eggs carried on the feet of bathing birds or as eggs or small snails stuck to aquatic plants.

Many snails, however, are just as eager to eat aquatic vegetation as algae and, for this reason, only the ramshorn can be recommended unreservedly for the garden pool. The ramshorn snail has a flattened shell like a catherine wheel which it carries in an upright position on its back. In addition to the normal black-fleshed variety there are those with red or white bodies. There is no point mixing the varieties: once breeding starts the black colour will dominate and within a couple of generations the red and white pigmentations will have largely disappeared.

Mussels The swan mussel is the largest and most common mussel. Up to 6in (15cm) long, it has a dull brownish-green oval shell and a white, fleshy body. The painter's mussel is less common, and has a yellowish-green shell marked with brown growth rings. Both are effective filters but will only prosper in an established pool which has a generous layer of debris on the floor. They rarely survive in the clear water of a new pool. Once settled they should remain undisturbed.

Frogs, toads and newts There is no need to introduce frogs, toads and newts as they come of their own accord. Most gardeners welcome frogs to their pools, although fish fanciers are less encouraging. This is because male frogs have been known to attack breeding fish, but this is an extremely rare occurrence and should not act as a deterrent.

The common frog is most widespread, and

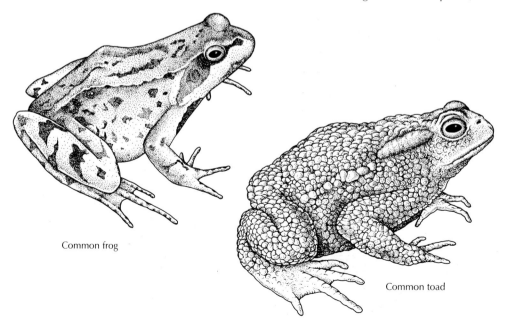

Common frog

Common toad

in localized areas the marsh and edible frogs are often seen. All three are superficially alike as they are the same dull muddy-green colour, but the marsh frog is longer than the common frog and the edible frog is more attractive, with a distinctive pale stripe down its back. They all breed during spring or early summer: the jelly-like eggs (frogspawn) turn into tadpoles which slowly develop into small frogs.

The toad only enters the water to breed, being content the rest of the time with a cool, damp corner out of the sun. It is a nocturnal creature and a great friend to the gardener because it devours large numbers of slugs, beetles and caterpillars. The common toad is mostly seen, and the natterjack, with an orangey-yellow stripe down its back, is of local occurrence.

Newts also gravitate to garden ponds, the brownish-olive common and palmate newts in particular. Like toads, they spend most of their time on land, only entering the water in spring to breed. The garden pool is also a refuge for threatened species like the great crested newt, which has a long, tapering crest and black and yellow body, and spends most of its time swimming in the water.

SPIRAL SNAILS

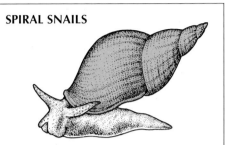

Any snail that has a tall, pointed, spiral shell (as opposed to a flat, disk-like one) is really a plant pest (see page 114) and should be avoided.

The great pond snail is the most common example. Although often sold as a pond snail, it should never be introduced to the pool as it vigorously attacks aquatic plants, leaving pieces of severed foliage floating around in the water.

It is easy to remove these snails. Take some lettuce or brassica leaves and float them on the water overnight. By morning the leaves will be covered with pond snails, and it is easy to remove them from the leaves and dispose of them.

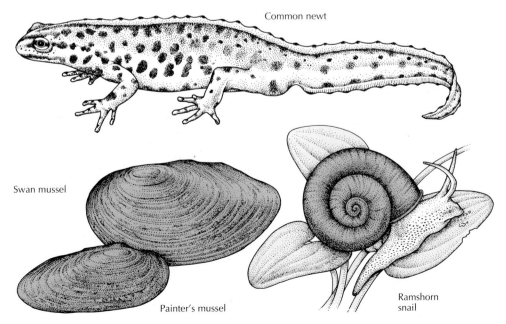

Common newt

Swan mussel

Painter's mussel

Ramshorn snail

Pool maintenance

SPRING
Pool cleaning and repairs
Any maintenance jobs requiring an empty pool are best carried out in spring. If necessary, clean out the pool and do any repair work needed (see pages 178 and 180).

Equipment
Once any danger of frost has passed, take out the pool heater and store it until next winter, making sure it is clean and dry. Check that filters and pumps are working and place them in the pool.

SUMMER
Topping up the pool
As spring turns to summer, the water in the pool starts to evaporate quite rapidly and will need topping up regularly with fresh water. If rain water is available from a water butt, use it to top up the pool, approximately once a week or more regularly in very hot weather. If only tap water is available, top up the pool more frequently, every evening if necessary. Tap water will be colder than rain water, and if used in large quantities will disturb fish, particularly the more delicate fancy types, which may lead to swim bladder disorders.

Large quantities of tap water will usually contain high mineral concentrations which will encourage water-discolouring algae. This is less likely to happen if the tap water is introduced little and often as the higher plants will absorb the minerals steadly, at the expense of algal growth.

Protection from falling leaves

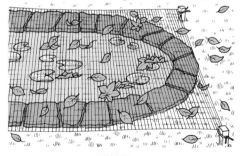

Secure a net over the surface of the pool, pegging it into the ground. This will catch falling leaves.

Maintaining clean water
Throughout the summer, it is important to keep the pool free of decaying foliage in order to maintain clean water. Flowers should be dead-headed as soon as they fade, and blanketweed and silkweed (see page 182) should be removed with a blanketweed remover, with a stick or by hand.

AUTUMN
Protection from falling leaves
Leaves dropping from neighbouring deciduous trees, and those blown from afar by the wind, pose one of the biggest problems for the pool owner in autumn. A net can be placed over the pond but, although it prevents leaves from falling into the water, it does not look very attractive and there are the practical difficulties of removing the leaves from the middle of the net. However, if there are trees growing directly over your pool this may be the only solution. Otherwise, a temporary low fence about 2-3 ft (60-90cm) high can be constructed around the pool using fine mesh wire-netting fixed to strong canes pushed into the ground every 2-3ft (60-90cm). This will prevent leaves from blowing in and is a more functional solution that is slightly less offensive to the eye than a net draped across the whole pool.

Avoiding water pollution
It is very important to remove waterside foliage as soon as it turns brown, otherwise it will decompose and pollute the water.

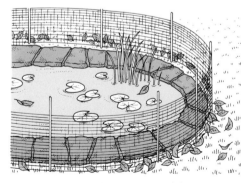

Alternatively, make a fence. Push strong canes into the ground and bend wire-netting round them, securing it with wire.

Winter care

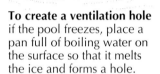

To create a ventilation hole if the pool freezes, place a pan full of boiling water on the surface so that it melts the ice and forms a hole.

Float a rubber ring in the pool; the water will freeze it in place. Pour boiling water into the centre of the ring to form a hole.

Alternatively, place a pool heater in the water. The heater will give off enough heat to keep a small patch of water free from ice.

Removing pool equipment
As autumn turns to winter, remove the pool equipment you are no longer using. Clean and dry pumps and filters, and store them until next spring.

WINTER
Concrete pool care
The pool itself needs winter protection, especially if it is made of concrete. In freezing conditions, the pressure exerted by ice can be sufficient to fracture the most expertly laid concrete. A piece of wood or a rubber ball floated on the surface will absorb some of the pressure exerted by the ice and, in most cases, prevent fracturing; alternatively, a pool heater can be used.

Using a pool heater (see page 14)
If a pool freezes over, gases produced by decaying organic matter will displace the air in the narrow void between the water surface and the coating of ice, causing fish to suffocate. The pool heater is a simple ventilation device consisting of a brass rod with a heating element in it, attached to a polystyrene float. This is placed in the water in icy conditions and, when switched on, the heat creates a small, ice-free area through which noxious gases can escape. It is economical to use and can be connected to the electricity supply at the same point where a submersible pump and filter might be plugged in during the summer months.

The hot pan and rubber ring techniques
Without a pool heater, it is possible to make a hole in the ice by standing a pan of boiling water on it and leaving the hot container to melt through. If the layer of ice is thick it may take several refills of boiling water before there is a complete melt-through. Although tedious, this is a necessary process as cracking the ice with a blunt instrument is very dangerous and can even kill the fish.

An alternative to this is to float a rubber ring on the surface of the water. This freezes in the ice and boiling water can be poured into the centre, thereby creating a small hole within the rubber ring. Once the ice has melted in the middle, regular introductions of hot water will ensure permanent ventilation.

CONCRETE POOLS

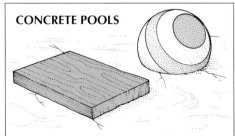

Drop a ball or piece of wood into the water. When the water freezes the ball or wood will absorb the pressure of the ice and this will stop the concrete from cracking.

Cleaning pools

Periodically all garden pools, even natural ones, will need cleaning out completely. Over a period of time, sediment builds up from soil spillage and decaying plant life; dead livestock will turn the water black, bluish or milky, and an oily scum will develop on the surface. If the pond is not cleaned out, it will silt up and the underwater plant population will grow into uncontrollable masses.

How often and when to clean

Many gardeners have a great urge to clean their pools every year, but unless something has gone seriously wrong (chemical pollution, for example) this is totally unnecessary and can damage the pool's ecosystem. Every time a pool is cleaned it takes a couple of years for the ecosystem to stabilize and take on a look of maturity. Large pools need cleaning only every ten years or so, while smaller pools need attention approximately every five years. Neglected pools will need total restoration (see page 184) as this is often the only way of sorting out the plants.

It is best to clean ponds in spring as this will give the plants time to re-establish themselves for summer. It is possible to clean in summer, but the plants will have to be cut back and they will not make a satisfactory display that year. Also, in the cool conditions of spring, algae are unlikely to be such a problem when the pond is refilled.

Draining the water

First, drain the pool by pumping, siphoning or bailing out the water into a storm drain or border. Siphoning is easy when part of the surrounding ground is lower than the pool. Lay a length of hosepipe no longer than 5ft (1.5m) in the pond, making sure it fills with water. Hold one end in the pool with a thumb over it, and quickly lift the other end up and out of the pool to a lower level. Providing the action is swift and the thumb is removed immediately the free end of the hosepipe is lower than the surface of the pool, then the pull of gravity will start and continue the flow. Siphon out most of the water, but bail out the remaining few inches, which will be full of debris, with a bucket.

Removing fish, snails and plants

Fish usually gravitate to the accumulated soil and debris on the pool floor, scavenging fish remaining until the very end, thrashing around in a minimal amount of mud. If you are bailing out water, be careful not to scoop out any fish and snails accidentally.

Fish can be removed whenever they are seen with a mug or a net. Have several buckets or saucepans full of clean water standing in a shady corner to accommodate the fish as soon as they are located; you can also use washing-up bowls provided they are clean and completely free from detergent.

Cleaning the pool

1 With a length of hose, siphon out the water, quickly removing the thumb from the submerged end to start the water flow.

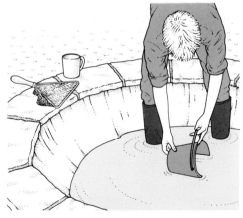

2 Next, use a bucket to carefully bail out the remaining dirty water, removing fish with a net or mug as you see them.

The containers do not have to be very deep, a minimum of 4-6in (10-15cm) is sufficient, but they should have as much surface area as possible to permit good oxygen exchange. Alternatively, use an aquarium. Include a clump or two of submerged plant to provide some shelter and a little green matter for food, but do not forget that the fish will need regular feeding with an ordinary dried food if the cleaning operation is to last several days.

Snails should be kept separately from fish, preferably in a large bucket with a handful of filamentous algae. In confined conditions fish will attack them, dragging them out of their shells and eating them. Only retain ramshorn snails as these are the ones that eat algae rather than pool vegetation; dispose of any snails with tall, spiral shells (see page 114) as these eat aquatic plants.

Once the pool is empty of water, sort out the plant life. Waterlilies can be kept in a bucket of water for a week or so, but after that they will need potting and placing in a tank. This is a good time to divide any waterlilies that have outgrown their containers. Leave marginal plants in their containers and put them in a shady spot, occasionally watering them, and place submerged plants in a bowl with enough water to cover them completely. They will only last for about half an hour without water before spoiling and so it is important to accommodate them quickly.

Removing the mud and debris

Once everything of any value has been removed from the pool, only the mud and debris remains. Dig this out with a spade; a natural pool will have a solid natural floor to dig down to. Be very careful not to damage the structure of the pool, especially if it is constructed with a liner of some sort, and on no account use a fork for fear of puncturing the liner. Take the mud and debris to another part of the garden and wait for it to dry out before incorporating it into the general garden soil. Never be tempted to use healthy-looking mud for propagating or re-potting aquatics because it will inevitably harbour the seeds of pernicious water weeds.

Cleaning the pool

With a stiff brush and bucket of clean water, scrub the sides and floor of the pool, removing all traces of dirt and algae. A solution of potassium permanganate will help to remove stubborn stains: add enough crystals to turn a bucket of water deep purple. Wear a pair of household rubber gloves while scrubbing as the solution stains the skin brown. Take care to siphon out the dregs of water from the pool when the job is complete. Never use detergent as it is difficult to rinse out completely and some of it may remain in the pool and cause minor pollution problems, affecting fish and plant life.

3 Place fish, snails and waterlilies in separate containers of water but leave marginal plants in their planting baskets.

4 Once you have dug out all the mud and debris, clean the pool with a stiff brush and clean water, wearing gloves if necessary.

Pool repairs

Once a pool has been cleaned out and is still empty, thoroughly check the structure for any damage.

A pond can be damaged in a variety of ways: it is possible to puncture a liner or crack unsupported fibreglass pools with heavy footsteps when cleaning them; the margins of polythene and, to a lesser degree, PVC liners can deteriorate if they are not covered with water and are exposed to sunshine; and concrete pools may develop crazed surfaces or cracks if they have not been laid properly and are exposed to frost and ice.

Repair kits are available for many types of liners, but not all types mend well. Polythene, plastic and PVC cannot be satisfactorily repaired even though repair kits are available. The repaired area will always be a source of weakness and will not remain watertight. Most polythene liners have a useful life of only three or four years; PVC will last for about ten years.

Once the pool has been mended, water, fish and other livestock can be introduced as soon as the repair work is dry.

Butyl rubber liners are worthy of repairing as rubber is easy to patch and will remain relatively watertight. Rubber repair kits, similar to bicycle repair kits, are widely available.

Locate the puncture and thoroughly clean the surface around it with a scrubbing brush and water. Once dry, roughen the surface a little with sandpaper. Cut a neat patch of liner one-and-a-half-times larger than the puncture. Spread the patch and the damaged area with a layer of adhesive and, once both surfaces are tacky to the touch, place the patch over the puncture and press it down firmly. The pool can be filled after 12 hours, when the repair is dry.

If you are using a repair kit the patches are already adhesive. Simply select a patch the right size, peel the back off and press it firmly over the puncture.

Fibreglass is tough enough to withstand most damage, even if it has been badly neglected. However, when damage does occur, it can be repaired with a motor repair kit containing fibreglass matting. This is not an easy job as repairs are seldom carried out on site: it is difficult to fix fibreglass while squatting down in the pool cavity, and most cracks are best repaired from underneath where they will not show. Fibreglass repair work also needs a warm atmosphere in order to cure quickly – a garage or outhouse with a heater is ideal.

First, roughen the surface around the damaged area with coarse sandpaper and

Repairing a butyl rubber liner

1 Thoroughly clean the damaged area. Make sure it is free from all dirt, otherwise the patch will not stick properly.

2 Sand the area around the puncture to roughen the surface and, using a paintbrush, spread adhesive on and around the puncture.

3 Spread one side of the patch with glue. Once both the surfaces are tacky, place the patch over the puncture and press it down.

thoroughly clean it with water. Once the area is dry, apply a patch of fibreglass matting, making sure that it is one-and-a-half times larger than the damaged area. Following the instructions, impregnate the fibreglass with resin using the ridged metal roller. Rub down with fine sandpaper once it has hardened, after about 24 hours.

Concrete pools are the most permanent, if properly laid. The majority of amateur-made concrete pools, however, tend to deteriorate quickly (usually because of an inconsistency in the concrete mix), developing cracks or flakes which are made worse by frost and ice. These may occur even after the first winter. Professionally constructed concrete pools should give years of trouble-free service.

If a concrete pool is flaking away then little can be done except line the shell with a butyl rubber liner. Do not use polythene or PVC because concrete is abrasive. Secure the rubber liner in the same way as in an earth excavation (see page 36), taking it up and over the edge of the pool and burying the edges in 4in (10cm) of earth; this will be reasonably permanent. Fractures or cracks in the concrete can usually be repaired, although even a good repair remains a point of weakness and may be a source of recurring trouble.

Clean the area with a scrubbing brush and water and leave it to dry. Using a cold chisel, chip out a "V"-shaped channel along the fracture line at least 1in (2.5cm) deeper than the crack itself. Roughen the surface by chipping it with a chisel; this enables the new concrete to key-in successfully.

Mix one part cement, two parts sand and four parts gravel in their dry states and add a waterproofing compound if you wish, according to the instructions. Without a waterproofing compound concrete will still be waterproof, but the compound will increase the chances of a waterproof repair. Add enough water to give a stiff, wet consistency. Carefully apply the fresh concrete using a plasterer's trowel, filling the channel and smoothing it over.

Leave the concrete to set: depending on the weather this could take from two days to a week, and if it rains take care to cover the area with polythene. If you prefer, use a quick setting cement, although this is more likely to develop hair-line cracks.

Once the concrete has set, treat it with a sealing compound (see page 40). This will prevent free-lime escaping from the concrete into the water, harming the fish and clouding the water. Water, plants and fish can be introduced as soon as the concrete is sealed.

Repairing a concrete pool

1 Make a "V"-shaped channel along the crack. The channel must be at least 1in (2.5cm) deeper than the crack.

2 Mix the concrete and add a waterproofing compound. Using a plasterer's trowel, fill the channel with concrete and smooth it level.

3 Once the concrete is dry, treat it with a sealant. Mix the powder according to the instructions, and paint it on with a paint brush.

Algal control

There are numerous forms of aquatic algae, but the most common two are the free-floating and filamentous types. The free-floating kinds comprise several hundred species, including suspended algae, which swarm in great masses and give water the appearance of pea soup. In addition to the common green kinds, there are rapid-growing brown and red algae which are mostly seen in spring. The filamentous kinds appear as floating silkweed or as thick, fibrous mats commonly known as blanketweed or flannelweed, all of which may be dragged from the pool using a stick, a blanketweed remover or by hand. Other filamentous species cling to plants and baskets and often coat the walls of the pool as well, but unless these become a nuisance they should not be removed as water snails graze upon them.

Algal growth is a natural phenomenon and algae continuously compete with higher plants for mineral salts in the water. These higher plants, floating and submerged aquatics in particular, also create shady patches of water, thus starving the algae out of existence. The gardener may strive to achieve crystal clear water devoid of algae, but chemical control is only temporary and the algae will be quick to return once the control is exhausted.

There is no real solution to algae, and it is a problem for most pool owners at some time, even if only for two or three weeks in late spring when warm water encourages algal growth and the higher plants have not yet started to grow. Algicides are useful at this time; alternatively floating and submerged aquatics can be encouraged into early activity if overwintered inside (see page 116). Filters also help reduce algae (see page 14).

The best permanent solution is to achieve a natural ecological balance of nutrients and shade, but once this is disturbed the algae will quickly return. It is also difficult to create a steady balance in small volumes of water as they heat up and cool down so rapidly. Furthermore, evaporation of water in summer is more of a problem in smaller pools because of the relatively large quantities of water needed to top them up. If this new water is nutrient-rich tap water, it will encourage a rapid proliferation of algae; use collected rain water if at all possible.

Algicides
It is possible to exercise some control over algae using algicides, available from garden centres. IT IS VERY IMPORTANT TO FOLLOW THE INSTRUCTIONS FOR ALL PROPRIETARY BRANDS. Algae are among the most primitive of plants and algicides are carefully formulated to be used in specific amounts to act on these plants without affecting higher plant life. Filamentous algae are more complex in structure than free-floating algae and so need different treatments.

Calculate the water capacity of your pool using the formula on page 10 and add the algicide as directed. When using proprietary algicides, follow the dilution rates carefully as each product will be different.

Potassium permanganate
Algicides based on potassium permanganate are effective against free-floating and suspended algae but not against filamentous types, because the solution needed to control the latter would be too strong for other plants and fish to survive.

These algicides must be used on a dull day when the water is not warm to the touch, otherwise the water will become de-oxygenated and turn a cloudy yellow. If this occurs, the pool must be cleaned out or the plants and fish will die. On no account should potassium permanganate crystals be used; the margin for error is very small, especially when fish are present, and an excessive dose of the crystals may damage or kill some kinds of water plants.

CREATING A NATURAL BALANCE

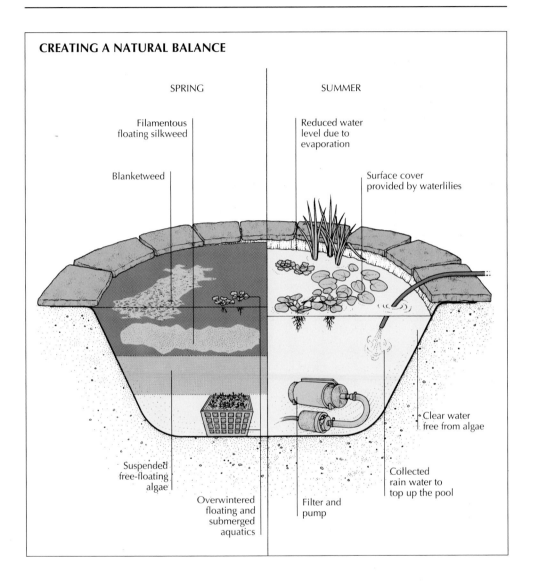

SPRING

SUMMER

Filamentous
floating silkweed

Reduced water
level due to
evaporation

Blanketweed

Surface cover
provided by waterlilies

Suspended
free-floating
algae

Overwintered
floating and
submerged
aquatics

Filter and
pump

Clear water
free from algae

Collected
rain water to
top up the pool

Other problems

In addition to the problems caused by algae and the various pests and diseases which may attack fish and plants, there are a number of other problems which may arise in a pool from time to time.

Birds

Although it is pleasant to see birds bathing in the margins of a pool, it is better to have a separate bird bath. This is because birds often carry pollutants, such as agricultural chemicals, on their feathers which wash off in the water and endanger pool life. In such cases, the pool must be thoroughly cleaned out (see page 178).

Muddy Water

There is no cure for muddy water other than cleaning the pool out completely. It is usually caused by fish nosing around the planting baskets in search of aquatic insect grubs. Once soil deposits have escaped from the containers, every passing fish will cause the particles to swirl in the water like a cloud of brown smoke. Large, boisterous carp are quite capable of tearing submerged plants from their containers and creating clouds of soil particles; the more fish there are, the worse the problem will be. If the soil in the planting baskets is covered with about ½in (1.25cm) of pea gravel, the fish can remove

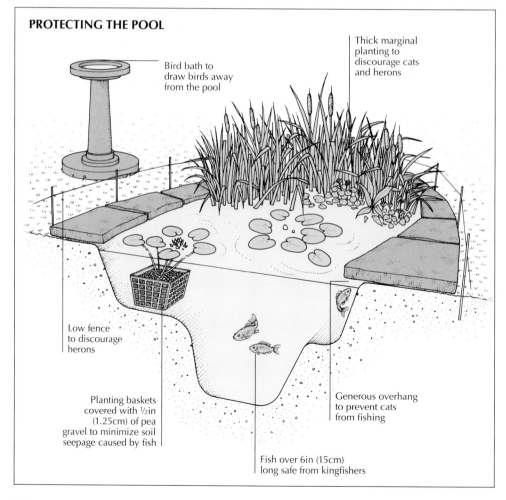

PROTECTING THE POOL

Bird bath to draw birds away from the pool

Thick marginal planting to discourage cats and herons

Low fence to discourage herons

Planting baskets covered with ½in (1.25cm) of pea gravel to minimize soil seepage caused by fish

Generous overhang to prevent cats from fishing

Fish over 6in (15cm) long safe from kingfishers

the larvae without disturbing the soil. Fewer fish will also help to minimize the problem.

Predators

There are several predators which cause problems for the inhabitants of pools, the most common being the heron. This bird is very adept at flying over an area and spotting garden ponds, however small, and once it has homed in on a pool, it will return again and again until all the fish have been taken. Herons often fish at daybreak before the pool owner is up and about, so they need to be deterred by artifical means.

Some pool owners find that a plastic heron positioned by the pool will discourage live herons as they are birds which fish alone, but this is not an infallible deterrent. Heron netting, which covers the entire pool, is available from some garden centres but, although it keeps herons out, it is messy and gets tangled up in the plants.

Alternatively, take a number of short pieces of cane, up to 10in (23cm) long, and push them into the ground at intervals of about 2-3ft (60-90cm) around the pool, taking special care where poolside vegetation is sparse. Wind a single strong strand of black garden cotton or fishing line round the canes to form a low fence about 4-6in (10-15cm) high. When the heron walks towards the water, its legs will come in contact with the thread and, discouraged after two or three tries, it usually leaves.

Kingfishers occasionally make themselves a nuisance, particularly where the garden is close to a river. They do not travel vast distances to feed, but they will prey on any brightly-coloured goldfish. The majority of pool owners are happy to live with them despite the fact that they eat the small fish. Fish over 6in (15cm) long will be safe as they are too large to be taken.

Cats can also be tiresome. In order to prevent them fishing from the poolside, plant as much of the marginal area of the pool as possible with strong-growing aquatics. Where the pool meets the surrounding ground, pave the edge with a 3in (8cm) overhang so cats' paws cannot reach the fish underneath.

ACIDIC AND ALKALINE CONDITIONS

Pool life is affected by high levels of acidity or alkalinity (see page 112). It is possible to measure the pH value using a pH test kit available from garden centres.

Alkaline conditions (above pH7) can be caused by improperly cured concrete, and are often a problem in new pools. If the water has a pH value of 8.5 or over, plants are not able to absorb certain nutrients and they may stop growing and develop a coating of limy deposit. Fish become vulnerable to gill disorders. Acid conditions (below pH7), caused by large accumulations of organic matter, may also cause problems: water with a pH level of 5 or below will lock up essential nutrients such as phosphates; fish will become more prone to diseases and snails will develop thin, pitted shells.

There is no solution to these conditions other than emptying out the pool and giving it a thorough clean, after which it can be refilled.

NEGLECTED POOLS

Restoring a neglected pond involves much work. Floating plants may have covered the water surface, marginal plants may be rampant and overgrown, many plants may have outgrown their containers and spread to other parts of the pool, and some aquatics may have seeded. The water will be dirty and full of filamentous and free-floating algae, and may be polluted with dead plant and animal matter. If the water level has been allowed to fall, the liner may be damaged by sunlight and will need to be repaired.

The solution is to clean out the pond thoroughly, inspect it for damage, and start again (see pages 178 and 180). It may be possible to save some of the old plants: waterlilies are almost always worth saving, especially good cultivars with mottled foliage. Few submerged plants are likely to have survived the neglect, but if there is suitable growth, cuttings can be taken.

Seasonal checklist

SPRING
Pool maintenance Clean out the pool every five to ten years (see page 178) Carry out any repair work (see page 180) Check that pumps, filters and lights stored in autumn are in working order and install them in the pond (see page 14) Remove the pool heater, dry it and store it for the summer (see page 14) Clear the water of dead winter foliage (see page 116) Treat the water with algicide (see page 182) Introduce overwintered floating and sub-merged aquatics early in the season to help combat algae (see page 116)
Plant care Propagate plants by means of cuttings, seed or division (see page 106) Introduce new plants (see page 100) Introduce any tender plants overwintered indoors (see page 116) Divide existing plants (see page 116) Feed plants as necessary (see page 112)
Fish care Start feeding fish (see page 160) Introduce new fish (see page 158) Introduce any tender fish overwintered indoors (see page 156) Take precautions against herons and cats (see page 184)

SUMMER
Pool maintenance Top up the pool regularly (see page 176) Remove clumps of algae (see page 182) Control algae with an algicide (see page 182) Keep the water free from decaying foliage (see page 176)
Plant care Dead-head flowers (see page 116) Tie up sprawling plants (see page 116) Thin out any plants which have become overgrown (see page 116) Weed the bog garden (see page 116) Remove seed heads (see page 116) Treat plants for pests and diseases if necessary (see page 114) Remove any disease-affected foliage (see page 114)
Fish care Increase the feeding of fish with high-protein foods (see page 160) Treat fish for pests and diseases if necessary (see page 164) Check spawning, removing fry to a separate pool if preferred (see page 162) Carry out stripping for fish breeding if desired (see page 162)

AUTUMN	WINTER
Pool maintenance Take precautions against falling leaves (see page 176)	**Pool maintenance** Insert a pool heater, or an alternative device (see page 176) Remove, clean and store pumps, filters and lights (see page 14)
Plant care Collect ripe seed (see page 108) Collect turions and bulbils for overwintering indoors (see page 116) Remove dying foliage (see page 176) Cut back frost-damaged foliage (see page 116) Cover half-hardy bog plants with straw (see page 116) Dry out containers and store plants if necessary (see page 116) Prepare any indoor plants for winter (see page 116) Remove tender plants to a frost-free environment (see page 116)	**Fish care** Reduce fish feeding (see page 160) Make provisions for protecting fish (see page 156)
Fish care Supplement fish diet with high protein foods (see page 160) Remove tender fish to frost-free aquarium (see page 156)	

Index 1

Index 2/Acknowledgements

Acknowledgements
The author and publishers wish to thank Peter Robinson and Robin Williams who have given invaluable help and advice during the preparation of this book.

Executive Editor: Sarah Polden
Editor: Emily Wright
Senior Art Editor: Mike Brown
Designer: Geoff Fennell
Artists: William Giles, Coral Mula and Sandra Pond
Production: Sarah Schuman
Planting plans: Alison Coleman

The Royal Horticultural Society and publishers have made every effort to ensure that all instructions given in this book are accurate and safe, but they cannot accept liability for any resulting injury, damage or loss to either person or property whether direct or consequential and howsoever arising. The author and publishers will be grateful for any information which will assist them in keeping future editions up to date. We specifically draw our readers' attention to the necessity of carefully reading and accurately following the manufacturer's instructions on any product.

Typesetting by SX Composing Ltd, Rayleigh, Essex
Origination by M & E Reproductions, North Fambridge, Essex

THE R.H.S. ENCYCLOPEDIA OF PRACTICAL GARDENING

EDITOR-IN-CHIEF: CHRISTOPHER BRICKELL

A complete range of titles in this series is available from all good bookshops or by mail order direct from the publisher. Payment can be made by credit card or cheque/postal order in the following ways:

BY PHONE   Phone through your order on our special CREDIT CARD HOTLINE on 01933 443863; speak to our customer service team during office hours (9am to 5pm) or leave a message on the answer machine, quoting your full credit card number plus expiry date and your full name and address.

BY POST   Simply fill out the order form below (it can be photocopied) and send it with your payment to: MITCHELL BEAZLEY DIRECT, 27 SANDERS ROAD, WELLINGBOROUGH, NORTHANTS, NN8 4NL.

ISBN	TITLE	PRICE	QUANTITY	TOTAL
1 84000160 7	GARDEN PLANNING	£8.99		
1 84000159 3	WATER GARDENING	£8.99		
1 84000157 7	GARDEN STRUCTURES	£8.99		
1 84000151 8	PRUNING	£8.99		
1 84000156 9	PLANT PROPAGATION	£8.99		
1 84000153 4	GROWING FRUIT	£8.99		
1 84000152 6	GROWING VEGETABLES	£8.99		
1 84000154 2	GROWING UNDER GLASS	£8.99		
1 84000158 5	ORGANIC GARDENING	£8.99		
1 84000155 0	GARDEN PESTS AND DISEASES	£8.99		
			POSTAGE & PACKING	£2.50
			GRAND TOTAL	

Name ....(BLOCK CAPITALS)

Address ....

....Postcode..............................

I enclose a cheque/postal order for £.................made payable to Octopus Publishing Group Ltd. or:

Please debit my: Access ☐   Visa ☐   AmEx ☐   Diners ☐   account

by £........................... Expiry date ....

Account no ☐☐☐☐☐☐☐☐☐☐☐☐☐☐☐☐

Signature ....

Whilst every effort is made to keep our prices low, the publisher reserves the right to increase the price at short notice.

Your order will be dispatched within 28 days, subject to availability. Free postage and packing offer applies to UK only. Please call 01933 443863 for details of export postage and packing charges

Registered office: Michelin House, 81 Fulham Road, London SW3 6RB. Registered in England no 3597451

THIS FORM MAY BE PHOTOCOPIED.